THE BLUE ANGEL

Ungar Film Library *Stanley Hochman*, GENERAL EDITOR

Academy Awards: An Ungar Reference Index,
edited by Richard Shale

American History / American Film: Interpreting the Hollywood Image,
edited by John E. O'Connor and Martin A. Jackson

The Classic American Novel and the Movies,
edited by Gerald Peary and Roger Shatzkin

Costume Design in the Movies / Elizabeth Leese

Faulkner and Film / Bruce F. Kawin

Fellini the Artist / Edward Murray

The Modern American Novel and the Movies,
edited by Gerald Peary and Roger Shatzkin

*On the Verge of Revolt: Women in American Films
of the Fifties* / Brandon French

Ten Film Classics / Edward Murray

Tennessee Williams and Film / Maurice Yacowar

OTHER FILM BOOKS

*The Age of the American Novel: The Film Aesthetic of Fiction
between the Two Wars* / Claude-Edmonde Magny

The Cinematic Imagination: Writers and the Motion Pictures,
Edward Murray

A Library of Film Criticism: American Film Directors,
edited by Stanley Hochman

Nine American Film Critics / Edward Murray

THE
BLUE ANGEL

The Novel by
HEINRICH MANN

The Film by
JOSEF
VON STERNBERG

Frederick Ungar Publishing Co.
New York

The Blue Angel in novel form was originally
published in German as *Professor Unrat* (1905).
The English translation was first issued in
London in 1932.

The Blue Angel film continuity is included here
by arrangement with Lorrimer Publishing Limited, London.
Introduction by Josef von Sternberg and
continuity translation: © 1968 by Lorrimer Publishing
Limited

Printed in the United States of America

LC 78-20934

ISBN 0-8044-2591-4 (cloth)
ISBN 0-8044-6468-5 (paper)

FOREWORD

The availability in a single volume of the continuity script of Josef von Sternberg's *The Blue Angel* (1930) and the complete text of the Heinrich Mann novel on which the film was based provides a unique opportunity to study the art of adaptation. There can surely be no more fitting way to mark the approaching 50th anniversary of this now classic film.

Generally conceded to be a triumph of cinematic storytelling—even by those who like Harry Alan Potamkin were to complain that in his cinematic "meditations" on life Sternberg had developed an "umbilical perseverance" that was to be fixed on the navel of Venus—the film bears little resemblance to the work Heinrich Mann originally published as *Professor Unrat* (1905). However, as Sternberg points out in his introduction to the script, it was never intended to.

In converting the novel into a series of images that would meet his "standards of visual poetry," Sternberg inevitably stamped the film with his own special sensibility and concerns. As a result, the German novelist's achievement in his gripping study of a small-town tyrant obsessed by hatred of his social betters has been overshadowed by the cinematic genius of the American film director—just as his overall literary production was to be overshadowed by that of his more famous younger brother, Thomas Mann. Sternberg transformed the novel into the story of "the downfall of an enamoured man *à la* Human Bondage."

Mann's Professor Rath—called Mud in this translation to echo the nickname of *Unrat* (filth) given him by his students—fashions the sluttish but essentially bourgeois Rosa Frölich into an instrument of social corruption. Sternberg's Professor Rath falls into the clutches of desire as incarnated in the amoral cabaret singer Lola-Lola—unforgettably played by the young Marlene Dietrich.

The truth is that Sternberg was always to be his own author and concerned only with his own vision of reality, whether in adapting Theodore Dreiser's *An American Tragedy* (1931), Pierre Louys' *The Woman and the Puppet* (*The Devil Is a Woman*, 1935), or Fyodor Dostoevsky's *Crime and Punishment* (1935).

When, for example, Paramount assigned him to "salvage" the projected filming of Dreiser's deterministic masterpiece, he eliminated all the "dull" parts, the sociological elements that in his opinion were "far from being responsible for the dramatic accident with which Dreiser had concerned himself." Dreiser, who had expressed great admiration for the script originally prepared by the Russian director Sergei Eisenstein, was furious, and he unsuccessfully sued to prevent the completed film from being released.

Sternberg may have been somewhat surprised by the novelist's angry response to the cavalier manner in which his original intentions had been disregarded. After all, when he had told Heinrich Mann of the changes he intended to make in *Professor Unrat*, Mann had expressed complete agreement and even flatteringly noted that he was sorry not to have thought of some of these alterations himself. No doubt these comments were not so much insincere as a sincere recognition of the fact that though the projected film was only minimally related to the novel he had written, it had an integrity of its own.

Heinrich Mann's embittered high-school teacher first ventures into the seamy cabaret known as The Blue Angel not to save his students from moral contamination but to "catch" them—just as he "catches" them by trick questions in the classroom. Caught himself in a struggle between love and hate, he sacrifices the former to the latter and becomes "haunted by the delectable vision of mankind at his feet, begging for mercy; of the town, shattered and laid waste; one mass of gold and blood running to grey, burnt-out ashes." The portrait foreshadows that of a petty bourgeois type who was to swell the ranks of the

Nazi party, and whose unleashed hatred was to convulse first Germany and then the world.

Sternberg's Professor Rath, however, is a prudish but loving man, and our sympathy for him is established in the opening scenes with the dead canary. His is the undeveloped heart; the late awakening of both heart and flesh overwhelms prudence and brings about his subsequent degradation, visually foreshadowed by the mute clown introduced into the film by Sternberg. His roosterlike cry of joy on his wedding night is brilliantly echoed by the despairing "kick-a-rick-i" with which he acknowledges his humiliation in the final sequences of the film.

In Mann's novel we tend to celebrate when Professor Rath is brought low by the fury of the townspeople; in Sternberg's film we are horror-stricken by the vision of an essentially honorable man destroyed by desire. As Lola coolly observes the film audience during a final and more menacing rendition of "Falling in Love Again," our hearts constrict.

STANLEY HOCHMAN

HEINRICH MANN

THE
BLUE ANGEL

(Translated from the German by
Professor Unrat)

THE BLUE ANGEL

CHAPTER I

His name being Mut, the whole school, of course, called him Mud. Nothing could have been simpler or more natural; the teachers were always given nicknames. Each new batch of scholars in a class-room, not finding the efforts of their predecessors sufficiently funny, seized on the chance of inventing a really ruddy nickname. Old Mud, however, had kept the same one for several generations of students, and the whole town knew him by it, even his colleagues using it out of school—and in the sacred precincts, when his back was turned. Those masters who took boarders and did coaching spoke of him as Dr. Mud before their pupils. The Head, roused to a watchful observation of the Fifth Form professor, could never manage to stamp it out; the joke was as popular as it had been twenty-six years ago. As soon as he appeared, one boy would call to another:

"Some mud about the place, ain't there?"

Or:

"Seems a smell of mud, what?"

On which Old Mud would shrug impatiently, and from behind his glasses he would dart a glance from his green eyes which the boys called sly, but which was really shy, though none the less vindictive; it was the glance of a tyrant with a bad conscience, cherishing a dagger in the folds of his mantle. He would work his jaws beneath his sparse, greying beard, his wooden chin jutting out, but he could not bring it home to the boys, and had to crawl impotently by, on his thin, knock-kneed legs, his greasy mortar-board on his head.

The school had arranged a torchlight procession for his jubilee the year before, and he had gone out on to the balcony and made a speech. As everyone was staring up at the speaker, a shrill voice had cried:

"Hot air—just stinks of mud!"

And the others had caught it up at once:

"It's muggy—muddy Mud!"

The poor man began to stutter, although he had expected it and was looking right down into his persecutors' open mouths. The other masters were standing near, but he felt once again that he could not bring it home to the guilty, though he made a private note of their names. A few days later Kieselack, the boy with the shrill voice, happening to confess that he did not know the name of the village where Joan of Arc was born, his teacher had a dire foreboding that he would not soon be quit of his impertinence, and indeed Kieselack was not promoted to a higher form at Easter, but remained in the doctor's class, with most of those who had created the disturbance at the jubilee. Von Ertzum and Lohmann, too, were among the laggards, though

Lohmann was not one of the enemy; he incited Dr. Mut to ironic mirth with his laziness, and his friend von Ertzum was downright stupid. During the following autumn, one morning in the interval before Dr. Mut's lesson on Schiller's *Maid of Orleans*, it happened that von Ertzum, who was still as distantly acquainted as ever with the Maid and knew he was in for trouble anyway, in an access of despair threw open the window and defying fate, yelled at the top of his lungs:

"Mud!"

He did not know or care whether the professor was near or not; he merely felt the need of self-expression for one short moment, before sitting down for two endless hours to stare at a sheet of blank paper, trying to cover it with words—words culled, moreover, from his own empty head. As it chanced, the doctor was crossing the courtyard and when he heard that voice from the void he jumped. Up above he spied von Ertzum's plump person; no other boys were below and there was no one to create an alibi—that is, to whom von Ertzum could have directed his remark except himself.

"This time I've caught you, my boy," thought the professor with glee. He was up the stairs in five bounds, threw open the schoolroom door, hastened through the benches and, clutching at the desk, mounted the steps of the rostrum. But there he had to stand panting, getting back his breath, while the Fifth Form stood up to receive him. Highly alarmed, the boys had sunk into a silence that could be felt. They looked at their teacher as one might look at a mad bull dangerous to the community, but whom they dared not slay and who had a momentary advantage over them. Dr. Mud's breast was heaving in the effort to get his breath, but at last he spoke in his customary deep voice:

"Once again I have been called by a name—an insulting nickname—and I am not minded to put up with it. I will not endure to be so treated by the kind of creatures I have only too good reason to know you boys to be. Mark that! I'll punish you for it whenever I get the chance. I warn you, von Ertzum, that I'll break that impudent spirit of yours like glass; it fills me with abhorrence. I'll report your impertinence to the Head this very day, and do my level best to free this school from the disgrace of your presence!" With that, he tore his gown from his shoulders and shouted: "Take your places!"

The class sat down, von Ertzum alone remaining standing. His round and callow head was now fiery red—as red as the bristles that stood on end upon it. He wanted to speak—but then gave it up and sat down with the rest. Then, at last, he made the effort:

"It wasn't me, sir!"

On this many others supported him in a spirit of steadfast and sacrificial comradeship:

"It wasn't him, sir!"

"Silence!" Dr. Mud stamped angrily. "And you, von Ertzum, just remember this: You aren't the

first of your name to come up against me! I've put
a spoke in the wheel of more than one—and I'll see
to it that things are difficult for you—if not impossible—as I did for your uncle. He never managed
to pass his exams, only scraping through to officer's
rank by favour, and he soon found even that career
at an end for him. Very well! Your uncle's fate
will be yours, von Ertzum, or something very like
it. I wish you luck of it! I formed my opinion of
your family, von Ertzum, some fifteen years ago,
and have never had occasion to change it. And
now——" He dropped his voice to a growl: "You
are not worthy to use your pen on the saintly Maid
whom we are now going to discuss. Out of the room
with you!"

Von Ertzum, long past understanding, was still
listening open-mouthed, and unconsciously mimick-
ing the movements that the professor's jaws were
executing. The doctor's chin, its upper portion
bristling with a yellow portcullis, rolled as if between
cart-rucks from one deep fissure of his cheek to the
other, and foam spluttered forth to the front bench,
as he cried:

"You dare to defy me, boy! Come here!"

Von Ertzum dragged himself up from his bench as
Kieselack whispered:

"Cave, old man!"

And Lohmann from the seat behind, added:

"We'll tame the tiger yet, old chap."

The condemned slouched past the rostrum to the
dark corner in which was the room where the class

hung up their coats, and as the door closed behind
his plump back, the professor's face cleared.

"And now let us make up for the time that rascal
has caused us to lose," he said.   "Here is the theme.
Write it out on the blackboard, Angst."

The head of the class held the paper close to his
short-sighted eyes and slowly began to write. All
the boys watched the piece of chalk forming the letters
with close attention, for much hung on what they
might prove to be.   If it should be a scene that they
had not prepared, it would be a case of "no luck this
time." From sheer superstition, before the words
were written, they kept repeating:

"I know—I know——"

At last the theme was written:

> *Joan :* You offered up three prayers, my lord
> Dauphin.
> Listen, and I will tell you what they were!
> *Theme :* The Dauphin's Third Prayer.

When the boys read this they all looked at one
another, for not one of them knew what to say.
Old Mud had had it in for them this time! He
leaned back in the arm-chair behind the desk with a
sly chuckle and began turning the leaves of his notebook.

"Well?" said he, without looking round, as if
everything must be clear and understandable.
"Well, any questions to ask? No? Get on with
it, then!"

Most of them bent over their exercise-books and

pretended to be writing, but some stared blankly before them.

"You've still got an hour and a quarter," said Old Mud, and his voice was carefully indifferent, although he was rejoicing inwardly. They wouldn't have been able to find that theme in their conscienceless cribs, which analyse every well-known scene for the benefit of the lazy lout.

Most of the boys remembered the tenth scene of the first act, and could rattle off Charles's two first prayers, but they could recall nothing about the third. It was as if they had not read it, and indeed the head boy and two or three others, among them Lohmann, felt certain that they had not. The Dauphin only allowed the Maid to repeat two of his nightly prayers; that had sufficed to convince him that Joan was an ambassador from God. The third prayer, worse luck, was not given; it must be somewhere else in the play unless they were supposed to deduce it from the context. Or was it fulfilled then and there, without anything being said? That this might have been the case and he had never noticed it gave the head boy, Angst, cold feet. He really must find something to say about this third prayer; oh, yes—and about a fourth and fifth too, if Old Mud insisted on it. Hang it all, there were so many themes about which it was easy to say the right thing—such as Duty—Our Loyalty to the Old School—the Call to Arms—every boy knew what he was expected to say about them, for they'd been in use for years. This blessed theme gave one nothing to go on. However, they all started writing. The result of their efforts might be appalling, but at any rate they wrote *currente calamo*.

They had been studying Schiller's *Maid of Orleans* since Easter and those who had stayed on in the form knew it by heart, and could have repeated it backwards. They had memorized scenes, studied notes, analysed it, paraphrased it, turned its verse into prose and then turned their own prose back into verse. For them all the lines, the brilliance and beauty of which had dazzled them at first reading, had become stale by repetition. However exquisite the lyre, the strings that are strummed daily lose their music. No one now responded to that pure Maid's voice, or thrilled when she raised her sacred sword; that armour had ceased to cover a human heart and angel's wings spread in vain around her head. The boy who once felt his breast yearn for that innocent Maid, rejoicing in the triumph of the Weak—weeping for the naïve spirit that, deserted from on High, became once more a helpless, bewildered girl—for him it was all lost now in mechanical drudgery and it would be at least twenty years before he could think of Joan again except as a dry-as-dust pedant.

The pens scratched on the paper, and Dr. Mud, having nothing else to do, peered at the bent heads. He felt it was a lucky day for him, to have caught one of the young scamps, especially in the very act of yelling out that filthy nickname. It cast a bright light over the whole year. He had not caught one

of them in the act for the last two years, and damned
bad years they had been. For a year was good or
bad to Old Mud according to whether he got his own
back on the boys or not. He knew that the boys
hated him, and that sometimes the hatred was a
family legacy, triumphing over even Loyalty to the
Old School. As he had passed the whole of his
life in school he could not view the boys and their
doings in true perspective. He was too near to
them, and yet was raised arbitrarily over their heads
to the tyrannical despotism of the rostrum. He spoke
and thought their language, using their slang, and
shaping his lectures into the style to which they were
accustomed—that is, into Latin periods interspersed
with phrases like: "And so on and so forth." "Yes, yes.
Quite so!" and certain well-worn clichés. Legacies,
many of them, of his own days in the Sixth Form—
when Homer and the affairs of the Greeks had to be
set down in correct and formal translation. Because
he himself had suffered from cramped limbs in these
hours of study he exacted the same from the present
scholars. The inherent urge of young limbs and
young brains to be up and doing—to hunt and make
a noise, to make rude jokes and hurt something, to
knock one another about and let off steam, releasing
some of that superabundant energy which was rebel-
ling against inertia—Old Mud had forgotten these
things, if he had ever understood them. When he
punished it was not with the implied admission:
"I've been a boy too, and boys are scamps, but
justice must be done." He punished in earnest, with

clenched teeth. The events of the school life seemed
to Old Mud as serious as anything in later years, laziness was to him equivalent to the worthlessness of a
ne'er-do-well and disrespectful laughing at a master
was a revolt against authority and law, while a boy
letting off a squib was an act of revolution, and an
attempt to cheat meant a ruined future. Such
things were life to Old Mud; when he sent any boy
out of the room, he was as proud of it as a detective
might be who sends a batch of criminals to gaol,
but he felt both triumph and grief, as if he knew he
had brought his highest powers to bear upon the
matter and yet—as if he felt a secret dread that something was gnawing at the roots of his being. And
those whom he sent out of the room and indeed all
who incurred his anger never forgot it. As he had
been at the school for a quarter of a century, the whole
town was full of his former scholars—boys whom he
had caught or had not caught yelling his nickname—
and all still called him by it! The schoolgrounds did
not end for him at the encircling walls; they extended
to the houses round about and included all classes of
inhabitants. Everywhere he saw unruly, depraved
boys, who hadn't done their preps and who were rude
to their teachers. Even a new boy, harmless in
himself, would have relatives who had laughed
at home at Old Mud as at a great joke of
their schoolboy days, and such a boy, if he had succeeded in getting into the doctor's form at the
Easter term, might be told, at the first wrong answer
he gave:

"I've had three of your family here before and I hate the whole lot of you!"

Old Mud was enjoying his fancied security from his rostrum, raised above those bent, industrious heads, but if he had only known it, there was more trouble to come. Its instrument was Lohmann.

Lohmann had quickly finished his essay and then had betaken himself to some private business of his own, but he did not wish to attract attention, for he had been warned by the fate of his friend von Ertzum. He had assigned to himself the rôle of menfor to the young aristocrat, and looked on his friend's backslidings as a slur on his own diligence. Whenever von Ertzum was about to make a stupid blunder Lohmann would whisper the correct answer to him and to the others he excused the amazing doings of von Ertzum as having been purposely ordained to "make Old Mud see red." Lohmann had black hair that fell over his forehead in a thick lock; he was as pale as Lucifer and a talented mimic. He wrote poems in the vein of Heine and was in love with a woman of thirty. He was giving only half his time to his schoolwork because he had joined a literary society. His teachers had begun to realize that he never started work until the term was nearly over and in spite of his satisfactory efforts at the end, they had twice insisted on his forfeiting his move to a higher form. This was why Lohmann and his friend, though both seventeen, were still with the boys of fourteen and fifteen, and if von Ertzum.

thanks to his hefty physical development, looked twenty Lohmann also seemed more than his age because of his obvious mental powers.

What impression could the wooden image in the rostrum make on Lohmann—suffering as he was from an obvious obsession? When Old Mud called him forward, he moved without haste from the bench, and wrinkling that broad brow of his in an unfriendly frown, he gazed from contemptuous eyes, through half-shut lids, at the embittered cross-examiner, at the dust on the schoolmaster's coat and the creases in his garments. Then he cast a glance at his own well-kept finger-nails. Old Mud hated Lohmann even more than the others, chiefly because of his insubordination, and almost as much because Lohmann did *not* use his nickname, for he felt vaguely that he thought of him by an even worse one. Lohmann met the old man's hate with quiet contempt, and even a spice of pity was apparent in his disgust. But he regarded himself as involved in the punishment of von Ertzum, and was the only one among the thirty boys in the class to feel that Old Mud's public reference to von Ertzum's uncle was dastardly. One could not allow the old tyrant up there to go too far. Lohmann therefore made up his mind; he rose, put his hands on the edge of the table, looked the professor in the eyes as if he were about to say something important, and then quietly remarked:

"I can't go on working in this room, Professor. There is such a smell of mud."

Old Mud jumped up, swore, stretched out a hand

and closed his jaws with a snap. He was not prepared
for this—and after he had punished one fellow for it
already! Was he to catch Lohmann at it, too?
He would have liked nothing better—but could he
do it? At that very moment, little Kieselack held
up his hand, blue with cold and with the nails bitten
right down, doubled it into a fist, rapped on the desk
and piped out:

"Lohmann won't give a fellow a chance to think.
He keeps grumbling about the smell of mud here!"

There was a sound of smothered giggling and
shuffling of feet, and Old Mud, catching the wind of
revolt, was seized with panic. He rose, bent this
way and that as if casting hypnotic glances at number-
less rebels, and shouted:

"Out of the room, do you hear? All of you!"

He would not take it calmly, for he believed that
he could only avert catastrophe with the strong hand.
Before anyone could interfere, he pounced on
Lohmann, seized his arm, shook it and cried:

"Get out of the room! You aren't fit to be in the
company of decent people!"

Lohmann followed him, distressed at the whole
affair. Old Mud pushed him up against the door of
the dressing-room with some violence, but failed to
make him lose his footing. Lohmann dusted himself carefully and then turned and walked quietly
into the dressing-room. The teacher then turned to
Kieselack, but while his back had been turned this
bright boy had managed to slip past and was already
hastening to the place of detention with an impudent

grimace. It fell to the lot of the head boy to tell
Old Mud where Kieselack had gone. Old Mud then
demanded that the class should not lose another
moment of the Maid through this regrettable inter-
lude.

"Why aren't you writing? You've still a quarter
of an hour. And I will not correct the unfinished
essays. You know my rule!"

As a consequence of this threat, most of them did
nothing, and faces took on an anxious expression. Old
Mud was too angry to take his usual pleasure in this
sight; he felt the need to break down every possible
insubordination and render vain any reprisals—to
bring about an even greater silence—the deep and
reverent silence of a cathedral. The three rebels had
been removed, but their exercise-books, lying open
on the desk, seemed to give forth the very spirit of
rebellion. He snatched them up and took them with
him to the rostrum.

The essays of von Ertzum and Kieselack were
composed of laborious, awkward phrases which proved
goodwill at any rate. In the case of Lohmann, it
seemed strange that he had not divided his thesis
into headings—A, B, C, etc. He had only written
one page which Old Mud read with growing indignation. It ran as follows:

THE DAUPHIN'S THIRD PRAYER
(Maid of Orleans, Act I *Scene* 10)

Young Joan, more apt than her years and her
peasant upbringing would lead one to expect,

arrived at court by means of a species of jugglery.
She gave the Dauphin information as to the three
prayers that he had sent up to Heaven the night
before, and her clever thought-reading made a
deep impression on the great lords, who had little
learning. I said—the three prayers: but, as a matter
of fact, she only repeated two; the Dauphin, convinced, let her off the third, which was lucky, for
she would have found it difficult to think of a
third, since she had mentioned in the two first
everything that a man *can* pray for—i.e. if his
father has committed a sin that is still unshriven,
to take himself as the sacrifice instead of his people;
and if he must lose country and crown, at least to
grant him content, his friend and his beloved. He
had already renounced the most important of all—
kingly power. What else could he pray for? We
need not seek the solution; he himself did not know
it. Nor did Joan. Nor did Schiller. The poet
kept back nothing that he knew and practically
said "And so on." That is the whole secret, and
there is nothing to be surprised at if one is to some
extent familiar with the superficial nature of the
artistic temperament.

That was all.
And Old Mud, who was almost trembling, realized
that to cast aside this scholar—to warn the others of
infection from a man of *this* quality—was a far
more serious thing than the expulsion of the simpleton
von Ertzum. He cast an eye over the following

pages, where there was some writing, the sheets
being half torn out. Suddenly, as he gathered its
meaning, something like a blush rose on the wrinkled
cheek of the teacher. Hastily and almost furtively
he closed the book, as if he wished he had not seen
that page. Then he opened it again, threw it down
with the two others and breathed heavily. He
thought to himself:

"I've caught the fellow. And it was high time!"

A fellow who could—who had—— An actress too!
Rosa? For the third time he picked up Lohmann's
exercise-book—— But the bell was already sounding.

"Time's up!" shouted Old Mud, afraid lest a pupil
who was not quite ready, might manage to finish in
that last moment. The head boy collected the note-
books, and some of the boys began to gather round
the door of the dressing-room. "Wait a moment!
Wait!" shouted Old Mud, in fresh excitement. He
would rather have kept that door closed and held
the three prisoners in close arrest until he had made
sure of their expulsion. But things could not be
hurried like that; one must be reasonable. Lohmann's
case seemed to him to betoken an excess of depravity.

Some of the smaller boys stationed themselves in
indignant complaint before the rostrum.

"We want our things, please, Professor."

Old Mud had to let the dressing-room door be
opened, and through the crowd came the three
culprits, already in their overcoats. Lohmann saw
at once that Old Mud had his book in his hands, and—
bored—foresaw the old fool's righteous indignation.

Now of course he would go and lay the whole matter before the Head!

Von Ertzum merely lifted his red-gold eyebrows— his friend Lohmann called them "garnished moons." Kieselack had made up his mind to apologize.

"It's not true that I said there was a smell of mud, sir. I only said *he* said there was a smell of mud!"

"Silence!" shouted Old Mud, shaking with rage. He twisted his neck this way and that, recovered his self-control, and added more quietly: "Your fates be on your own heads. Go!"

The three went off to get some food, each meditating on what that fate would be.

CHAPTER II

OLD MUD had his own meal and then lay down on the sofa; but, as usual, just as he had dropped off his housekeeper must needs make a racket. He rose and took up Lohmann's notebook again, and the colour mounted to his cheeks once more as he read through the shameful things he found in it. But he would not let himself put it down, so difficult was it to decipher, especially that page with the verses:

"Homage to the great artist, Rosa Fröhlich."

Some illegible lines followed that title—then a space—and then:

> "Her virtue truly is to seek,
> But she's an artist to the bone,
> And when she comes to me next week——"

The poet had still to find his rhyme, but that third line hinted many things, seeming to imply a personal interest and to put this into plain words was probably the intention of the missing fourth line. Old Mud beat his brains to imagine this missing line with as much stringent effort as his class had displayed in their effort to discover the Dauphin's third prayer. He felt as if Lohmann were laughing at him, and he wrestled with the problem with a growing passion, determined to show the rascal that he was the better man of the two. He wanted to send him out of the room again!

Still undefined, an outline of the coming artistic achievement began to form in his mind and he felt he could not stay quiet, but seized his old gown and went out. It was raining and very cold and he slunk along, his hands behind his back and his head sunk on his breast, a malicious smile curving the deep ruts by his lips. He came across a coal wagon and a couple of children, but met no one else. Outside the shop at the corner a poster of the coming programme at the theatre was hanging; the play advertised was *William Tell*. Seized with an idea, Old Mud stumbled up to it—no, there was no Rosa Fröhlich among the cast, but then—any woman in that vile place might be concerned. Of course Dröge, the shopkeeper in whose window the bill was hanging, knew all about such things. Old Mud had put his hand on the door-handle—then he started back, horrified, and hurried away. Was he to be asking questions about an actress in his own street? He must be careful not to let any gossip of that sort get round among these ignorant tradespeople. He would have to go to work with diplomacy in this matter of unmasking the depravity of that boy Lohmann. He turned up the alley on his way to the town itself.

If he could only find out—then Lohmann would certainly be expelled, and von Ertzum and Kieselack

with him. He did not want any tales to be carried
to the Head with his name mixed up in them until
he was ready. He must be prepared to prove that a
boy who could behave like that might be guilty of
anything. Old Mud knew that this was so, for he
had had experience with his own son. The boy's
mother was a widow who had provided him with
funds to enable him to pursue his studies when he
himself was a youngster, and whom he had married
in conformity with their agreement as soon as he
was in a position to do so. She had been a big, raw-
boned woman and was now dead. Her son was no
better-looking than herself and had only one eye.
Nevertheless, when he was still a student he had been
seen by the whole town with two women of doubtful
character. Then he had got through a lot of money
in bad company; and, moreover, had failed four times
in his exams, so that he had had to take a berth as
a mere clerk, a fairly useful public functionary, though,
in his way, but he only got the post because he had
struggled through his finals after all, and naturally
he was painfully behind those worthier scholars who
had passed the Civil Service exam. Old Mud had
firmly refused to have anything more to do with
him, and had foreseen it all; had he not once caught
his own son calling him by that hateful nickname
when speaking of him to other schoolfellows?

He felt that a similar evil fate awaited Kieselack,
von Ertzum and Lohmann, and especially Lohmann,
who had evidently already begun to take the down-
ward path, thanks to this actress woman, Rosa

Fröhlich. Thinking of his coming revenge on Lohmann, Old Mud began to hasten; those two other boys were nothing compared to this rascal, with his profligate ways, and that impertinent curiosity with which he watched one when one fell into righteous anger. What sort of scholar would he ever be? Old Mud was filled with fiery hatred of Lohmann. Suddenly halting before the gate of the town, he cried:

"He's the worst of them all!"

A schoolboy was a dirty, sly, despicable creature, always plotting some mischief against his teacher; Kieselack was that sort of boy. Or if not, he was a stupid lump of flesh, like von Ertzum, and that type the professor could soon plunge into trouble by reason of his superior brains. But Lohmann—why he didn't seem to believe his teacher! Old Mud began to rage at the humiliation of authority, so badly paid that a well-dressed cub of that sort, with money in his pockets, thought he could swagger and strut in front of his betters. Of course—it was clear —he was capable of any audacity. That Lohmann's clothes were never dusty and that he always had clean linen and looked so—so spick and span—it was shameful! That business this morning and the acquaintances these schoolboys made out of hours— of the type of this Rosa Fröhlich—it was shameful! And the most shameful thing of all was—that Lohmann never called him by his nickname!

Old Mud climbed the rest of the steep street, lined each side with old, gabled houses, reached the church round which the wind was raging and went on a little further, clutching his old gown about him. A side turning met the road here and Old Mud came to a standstill before one of the first houses down this street, for right and left of the door hung two wooden frames in which were inserted two programmes of *William Tell.* Old Mud read through first one programme and then the other and at last, with some anxiety, he went in at the door. A man was sitting behind a little wicket, a lamp beside him, but Old Mud was so excited that he could scarcely see. He had not been in at this door for some twenty years, and he felt like a king who has long been absent from his country; he might be misunderstood; they might be impertinently familiar and remind him that he was but a man after all. He stood in front of the little wicket and softly cleared his throat. Then as no notice was taken of him, he rapped with the tips of his crooked fingers. On this the man behind the wicket lifted his head and leaned forward over the counter, past the little shutter.

"Yes?" he said. "What do you want, please?"

Old Mud's lips moved, but no sound came from them. They stared at one another, he and the old actor, with his blueblack chin, and his flat nose on which the pince-nez sat so tightly. Then Old Mud managed to find words:

"So you're putting on *William Tell?* That's good."

"If you think we do it to amuse ourselves——" began the box-office attendant.

"I didn't say that exactly," replied Old Mud, worried at this suggestion.

"No one will come to see it; but it is one of the conditions of our contract here that we put on certain of the classics."

Old Mud thought it was time he made himself known.

"I am Old—er—Dr. Mut," he said. "I take the Fifth Form at the college here."

"Pleased to meet you. My name's Blumenberg."

"I should like to bring my boys to see one of the classics."

"Jolly nice of you, Professor. I am sure our manager'll be delighted to hear that. No doubt of it."

"But "— Old Mud raised his finger—"of course it must be the play that my scholars are studying; the one we're taking in class—Schiller's *Maid of Orleans*."

The old actor's mouth fell; he dropped his head and threw a reproachful glance over his glasses.

"Sorry—very sorry," he said. "We should have to put it into rehearsal, you see. Won't *William Tell* do? It's quite a good play for boys."

"No," said Old Mud decidedly. "That's no good to me at all. We must have the *Maid of Orleans*. And mind this——" He took a deep breath and could hear his heart beating. "It is important to know who is to play Joan of Arc. She must be a woman of some dignity, to help the boys to realize the holy nature of the Maid."

"Of course, of course," agreed the actor.

"I was thinking of one of your cast whom I have heard—I am sure with justice—very highly praised——"

"Who is that?"

"Miss Rosa Fröhlich."

"Who did you say?"

"Rosa Fröhlich."

Old Mud held his breath for the reply.

"Fröhlich? No one of that name here."

"Are you sure?" asked Old Mud, surprised.

"I beg your pardon, I'm not in my second childhood yet."

"Then you can't——"

Old Mud dared not look the man in the face but the other came to his help.

"Must be some mistake."

"Yes, yes," said Old Mud, childishly thankful for the suggestion. "I'm sorry——"

With a little nod he turned to go. The box-office attendant, surprised, called after him:

"But Professor, let's talk this over. How many tickets would you be taking? I say—Professor——"

Old Mud turned again with an anxious smile.

"Sorry—sorry——" he said, and fled.

He walked right down the street to the harbour without being conscious of the fact. Round him were men carrying loads, calling out to others up at the dormer windows. There was a smell of fish, ta , oil and alcohol. The masts and funnels on the water were already shrouded in twilight mist, and in the midst of the activity which still reigned in spite of the coming darkness, Old Mud went along, lost in thought. How was he to catch Lohmann? How discover where this Rosa Fröhlich was to be found?

Round him men were running about with bills of lading, and others kept bidding him "Take care!" The general hurry took possession of him too, and before he had time to think he had seized the handle of a door over which stood a Swedish or Danish sign. In the shop lay coils of rope, ship's biscuit and small, smelly kegs. A parrot cackled: "Putrid! Putrid!" Sailors were drinking in there, some of them talking, hands in pockets, to a big, red-bearded man. After a bit, the shopkeeper detached himself from the smoky background and came to the counter, where the light of the lamp shone full on his bald head. He leaned his fists on the counter.

"What can I do for you, sir?" he asked.

"I want a season ticket for the Summer Theatre," replied Old Mud.

"You want *what?*"

"A season ticket for the Summer Theatre. You have a notice in your window that you sell season tickets for the Summer Theatre."

"What say?" gaped the man. "You can't have a ticket for the summer season now. It's winter!"

"But you've got the announcement in your window, man," cried Old Mud, standing up for his rights.

"And there it can remain, mister!"

That was curt; but the shopkeeper recovered his

respectful attitude towards this gent in specs. He tried his hardest to think of some way by which he could convince this stranger that the summer season was over. To assist the strenuous task of thought, he kept hitting the counter with his red and hairy hand. Then at last he had an idea.

"Why, even the schoolboys know that the Summer Theatre isn't open through the winter!"

"I beg your pardon, sir——" began Old Mud, defending his position obstinately.

"Here, 'Enery—Larry!" called the man, feeling in need of help. The sailors drew closer. "I don't know wot's the matter with this old bloke, but 'e wants to go to the Paviliong."

The sailors rolled their plugs from one cheek to the other, staring at Old Mud as if he were some sort of curiosity—a Chinaman, or someone equally difficult to understand. Old Mud endured this, for it suited him to take advantage of this place.

"At least you can tell me, surely, whether there was an actress called Rosa Fröhlich playing with the company last season?"

"How do I know, mister?" The man was quite confounded. "You don't fink I mixes meself up with them circus folk, do yer?"

"Or perhaps you can tell me if the lady will be here in the coming season, to give us the pleasure of her remarkable talent?"

The marine storekeeper stared; he couldn't understand a word of this. One of the sailors answered for him:

"''E's barmy, that's wot 'e 'is," he cried; and, putting his head back, he burst into a roar of laughter; the others all joined in. The poor storekeeper could not make out whether this stranger was having a joke with him or not, but he saw that the respect his customers ought to feel for him was being jeopardized; these poor ignorant seamen, whom he hired out, selling them to the captains with barrels of biscuit and Geneva rum! So he promptly lost his temper, raging and striking the counter with his fists, stretching out a domineering finger.

"Get out of this, please. I've other things to do besides answering silly questions!"

And as Old Mud still did not budge, he moved as if he were about to come round from behind that counter, on which the professor made quickly for the door. "Putrid!" shrieked the parrot by way of farewell. The sailors roared with laughter as Old Mud slammed the door.

He turned sharply round the next corner and left the harbour for the quiet streets. He blamed himself for what had happened.

"It was a mistake. Yes—yes—it was a mistake!"

He would have to find this actress woman in some other way. He peered at the passers-by as if they must know something about her, but they were errand-boys, servant girls, lamp-lighters, and newspaper boys. He could not speak to people of that kind; he had tried that sort of thing already, and his recent experience had taught him to be careful of speaking to strangers. It would be wiser to look for

someone he knew. At the very next corner he ran
into someone at whom he had screamed Latin verse
in a raging temper only the year before. This former
student, who never did his prep properly seemed now
to be an apprentice to some business. He was coming
along with a number of letters in his hand and had
become quite a fop. Old Mud went up to him and
had already opened his mouth to speak, but waited
for the youngster to greet him first. The youth,
however, did nothing of the sort. He stared disdainfully at his former teacher and went his way,
thrusting him aside with a broad grin on his face.
He managed, too, to push against the professor's
deformed shoulder.

Old Mud vanished quickly down the alley from
which the youth had come; it was one of the streets
running down to the harbour, and as it was steeper
than the others, there were innumerable children at
play in it, rolling up and down the slope in little carts
with great wheels, which squeaked as they turned
round. Mothers and nursemaids stood about on the
pavement, calling out that it was time for supper;
but the young folk took no notice, kneeling in their
little carts, or lying with their legs in the air, their
neckcloths waving, their caps drawn right over their
ears and their little mouths wide open—shouting for
joy as they jolted over the rough stones. To get
across the street, Old Mud had to jump more than
once, or he would have been in the gutter. They
began to whistle and jeer, and from one of the carts a
voice suddenly sang out:

"Mud! Mud!"

He started as others took up the word. These children must have heard his nickname from the students; even those who did not know what it meant were screaming out the name. He had to go right down the steep street through the storm of shouts. He was trembling when at last he reached a quiet churchyard.

This sort of thing was only too familiar to him; former students who did not greet him but only grinned at him; and street children who yelled that hateful nickname after him. In his eagerness he had forgotten these things to-day, for now he wanted an answer of some sort from these people. They might not have known their Virgil in old days, but they could probably tell him something about Rosa Fröhlich, the actress woman.

He came out into the market-place and saw a tobacconist's shop kept by a man who had been a student of his twenty years ago. He sometimes made small purchases at this shop—only sometimes, for he smoked very little and seldom drank; he had none of the customary weaknesses. This man Meyer's accounts had always shown the same corrected mistake; Dr. Mu— and then the d turned into a t. Whether this was ill will or merely carelessness Old Mud had never determined; but he felt he had not the courage to cross the threshold of the shop, although he had already started to do so. Meyer was a boy whom he could never hope to "catch."

He went on his way in haste; it was no longer

raining, for the wind had driven the clouds away.
The street lamps shone red in the slight mist and the
moon hung faintly yellow over a gable; it looked down
on him contemptuously and then dropped a lid over
its eye, so that he should not spot its impertinence.
As he turned into a broader street, the lights of the
Central Café were blazing away gaily, and he felt an
unusual desire to go in and have a drink. To-day he
had deviated in a marked manner from his usual
habits, and in there surely he would hear something
of this actress woman; for in such a place she would
be sure to be talked about. He knew this from the
old days when his wife was alive, for he had passed
many a free hour in this very café. Well, not many
perhaps—rather seldom, as a matter of fact. Since
she had been dead he had as much quiet as he wished
at home and went to the café no longer. Moreover,
the place was closed to him since it had changed hands,
for the new proprietor was also a former student of his.
He had received his former teacher with the utmost
courtesy and served him himself so that Old Mud
could not possibly lay hands on the slightest proof
that he was always referred to as "Old Mud." The
guests in the place all showed signs of interest and he
had a feeling that if he went there more often he
would serve as an advertisement for the place.

He therefore turned away and sought for some other
place where he might put his question, but he could
not think of any. All the people he called to mind
seemed to be grinning at him, like that rascally
young apprentice. Those gaily-lit shops—the cafés

and tobacconists—would be full of rebellious students
—noisy rascals! His anger grew, and he began to
feel tired and thirsty. On the shops and houses that
bore names of former students he threw that green,
malicious glance from behind his spectacles—the
glance his scholars always termed "poisonous." They
all seemed to be throwing down a challenge to him.
Even this actress woman—Fröhlich—who must be
hidden in one or other of those houses, had been busy
with one of his scholars, and defying him! He came
upon the door-plate of Professor Hübbenett; he turned
his eyes away, for that man had actually called him
by his nickname before his own students and though
he had hastily corrected himself that did not mend
matters. Hübbenett had seen his son going about
with a woman of doubtful character and talked of it to
others. On every side enemies seemed thronged as
Old Mud passed along the streets, slipping past the
houses with a strange feeling of excitement, for at any
moment a pail of dirty water might be emptied over
his head and that hateful nickname sound in his ears,
called from an upper window. And as he could not
see who it was, he could not "catch" the rascal. It
seemed to him as if a class of some fifty thousand
mutinous scholars was shouting round him.

Almost unconsciously he took refuge in the quiet
street where the Home for Indigent Gentlewomen was
situated. It was quite dark in this place; a couple of
figures in shortish cloaks with a shawl over their heads
slipped passed him, returning home after an evening
service or meeting at a club, to ring a doorbell fur-

tively and disappear quickly within the opening door.
A bat flew round his mortar-board and he bethought
him and turned back to glance once again at the town.

"I haven't a friend!" he cried. "But I'll catch
them all yet!"

Even as he felt his impotence his hate raged the
more, tearing him to pieces; he hated all those
thousands of stupid, rebellious scholars, who were
always calling him by that disgusting name—always
kicking up disturbances; he associated them now with
that actress woman, Fröhlich; she and that rascal
Lohmann behaving together like common street-
walkers—holding together, all of them, against their
teacher. There they were, all sitting down to their
suppers and yet all ready to sneak round after him.
And yet here he was, wanting to speak to them—to
question them—and they cherished those evil
thoughts, all these long years!

He had been teaching for twenty-six years, and
there were always the same faces—just as mischievous and unruly. No one else seemed to
notice how the same faces persisted, and soon the
newcomers, too, would be quite indifferent to their
teacher. In the constant fight he had never managed
to do anything that would lead the elder men, even
if the nickname sprang to their lips, to keep it back
unspoken; to wish not to wound him, for the sake
of old remembrance, and to greet him with cheerful
faces. He was a figure of fun in that town, but for
many there might have been a sort of tenderness in
their amusement. He did not hear the talk between

two old students who met at a street corner and looked after him, as he believed of course with the usual contempt.

"What's up with Old Mud? He's growing old."

"He's dirtier than ever."

"I never knew him otherwise."

"Oh, that's not so. He was quite smart when he was an assistant teacher."

"Was he? A nickname's responsible for much, isn't it? I simply can't fancy that man looking clean."

"Do you know what I think? *He* can't fancy it either. Give a dog a bad name, you know—Mud sticks, doesn't it?"

CHAPTER III

OLD MUD went hastily along the streets again, for a thought had come to him, and he wanted to put it at once to the test. He had suddenly got the idea that Rosa Fröhlich must be the barefoot dancer of whom there had been so much talk of late. She was to give an exhibition of her dancing in the Town Hall for the members of the Æsthetic Club; he remembered clearly now how Professor Wittkopp, a member of the club, had spoken about it. He had gone to his cupboard in the schoolroom and taken out a bundle of newspaper cuttings.

"We're going to have Rosa Fröhlich here soon. You know, she does Greek dances—barefoot."

He remembered how Wittkopp had given himself airs of importance, glanced round, adjusting his pince-nez and pouting out his lips, as he spoke the name "Rosa Fröhlich." Yes, he had certainly said Rosa Fröhlich; Old Mud could still hear the four syllables pronounced in Wittkopp's pedantic manner. Why didn't he think of it before! No doubt she had arrived by now and Lohmann would be with her. Old Mud thought he would be able to "catch" them both! He reached the street where the hall stood and hurried half-way down it, when a roll of drums came thundering from a shop-window, and he stopped dead. He knew it came from the music shop, whose owner, Kellner, sold tickets for all the entertainments in the place and knew everything there was to be known about them. Old Mud began to think that he would get no information that day, and yet he could not bring himself to go home, and have his supper. He had been seized with a passion for the chase, and he decided to stay out still a little longer and make one more attempt.

In the next street he stopped, trembling, before some wooden steps which led to a small door over which was the sign: "Johannes Rindfleisch, shoemaker." There was no trade entrance; flowers were standing in the two small windows; and Old Mud bewailed his stupidity in not coming here before, for he knew that it was the home of an honest, harmless man, a God-fearing man who would not think of speaking any offensive word, or hurting anyone's feelings, and who would certainly know all there was to be known about Rosa Fröhlich.

He opened the door and a bell rang, its tone sounding friendly. The workshop in the half dark looked clean and inviting, and framed in the open door that led into the next room was to be seen the shoemaker's family having their evening meal, the journeyman sitting beside the daughter of the house. The mother was serving the children with sausage and mashed; and their father, having placed the brown jug of beer near the lamp, rose to see who had come in.

"Good evening, sir." He swallowed his mouthful of food in some haste. "What can I do for you, please?"

"Hullo," replied Old Mud, rubbing his hands together nervously, He swallowed, for his throat was dry.

"Please excuse the darkness, but we shut up at seven o'clock," interrupted the shoemaker. "The rest of the evening belongs to Our Lord. No blessing can rest on work done on the Sabbath."

"Yes, of course—I mean of course not," stammered Old Mud. The shoemaker was a head taller than he was, and had brawny shoulders and something of a corporation beneath his leather apron. His hair was going grey and was a trifle oily, arching above his long pale face. A wedge-shaped beard adorned his cheeks and he had a peculiar, slow smile. He kept linking his hands over his stomach, separating them and then linking them again.

"But I didn't come about work," explained Old Mud.

"Good evening, sir," cried the shoemaker's wife from the doorway. "Bring the gentleman in, John. You won't be offended if we ask you to have a bit of supper, will you, sir?"

"Certainly not, my good woman," replied Old Mud, resolved on a sacrifice. "I'm sorry to interrupt your meal, Mr. Rindfleisch, but I was just passing and it occurred to me that you—er—might measure me for a pair of boots."

"At your service, sir," replied the woman, but Rindfleisch thought for a moment, and then took up the lamp. "Now we shall all have to eat in the dark," remarked his wife cheerfully. "Come along in, sir; I'll put a light in the blue room for you."

She went into a room that struck very cold, and in Old Mud's honour lit the two wax candles of rosy hue, each with its little frill, that stood one on each side of the pier-glass, flanked by two large shelves. Along the blue walls the family mahogany was ranged in sabbatarian stiffness and on the crochet table-cover a Christ in biscuit china spread His arms upon the Cross. Old Mud waited until she had left the room and when the shoemaker had closed the door and stood face to face with him, he sat down.

"On with the good work, my friend. I am sure you won't mind making a pair of boots for me, will you now?"

"Oh, no, sir, no," stammered the shoemaker, as humble and zealous as a head boy.

"I have two pairs already, but in this wet weather no one can have too many of your good boots." Rindfleisch had knelt down and was taking a note of the measurements. "Moreover, this is the time of year when something fresh usually happens in this old town—some—er—refreshing novelty or other. It does one good——"

"Say that again, sir," cried the shoemaker, looking up. "It does do one good, doesn't it? That's what we say in our Christian Brotherhood."

"I was thinking of—er—visits to the town from— er—people of outstanding notoriety——"

"So was I, sir, and that's why our Christian Brotherhood have called a meeting for to-morrow evening. A prayer-meeting, you understand, to greet a famous missionary."

Old Mud found it rather difficult to mention Rosa Fröhlich after this. He tried to think of an opening but as nothing occurred to him, he took the plunge.

"The Æsthetic Society have a celebrity coming to visit them too. An artist. I presume you have heard about it, my friend?"

But Rindfleisch did not reply and Old Mud waited in suspense. He was convinced that the man at his feet had the information he wanted and the only difficulty was to extract it from him. The Fröhlich's name had been in the papers, and had been mentioned in his own classroom; it was hanging in Kellner's window. The whole town must know all about her—everyone but Old Mud himself, but then they all had more knowledge of the world than he had; he lived in his thoughts without realizing the fact and he turned in all confidence to a God-fearing shoemaker to give him news of the arrival of a dancer.

"She dances, you know. She's dancing for the Æsthetic Society. Everyone's flocking to see her."

"People will run to see anything, sir," nodded Rindfleisch gloomily.

"Yes, and just think—barefoot! She dances bare-foot. Isn't that amazing?"

"Barefoot?" repeated the shoemaker. "Oh, dear! So did the women of the Amalekites, when they danced before their gods." His smile was arid, expressing his sense of his unworthiness to thus make use of the words of the Holy Book. Old Mud began to fidget, as he did when a scholar was translating very badly, stumbling and stopping and seeming about to dry up altogether. He grasped the arms of his chair and rose.

"Never mind the measurements, my friend. Just tell me—has the little dancer arrived yet? Fröhlich, you know. You must know all about it."

"I, sir?" Rindfleisch stared. "I—know all about a dancer!"

"It wouldn't do you any harm," said Old Mud impatiently.

"Oh, I hope I am not blown out with self-righteousness and pride! Even my barefooted sisters, sir, I must cherish as sisters in the Lord—Oh, glory!— and pray that Our Blessed Jesus, in His own good time, will do for her even as He did with Mary Magdalene."

"Magdalene? What makes you think this Fröhlich woman is a Magdalene?" asked Old Mud sharply. The shoemaker looked down modestly at the stained and beeswaxed floor. "Oh, of course," Old Mud went on, more and more annoyed with the man. "If your wife or daughter had to get their living as an artist you wouldn't talk like that. But business and morals are two different things." He made an angry gesture as if to say that this antagonist was ignorant of the very beginnings of logic.

"My wife is a sinner too," said the shoemaker softly and he clasped his hands over his stomach and looked knowing. "Even I myself, Oh Lord, am a sinner in Thy sight! We all hunger after the sins of the flesh."

"You and your wife? But you are married,"
cried Old Mud, astonished.

"Oh, yes, of course! But it is a sin of the flesh
for all that, sir, and Our Lord does not permit—He
only sanctions it when——" He towered to his full
height and his eyes grew round and his cheeks
whitened.

"Well?" prompted Old Mud.

"Other men don't know it," whispered the other,
"but Our Lord only sanctions the act when He wants
more angels for His heavenly mansions."

"Oh, that's it, is it?" said Old Mud. "Yes, that's
a remarkable idea." He smiled slyly up into the
face of the God-fearing shoemaker. But he soon
tired of the joke and turned to go. He began to
think that Rindfleisch really knew nothing about
Rosa Fröhlich, but the man condescended to dismiss
the things of this world so far as to ask how long the
boots were to be in the leg. Old Mud answered
indifferently, took a hasty farewell of the family
and hurried out into the street again, bending his
steps towards home. He had a contempt for Rindfleisch; for his blue room, his narrow brain, his
humble soul, his hypocritical exaggerations and his
moral bigotry. It was dreary enough in his own
home, but he could always seek entertainment from
the Princes of the Mind, and had they returned to
earth could have conversed with them in their own
language and discussed their works even with the
old Grammarians. He was poor and unknown; and
no one knew of the serious work he had undertaken

these last twenty years. He went about among these people unwelcome, laughed at, but he belonged, by virtue of his learning, to the Immortals. Neither banker nor king was better qualified for power, or more interested in the maintenance of existence than Old Mud. He was zealous for all forms of authority and raged in the privacy of his study against the proletariat, who if they had achieved their end, might have seen to it that Old Mud himself had a little better pay. Young assistant teachers even shyer than he was, to whom he ventured to speak, he would warn against the wasting disease of the modern spirit, striking at the foundations of everything. He would have had them strong; one influential church, one steadfast sword, strict obedience and severe morals; yet he was an unbeliever and would venture on the boldest free thought when alone. But as a tyrant he knew how slaves should be treated; how the people, the enemy, the fifty thousand students who surrounded him should be coerced. This Fröhlich seemed to have relations with Lohmann, and Old Mud blushed at the thought, because he could do nothing to prevent it. But Lohmann's chief sin was that he broke through the teacher's harsh discipline by indulgence in these forbidden sins. Old Mud's anger was not due to a narrow code of ethics.

He reached his home and tiptoed to the kitchen, where his housekeeper, annoyed at his unpunctuality, was clattering her pots and pans. She gave him sausages and mashed to eat, overdone and left to get cold, but he was careful not to grumble, for she was standing over him with her hands on her hips, and he did not want to encourage her to turn against her master.

After supper he sat down at his writing table, which was unusually tall to suit his shortsighted eyes. It was the strain of reaching up to lay his right arm across this desk which had caused that shoulder to grow out of proportion.

"Friendship and literature are the only things that are real and true," said he to himself as usual. He was so accustomed to saying this that he did it mechanically when sitting down to work. What he really understood by friendship he never sought to discover; the word satisfied him. But literature! That was indeed important, and here was a work of which no one had heard but which had been pursued in silence now for many years and some day, perhaps, would come out into the light to astonish the world. The great book was concerned with the particles of Homer! But Lohmann's exercise-book lay to his hand, and he could not get it out of his thoughts. He had to take it up again and think of this woman Fröhlich. There was something about this affair that unsettled him; he was not even sure now that the barefoot dancer was called Rosa Fröhlich. It might be some other woman. Yes, it must be; he began to be convinced of that. But of course he must run her to earth if he was to "catch" that rascal Lohmann. Once again he threw himself back in his chair to go through the

struggle with that scamp all over again and he
gasped with agitation.

Suddenly he threw on his gown again and rushed
out of the house. The chain was already up on the
front door, but he took it softly down like a burglar.
His housekeeper was coughing and stamping about,
and in his anxiety he took the door-handle in a firm
grip and it turned. The door opened and he was
out in the street. He walked to the gates of the city,
now hurrying, now loitering; then he pulled himself
together to a certain extent, but his heart still continued to beat loudly; he felt so strange, as if about to
do something forbidden. Through the deserted
streets he went, up hill and down dale, always on
the move. He hung round the alleys, lingered before the hotels and looked up suspiciously at the windows if a gleam of light were to be seen through their
curtains. He walked always on the dark side of the
road; for the moon was clear and bright. The stars
were shining and it was no longer stormy; his steps
resounded on the pavements. At the town hall he
turned off to the market-place and made the round
of the leafy streets; the bridges, towers, streams
spread out in an arabesque before him in that moon-
light night. He was swayed by a puzzling agitation
and kept saying, over and over again:

"Yes, yes. Yes, yes. Quite so. Quite so!"

He scanned every window at the post office and
police-station, but as it did not seem likely that
Rosa Fröhlich could be in either building, he went
back again through the deserted streets. A few

steps farther and he saw the lighted windows of a
place where many of his colleagues would sit all
night, drinking beer. Against the blind he could
see the clear black silhouette of that fellow Hübbenett,
his mouth wide open. Old Mud had no respect for
him for he let down the discipline of the school with
his slackness, and yet he had sat in judgment over
Old Mud's son. Old Mud glared at him now; how
his beard wagged when he talked and what a beer-
swiller he was! A common boozer! Those fellows in
there had nothing in common with him—nothing
at all; luckily he was quite clear about that. They
hung together, which was right enough; he, however,
outlawed in a way as he was, could analyse himself. He no longer felt sore about those fellows
in there; he nodded to Hübbenett's silhouette
slowly and with some contempt, and then went his
way.

He was at the end of the town, so he turned and
walked back through the main street. There was
evidently a ball on at the consulate; the Breetpoots'
big house was all lit up, and carriages kept driving
up and away. The servants and hangers-on sprang
forward to open the doors and help out the guests;
silk frocks rustled across the pavement. One woman
stopped to offer her hand with a smile to a young
man who was coming along on foot, and Old Mud
recognized in this smart young fellow with the top
hat the assistant teacher, Richter. He had heard
it said that Richter was courting a rich wife, a woman
of a family that even a full-blown teacher might

have hesitated to lift his eyes to. Down in the darkness, Old Mud glowered.

"Pushing young fellow that!" he said.

He hugged his old gown closer about him and grimaced at the well-dressed, well-groomed young man like a mischievous sprite that looks from the shadows over the unconscious world, plotting to end it with the swiftness of a bomb. He felt himself in every way superior to Richter, and the thought made him laugh; but he stopped enjoying his grim joke and said, without himself understanding why:

"I'll punish you for it when I get the chance. Mark that!"

Starting off on his walk again, he behaved with the utmost propriety and when he passed a door-plate with the name of a colleague on it, or that of a former pupil, he would rub his hands and think:

"I'll catch that fellow yet!"

He smiled that secretive smile up at the old gabled houses, because he felt sure that Rosa Fröhlich the actress was to be found in one of them. She had caused him trouble enough bringing him out of his house like this. He felt that this night's agitation made a sort of bond between them. That schoolboy Lohmann was quite another thing—somewhat Byronic; a strain of Indian blood perhaps. When Old Mud escorted his class to the school breaking-up, he often had to take a hand in their games. He would stand on a hill, lift one hand to heaven and cry: "Stand firm, my

men!" and egg them on to do their best in the
skirmish that followed. But that skirmish was a
very real thing to him, for school and its games were
his life. And to-night he was playing the school's
game out here in the streets.

His eager excitement grew. The forms dimly dis-
cerned in the shadowy darkness awoke in him both
fear and expectation; each street corner had its
ghoulish fascination. He turned into each narrow
alley as the beginning of an adventure and a whisper
from a window would bring him to a halt with beating
heart. As he approached a door here and there
would softly open and once an arm clad in some
rosy silk was stretched out towards him. He fled,
quite overcome, and found himself down by the
harbour for the second time that day. He had not
been that way for years. The ships looked black
against the moonlit sky, floating there on the river-
bed. Old Mud got the idea that Rosa Fröhlich
might be on one of them, sleeping in a cabin, and
before the dawn the syren would sound and she would
sail away again to far distant lands. At this thought
the desire to do something—to take some action—
became uncontrollable. He heard the footsteps of
two workmen coming, the one from the right and the
other from the left. They met quite close to him
and one said to the other:

"How are things, Klaus?"

"Putrid," growled the other.

Old Mud began to wonder where he had heard the
word before to-day and how it came to be used in

that capacity, for he had not learned the intricacies
of argot in his twenty-six years of study. He
followed the two men and heard other choice phrases,
picking his way after them through various byways
until they halted in front of a rambling old house
with a huge porch, over which hung a lantern, lighting up the sign—that of The Blue Angel. He heard
music and the workmen vanished within, one of them
singing the refrain. Old Mud saw a brightly-coloured
poster just within the door and stopped to read it;
it announced the evening's entertainment. He had
got about half-way through the announcement when
something caused him to choke and a perspiration
broke out on his forehead. Fear and hope combined
made him begin to read from the beginning all over
again—and then, suddenly, he turned and rushed
into the house, as if plunging over an abyss.

CHAPTER IV

THE hall was unusually broad and long, the noble hall of a fine old house, in which small talk could be gracefully exchanged. From a half-opened door on the left came the glow of firelight and the rattle of pots and pans. Over the door to the right was the word Concert-Hall, and from it came a subdued murmur of sounds, among which one shrill voice often made itself heard. Old Mud hesitated before he pressed the bell for he felt that the action might have serious consequences. A fat, bald little man, carrying beer came towards him. He stopped him.

"Excuse me," he stammered, "but can I speak to Miss Fröhlich?"

"What you want to speak to her for?" asked the man. "She never speaks to nobody, she don't. She sings. Can't you wait a bit?"

"Are you the landlord of the Blue Angel? Ah, that's good. I'm Dr. Mut, from the college here, you know, and I've come here to look for one of my students. Can you tell me where he is?"

"You'd better get along to the artists' room, sir. That young fellow's always in there."

"I thought as much!" cried the professor, sternly. "You must admit, my good man, that it is not quite the thing——"

"It's all one to me who pays for the girl's supper,"

said the landlord with a lift of his brows. "That young fellow always brings his own wine, ours not bein' good enough for him. I have to put up with little things like that if I want to keep my customers."

Old Mud slipped a coin into his hand.

"Just go in and bring the young fellow out as quietly as possible, will you, please?"

"Go and do it yerself!"

But Old Mud's adventurous spirit had disappeared and he began to wish that he had not discovered the whereabouts of Rosa Fröhlich.

"Must I go through the concert-room?" he asked with some anxiety.

' It's that little room down there, with the red curtain in the window." He went a few steps towards the back of the hall with Old Mud, and pointed out a fair-sized window with red hangings. The professor tried to look in, while the landlord went back with his beer and opened the door of the concert-room. But Old Mud ran after him and begged with a note of real anxiety:

"Bring the boy out for me, please!"

"Which of them is it?" asked the host, turning in the doorway. "There's three of them in there. Old fool!" he growled and went his way, leaving Old Mud in the lurch.

"Three?" He wanted to ask questions, but he found himself in the concert-room, deafened by the noise and blinded by the white powder and dust which settled on his glasses. That other door must be the one he wanted.

"Someone at the door!" yelled a voice. He knocked, but without force, and heard laughing. "He's having a game at Blind Man's Buff," cried the same voice.

Old Mud took off his spectacles and found that the door of the concert-room was shut again. He saw that he was a prisoner and looked round hesitatingly.

"I say, Larry, that's the old josser who came and paid us a visit this afternoon. I wish the old store-keeper was here.

Old Mud didn't understand, but he felt the commotion in the audience was inimical. While the others there were all talking at once, he spied a table with an empty chair; he could sit down. He raised his hat and said:

"May I?"

He waited for an answer, but as none came he took his seat. He felt lost in the crowd and his feeling of painful conspicuousness died down. No one was paying any attention to him now, for the music had begun again and his neighbours were all singing the refrain. Old Mud wiped his glasses and tried to take stock of his whereabouts. Through the smoke of innumerable pipes, the steam of hot grog and warm human bodies, he counted numbers of heads, all apparently in the same state of besotted bliss, and here and there they were swaying to the music. All were sunburnt, both as regards skin and hair—yellow, brown, brick-red—and the swing of their multi-coloured heads to the music was like the swaying of a great bed of tulips in the wind. It swept through the room, to lose itself with the smoke in the hall outside. And then something appeared through the smoke— arm, shoulder or leg—a bit of white flesh in strong contrast to the murky smoke, shining in the light of a reflector, and then a mouth was opened wide. What she sang the piano did its best to drown and the voices of the guests completed the uproar. But the woman herself seemed to Old Mud a personified shriek, for a noise that no peal of thunder could have reduced to quiet came from that open mouth.

The landlord placed a glass before him and was going off again, but Old Mud seized his coat.

"Listen, my good man. Is that woman who is singing Miss Rosa Fröhlich?"

"'Course it is. Enjoy yourself now you are here, sir." He freed himself and disappeared.

Old Mud was hoping against hope that this could not be the woman—that Lohmann had never set foot in this place—that he might not have to interfere in an affair of this sort. He thought it likely that the poem in the youngster's book was pure imagination and had no foundation in fact—that the actress, Rosa Fröhlich, did not exist. He clung to this belief and wondered that it had not occurred to him before. He took a sip of the beer and his neighbour waved his glass towards him; he was an old fellow in a woollen shirt, his waistcoat unbuttoned over his paunch. Old Mud watched him from the corner of his eye as he sat drinking and stroking his beard with his horny hand; it was a streaky yellow colour. At last Old Mud ventured to speak:

"Is that Miss Fröhlich who is singing, sir?" But he could not make himself heard and had to wait until the song was ended, when he repeated his question.

"Fröhlich?" said his neighbour. "I'm sure I don't know the names of the little dears. They go on singing all night long here."

Old Mud was about to explain that the programme was given outside, but the piano began again, somewhat less loud than before, and he found himself able to understand what was being sung; a few words, as a cue for the girl to lift her frock and with a sly pretence of bashfulness cover her face with it.

"I'm such an innocent little thing!"

"Piffle," thought Old Mud; on a level with the idiotic answer his neighbour had just given him. He grew angry again, feeling himself imprisoned in this world which seemed the negation of himself, and a contempt rose from his innermost heart for these men who did not read, but went to a concert without even running through the programme. It irritated him to think that there must be over a hundred people gathered together here, who observed nothing, thought of nothing clearly, and spoke of intimate things openly and without shame. He took a pull at his glass.

"If they knew who I am," he thought and his cross-grained mood fell from him to be succeeded by a feeling of mild sentimentality. He was stirred by the atmosphere of warm humanity about him, and

the world seemed to beckon to him through the smoke
with unwonted charm. He passed his hand over his
forehead; surely that woman had told them she was
such an innocent little thing quite a number of
times by now! Oh, now she had finished and the
audience were clapping and shouting "Bravo." He
suddenly found himself clapping, too, and he looked
down at his hands with astonishment. He felt a
singular desire to stamp on the ground with his feet.
Luckily he had the strength of character to resist
that folly, but he was not annoyed with himself for
having felt like that; on the contrary, he smiled and
thought himself a bit of a dog.

"There's life in the old dog yet," was the way he
put it.

The singer then came down into the room. There
was a door near the platform which now opened and
Old Mud could see that someone inside the room was
looking at him. This person's face was turned towards him and now he stood up and laughed and then
Old Mud saw that—it was unbelievable—that it was
that schoolboy, Kieselack!

As soon as he was sure of this, Old Mud rose. He
had the feeling that he had forgotten himself for a
moment, and that his scholars would take advantage
of this. He pushed aside two soldiers and made his
way through the crowd, though some of the audience
resisted his passage and one workman knocked his
hat from his head. He sat down again, dishevelled,
amidst the shouts of those around him.

"Nice old party, ain't he?" yelled one man and

Kieselack laughed so much that his body rolled with
it. Old Mud made another effort, his jaws working,
but they seized and held him. He had knocked
over one man's drink and must pay for it. He did
this and then found that he could get along a few
steps further and raging, keeping his eyes fixed on
Kieselack, the thought of whose abandoned conduct
was inexpressibly painful to him, continued to make
his way towards the door. Kieselack was still
laughing when Old Mud pushed up against something soft, and a fat woman, whose evening cloak
had opened, showing her abominably-dressed figure,
threatened him angrily, while a man with exuberant
personality and oily hair, clad in a jersey and old
coat, joined in. Old Mud had knocked over the
woman's collecting-plate and coins were rolling about
everywhere. They all began hunting for them, Old
Mud with the rest, aimlessly, abstractedly. His
head, bent down to the carpet, got many a knock
from the people's feet, while complaints, offensive
jokes, curses, and fists assailed him from all sides.
He rose, his face flushed, with a small coin in his hand;
he was panting, and glared round at the inimical
faces. For the second time that day he felt the
breath of revolt in his face, and began pushing and
shoving his way as if fighting a mob of adversaries,
and as he did so, he saw Kieselack lying over the
piano, shaking with laughter. He even heard him
laughing now! He felt as a tyrant feels when in a
panic he sees the mob enter his palace and pull everything down, and for the moment any high-handed

act seemed justified. His rage broke all bounds and he shouted out, his voice ringing through the place: "Out of the room with you!"

Kieselack saw him coming and heard the words, vanishing through the door near the platform. He was inside before Old Mud had time to see what he was doing, but he caught a glimpse of the red curtains and an arm that reached up to it. He wanted to go in there too and took a bound forward, but even as he watched, Kieselack ran across the room and Old Mud saw a second figure vanishing with him. He had time to recognize it; it was Count von Ertzum. He reached up on tiptoe, but the window was too high; he then tried to climb up, and while he was using his elbows to lever himself up, he heard a shrill voice behind his back:

"Go it, young 'un! You're a fine fellow, aren't you?"

He dropped down again and turned, to find the gaily-dressed singer standing there.

He stared at her, his jaws working; then he brought out:

"Are you—er—Miss Fröhlich?"

"That's right," said she.

"You—you perform in a place like this?" He knew it, but he wanted to hear it from herself.

"Full of original remarks, aren't you?" she replied.

"But then——" he paused for breath, throwing a glance towards the window, through which Kieselack and von Ertzum had vanished. "But surely—you—ought you to do it?"

"Do what?" asked she, surprised.

"Those schoolboys," he said and added, in his deepest tones: "They're just—boys, you know."

"Can't help that, can I?" laughed she, but he interrupted, horrified:

"You make them forget their duties! You lead them astray!"

"I do?" said she, and touched herself on her breast. She had stopped laughing. "Isn't it a bit your own fault?"

"You're not trying to deny it?" demanded Old Mud, belligerently.

"Why should I? It isn't my business, thank God. I'm an artist, am I not? Have I got to ask your permission when people give me flowers and things?" She pointed to a corner, where two huge bunches of flowers stood one each side of the glass. "What business is it of yours, I say? What are you, anyway?"

"I? I am their teacher," replied Old Mud as if that settled the matter.

"There you are, then!" said she in more conciliatory tones. "What's it got to do with either of us what the boys get up to?"

But this view of life did not fit in with his ideas at all.

"I advise you to leave this town," he said. "Get out of it as fast as possible and take your company with you. If you don't——" His voice rose. "I'll do everything in my power to make things difficult for you—if not impossible. I'll put the police on your track."

At this, her face expressed the utmost contempt.

"You can do as you like about that; I'm not afraid of the old police. Oh, you make me tired!" But fatigue did not seem to soften her temper. "So I'm not to perform where you are, ain't I? Haven't you made a big enough fool of yourself already? Off with you to your friends at the police station! They'll shut you up all right. What a funny little man it is! I'm used to gentlemen! How would you like it if I told one of my soldier boys about you? Why, they'd wipe the floor with you!" And at this she looked almost sorry for him.

Old Mud kept trying to interrupt her, but the force of her personality seemed to imprison his thoughts, driving them down to some innermost place where even he himself could not distinguish them. He stared at her; this was no naughty schoolboy, disobedient and meet for punishment, as were to him the inhabitants of the little town. No, this was something new. He managed to collect the gist of what she had been saying and weighed it in his mind; he found it confusing. She was a new experience and she seemed utterly indifferent to him. He did not know how to answer her and something began to stir in him—a certain respect for her.

"So that's that," said she and turned her back on him. The piano was again sounding and the door opening, the fat woman with whom Old Mud had collided entered the room, followed by her husband. She sank into a chair, throwing back her evening cloak angrily and slamming the collecting plate down on the table.

"Not a silver bit among them," said the man. "Miserly swine!"

"This gentleman is going to set the police on us," said the Fröhlich bitterly. Horrified at this exaggeration, Old Mud began to stammer, while the fat woman turned round in her chair and looked him up and down. He found her contemptuous glance unbearable and flushing he dropped his eyes which fell on her fleshy calf, embarrassing him still further. Meanwhile her husband was stating his views in no measured tones:

"One of those swine, is he? I told you, Rosie, long ago, that I wouldn't have any of that sort about here. Jealous, I suppose! Just because they're younger'n what he is, eh? I expect he's known to the police all right, all right!"

His wife interrupted him, for she had formed quite a different idea of Old Mud.

"Shut up," she said. "You don't know what you're talking about." Then she spoke to Old Mud herself: "Blowin' off a bit of gas, ain't you, dearie? Ah, I know what it is! Kiepert here makes life a perfect hell when he gets it into his head I'm taking up with some other man. Now sit down and let's have a drink." She cleared a chair of the clothes and stockings that were lying on it, took a bottle from the table and poured him out a glass. He drank to avoid further discussion.

"Known Rosie long, dearie?" she asked. "I don't think I've seen you about before, have I?" He tried to reply but the piano drowned his words.

"He's those boys' teacher," explained Rosa.

"You know—they're hanging about after me all day long."

"Teacher, is he?" said the fat woman's husband; he emptied his glass, snapped his fingers and became good-natured again. "I say, you and I ought to get on. A Social Democrat, I suppose? If we get in, you know, we mean to see to it that you chaps get better pay. If we don't—you'll have to wait till Doomsday. Its the same with all us artists. Always got the police on our heels and never a ha'penny to call our own. Science"—(he pointed to Old Mud) "and Art"—he pointed to himself—"well, what I mean is—we're all in the same boat, aren't we?"

"That may be so or not," said Old Mud, "but you're wrong about one thing, my man. I'm not a board-school teacher, but a professor at the college—Dr. Mut——"

"Oh—oh, well, here's how," said the man and drank. After all, if the chap liked to call himself a doctor, that was his business.

"A professor, are you?" said his wife in quite a friendly tone. "That's fine, ain't it? How old are you, sonnie-boy?"

"Fifty-seven," replied Old Mud obediently.

"My, haven't you made yourself in a mess! Give me your hat now and let me get some of that dust off it."

She took his mortar-board from his knee, brushed it, straightened the brim and stuck it back on his head. Then, admiring her handiwork, she laid her hand on his shoulder.

"Thank you," said he, smiling shyly. "Thanks—er—very much." But he experienced something more than the usual tame gratitude for a slight favour. He felt that he was among people, who in spite of the fact that he had told them his name, knew nothing about him, and were receiving him with sincere friendliness. He did not mind their lack of respect; he excused it because they had no intention of offending. He was enjoying this respite, even if a short one, from the accustomed malice of his world.

The fat man produced from his trousers pocket a couple of flags and winked at Old Mud as if they had a secret understanding. The fat woman had lost all her fear of him and Old Mud had to keep telling himself that the softness of her glances in his direction were due to make-up. Only the Fröhlich still held off; she was standing a little distance away, busy with her own affairs, sewing on to a coat that she had picked up a bunch of artificial flowers.

The piano stopped with a bang· a bell rang and the big man said:

"Our call, Gussie." Then he added to Old Mud, genially; "we have to work, you see, dear boy." He threw off his coat and his wife took off her evening cloak. She shook her finger at Old Mud.

"Now don't you get too fresh with Rosie, dearie."

The door was left half open and he saw with surprise the fat couple break into a lively dance, with outstretched arms and a smile on their lips that simply invited the audience to join in. Directly they appeared a burst of clapping greeted them.

The door closed again and Old Mud found himself alone with Rosa. He felt embarrassed and his eyes glanced round the room. Dirty handkerchiefs lay about on the floor and on the toilet-table among the flowers, near which he was sitting. The table had various glasses and pots on it, besides the two bottles of wine, and smelt of grease-paint. The wine-glasses were standing on some sheets of music; Old Mud removed his from the close neighbourhood of a pair of corsets which the fat woman had put down there.

The Fröhlich had put her foot on one of the chairs with its romantic burden of underwear and continued her sewing. He did not dare to look at her, but he could see her in the glass which she was facing. He then noticed that her long black stockings had blue embroidery on them. For a time he dared look no further, but then he made the agitating discovery that the black net over blue silk frock she wore did not quite come up to her armpit, and that each time she drew out the needle and thread a glimpse of some light-coloured under-garment was visible there. After this he did not look again.

He found the silence oppressive; it was quieter in the other room than it had been. There were short, muffled noises, as of fat people hard at work in the most cheerful mood. Then there came a complete silence and after that the noise of something metallic being bent; something difficult to define, like the breathing of a crowd. Then, suddenly, the word "Go!" followed by two heavy plops, one after the

other. And as the applause broke out, he heard
exclamations: "My Gawd!" "See that now!"
"That's done," said the Fröhlich and took her foot
from the chair. She was ready. "Well? Haven't
you anything to say?"

Old Mud would have liked to turn and look at
her, but her cheerfulness made him feel nervous.
Her hair was reddish with almost a lilac sheen in
parts, and she wore a sort of tiara of green paste.
Her brows looked very black above her blue eyes;
the eyes were intelligent. But her make-up had
suffered from the dust of the place and her hair was
somewhat untidy; it was as if she had left something
of her brilliance behind her in the noisy concert-
room. The blue bow at her neck was limp, the
flowers in her frock nodded limp heads. The blacking
was coming off her shoes, two dirty marks disfigured
her stockings and the silk frock, all too short, hung in
creases. On the soft, rounded flesh of her arms and
shoulders the white make-up was peeling off with
every hasty movement, and her face he knew to be
haughty and disdainful, but this suited her personality, and she seemed to throw off her moods and
forget them. She laughed at everything, including
herself.

"You were so chatty to start with," she teased,
but Old Mud was listening to something else. All of
a sudden he sprang up like a cat. She fell back with
a little cry, but he pulled back the red curtain.
The face he had seen at the window had already vanished, and he came back to his seat.

"A bit sudden, aren't you? Quite frightening," said she, but he did not trouble to excuse himself.

"You know a number of young men in this town?" he asked sharply.

"I have to be polite to people, you know," she replied, her hips swaying slightly.

"Of course. The schoolboys—students from the college—they behave themselves?"

"You don't think I have the whole of your silly school in here, do you? I don't keep a kindergarten!"

"No, of course not." Then, to assist her, he added, but in somewhat peremptory tones: "Most of them wear caps."

"Oh, I know the school cap. I do know some things, old dear."

"I've no doubt you do," he replied grimly.

"And what do you mean by that, pray?" she demanded.

"I meant—you must have had some experience of men——" Startled, he saw her lift her hand and hastened to add, apologetically:

"I mean—you must have some knowledge of human nature. Not everyone has that; it's rare. And sometimes bitter." In his desire not to lose her again now he had found her, he showed her something of himself that others never saw. "Yes, it's bitter to know people. But the way to obtain power is to make oneself useful—and to despise them."

"Yes," she agreed. for she understood. "It's an

art, isn't it, to make something out of life." She
drew a chair forward. "You've no idea what this
life's like; everyone who comes here thinks he's the
only pebble on the beach. If you don't give them
what they want they threaten you with the police!
Why, you yourself——" She was rubbing her finger-
tip round and round on her knee. "You were just
as bad as the others. So there you see!"

"I certainly greatly regret having hurt a lady's
feelings," said he and not insincerely. She was
speaking of things that he did not seem to follow
with his usual mental clarity; and then, as she leaned
forward, her knee touched his. Afraid she might be
displeasing him, she conjured up an expression of
quiet intelligence.

"But of course one must keep clear of muck of
that sort." Then, as he didn't reply, she asked:
"Wine pretty good? Your schoolboys brought that.
They've got a cheek, I will say that for them.
One of them made a quick enough get-away."
She filled his glass again. Flatteringly, she murmured: "It would be a joke, wouldn't it, if they
came back and found you'd drunk it all? I should
laugh!"

"No doubt," stammered Old Mud; and though he
took up the glass he felt humiliated to think he had
drunk Lohmann's wine. For of course it was
Lohmann who paid for it. He had been here, but had
left before the others, though he might still be near at
hand. Old Mud glanced again at the window; the
red curtain again seemed to be veiling a face, but

he knew, if he sprang up, it would be gone as before.

Of course it was Lohmann; he had no doubt of it. Lohmann, the worst of them all, irremediably antagonistic, who yet never used his nickname. His was the unseen spirit with which Old Mud had to contend.

The other two had no brains; and Old Mud felt that for neither of them would he have come to this place, where he met with such unaccustomed treatment, sitting in a room which reeked of cosmetics and cast off garments—this room in which Rosa Fröhlich was to be found. But for Lohmann's sake he must remain here, for if he went Lohmann would be back again, gazing into the eyes of this woman whose chair was so close to his own. At the thought that that was now impossible, Old Mud emptied his glass before he realized what he was doing. The wine warmed him.

The fat couple had finished another number with labouring breath, and now the piano broke into something martial and their voices shouted a patriotic song with convincing force and enthusiasm. "That's their exit number," said the Fröhlich. "You must listen to this."

She opened the door carefully so that neither she nor Old Mud should be visible to the audience and showed him how to look through the crack. He could see the two plump creatures, each with a flag spread gaily over a fat chest, standing on the steps of a horizontal bar. They leaned against the

posts in heroic attitude, and with victorious gestures
shouted their patriotic boast:

> For everywhere upon the seas
> A proud white mast is seen,
> The German flag salute receives,
> Of Ocean's kingdom queen.

The audience received this with intense enthusiasm,
clapping in time with the tune. After each verse
caution demanded that the applause should be somewhat subdued, but at the end of the song they shouted
themselves hoarse. From behind the door Rosa made
a wide gesture, embracing the whole concert-room.

"Now you see!" she said. "Any one of that audience could sing that old song better than our Gussie
does, or he'd think he could, anyway. Kiepert and
Gussie know that well enough; they know they're
only doing their best to turn an honest penny.
They've no voice and no reputation, but they spread
their silly old flags on their fat old tummies and kid
the audience that they're giving them something
special. You can see for yourself!"

Old Mud agreed with her and they nodded
to one another in their mutual disdain of human folly.

"What's up now?" she then said and before the
fat couple could begin their encore, she stuck her
head through the door.

"Hullo, hullo, hullo!" yelled the audience, and she
withdrew again.

"You heard?" she cried, gaily. "They've been
listening to me the whole evening, but no sooner do

I show myself when I'm not wanted than they begin
mooing like a lot of silly cows."

Old Mud thought of the noise that would always
arise in a classroom when something unexpected
happened.

"They are all alike," he decided.

"Well, now it's my turn again," she sighed. "Shut
the door!" He did so.

"We haven't finished our discussion. You must
admit the truth of that matter with regard to young
Lohmann. Denying it will only make matters worse
for him."

"You're not going to begin that all over again?
Well, I do think you might let up on him a
little."

"I am his teacher and he has deserved the utmost
punishment. It is your duty to see that no wrong-
doer escapes justice."

"My God, you don't want to make sausage-meat of
the poor boy, do you? What's his silly name? I
never can remember people's names. What does he
look like?"

"Somewhat sallow skin—a good forehead, which he
is always wrinkling into a frown—black hair. Fairly
tall—moves with a certain careless grace which
betrays the undisciplined nature of his character——"
He was drawing a picture with his hands as well as
his words; hate made him a subtle portrait painter.

"Well?" prompted Rosa, finger to mouth, but she
had recognized Lohmann long ago.

"He is well-dressed, and seems to imagine it is the

thing to put on an appearance of Byronic melancholy, despising wisdom in a kind of pride——"

"That's enough," she interrupted. "Sorry I can't help you in the matter."

"But my dear girl——"

"Sorry. Nothing doing." She screwed up her face.

"But I know he has been here. I've proof."

"Then you can manage the business yourself and don't need me."

"I have his notebook in my pocket; if I show you that, you will admit, I am sure, that you know him. Let me show you."

"Oh, if you like"

He felt in his pocket, flushed, drew back his hand empty, tried another pocket. At last he gave her Lohmann's verses to read and she seemed to spell them out, like a child with a primer. She lost her temper.

"Impudence!" she cried.

"'And when she comes to me next week'—

Who came to him this week, I'd like to know?" Then, thoughtfully, she added: "But he's not such a fool as I thought he was."

"So you do know him?" he pounced, but she caught him up quickly.

"Who says I do? Get that out of your head, old dear. I haven't said so."

He glowered at her and stamped his foot. This stubbornness robbed him of all self-control. Without realizing what he was doing, he too told a lie.

"I know, for I've seen him here."

"Then that's all right, isn't it?" she said. "In that case, I may as well get to know him better." She bent forward, tapped Old Mud under the chin, scratching the bare skin between his beard, and drew in her lips with a sucking sound. "You'll introduce him to me, won't you, old dear?" And then she had to laugh, for he was looking as if her two small fingers were strangling him. "Your students are rather nice boys, aren't they? But of course it's because they've such a duck of a teacher."

"Which of them is your favourite?" asked he, awaiting her answer with some suspense.

She released him and her face again assumed its expression of quiet intelligence.

"How do you know I've got a favourite? If you want to know I'd give the whole boiling of those youngsters for one sensible older man, someone who doesn't want merely to amuse himself, but with whom I could have a good, sound, heart to heart talk. Men never understand that," she sighed.

The fat old couple came back and even before she nad got back her breath Gussie was asking:

"Well, how did he behave?"

But the piano was already playing the introduction to the next turn.

"Oh, he's all right." The Fröhlich was putting on a gaily-coloured shawl. "Are you off home?" she asked. "Well, I don't blame you. This place is no paradise. But you must come again to-morrow,

Professor, or your schoolboys will be getting up to mischief, I promise you!" With this she departed. Old Mud was so confused at this abrupt ending to their talk that he could think of nothing to say. Kiepert was standing with the door open.

"You can slip out quietly this way, dear boy."

Old Mud followed him round the concert-room along a free gangway that had escaped his notice before, and when they reached the door the actor left him. Once again Old Mud saw through the mists of smoke a pair of arms, a glimpse of a white shoulder, a flash of a bright frock. Then he was outside, away from the noise. The landlord was again passing with beer and called out to him:

"'Night, Professor. Come and see us again soon!"

He stopped in the porch and tried to analyse his feelings. He felt the cold wind on his head and came to the conclusion that had it not been for the beer and wine at an unaccustomed hour the whole experience would have been difficult to account for. He took a step along the street and started. Three figures were leaning against the wall. He glanced at them from behind his glasses; they were Kieselack, von Ertzum and Lohmann. He turned hurriedly away and heard a snort of indignation behind him which could only come from von Ertzum's broad chest. Then Kieslack's shrill voice rang out:

"See that house that chap came out of? There's a snifty mess of mud in there."

Old Mud started and his teeth clenched with rage.

"I'll smash the lot of you! I'm going to bring

the whole matter before the Headmaster to-morrow morning."

No one replied. He turned again and went his way in a menacing silence. Then, slowly, Kieselack spoke again and to Old Mud each word was like a whiplash.

"So are we!"

CHAPTER V

LOHMANN, von Ertzum and Kieselack walked down the concert-room and when they came in front of the platform, Kieselack gave a shrill whistle.

"Out of the room with you!" he piped and they all three rushed into the artists' room. The fat woman was mending a garment of sorts.

"Hullo? Where have you been?" she asked. "Your teacher's been giving us the pleasure of his company."

"We don't associate with people of that kind," explained Lohmann.

"But he's quite a good old sort and as easy to turn round your little finger as a baby."

"Rather you than us!"

"Oh, I haven't been trying it, but someone else has——"

She didn't finish her sentence for Kieselack started tickling her on the sly.

"Now don't you do that, you naughty boy." She took her glasses from her nose. "If Kiepert caught you doing that he'd smash you into smithereens."

"Does he bite?" asked Kieselack and the fat woman nodded solemnly, like an old Nannie telling her nursling that the Black Man will have him.

Lohmann, hands in pockets, was lounging in a chair by the toilet-table.

"Kieselack, you chump," he said. "I think you went a bit too far with Old Mud. What did you want to stir him up for when he came out of this place? He's evidently human, like the rest of us, and you shouldn't have thrown that in his face. Now he'll kick up a devil of a dust."

"So can we!" piped Kieselack.

Von Ertzum was sitting with his elbows on the table. He growled out something and his red face below the bristling red hair on which the lamplight was shining was turned immovably to the door. Suddenly he thumped upon the table with his fist.

"If that swine shows his nose here again I'll break every bone in his body!"

"Righto!" piped Kieselack. "That'll stop him setting us any more of his beastly themes. Bally nonsense!"

"Imitation's the sincerest flattery," smiled Lohmann. "The kid's yours to command, Ertzum."

The applause broke out and the door of the dressing-room opened.

"My dear lady, these kids are prepared to do battle for you. Murder and sudden death!"

"Oh, shut your nonsense," replied she ungraciously. "I've been having a talk with your teacher about you; he hasn't much opinion of you either."

"What did the old beast want?"

"He means to make sausage-meat of you, what?"

"Miss Rosa," stammered Ertzum; he had looked the picture of humbleness since she had come into the

room and his eyes followed her with the wistful look
of a dog.

"Oh, it's nothing to do with you," she explained.
"It would have been far better if you'd all stayed in
the concert-room and behaved yourselves. There are
lots of curmudgeons who'd like to get me into trouble."

"Who are they?" shouted von Ertzum. "Who
are they?"

"Now, now," she calmed him. "You shut up or
I'll leave the town this very night. Will you kindly
place your palace at my disposal, Count?"

"You are unjust, my dear lady," said Lohmann.
"He went to see his relative, Consul Breetpoot,
about you to-day, but that respected official has no
sympathy with love's young dream and he isn't
giving a ha'penny away. Ertzum would lay everything he possesses at your lovely feet; his name, his
brilliant future, his purse. He's quite simple enough
for that, God knows. So don't be so unjust as to cast
disdain upon his passion, there's a dear. Be kind to
him!"

"What I want to know is, what I'm to do about it.
Your friend may'nt have your lip, but he's got a
position, hasn't he?"

"Loyalty to the Old School——" began Kieselack.

"Oh, I know your sort, my child." She went up to
Lohmann. "You behave as if the whole world
belonged to you here, but you have to sing small
enough back there, don't you?" Lohmann tried to
smile, but she went on: "What do you mean by
implying that I'd come to you next week? Neither

then nor any time, understand? You're the last person I'd choose. Understand? The very last."

"The last, eh? That means I'll have to wait a bit, doesn't it?" drawled Lohmann, and as she promptly turned her back on him he stretched out his long legs and gazed up at the ceiling. He continued to sit like that as if he had no further personal interest in the conversation but was merely a somewhat ironical spectator. It seemed as if he were indifferent, but really his pride was far more engaged—far, far more —than anyone would have imagined. He brought his sense of humour to his aid, making of it a coat of mail.

The piano was going again.

"Rosie, that's your favourite valse," cried the fat woman.

"Who'll come and dance?" asked Rosa. She began to sway from foot to foot and smiled at von Ertzum, but Kieselack pushed in front of the bigger boy. He seized her in true guttersnipe fashion, twirled her round and suddenly let go of her, so that she almost fell, on which he put out his tongue at her and gave her a sly pinch. She screamed.

"If you behave like that again," she whispered, annoyed, "I'll tell him and he'll skin you alive."

"You do," he whispered back, "and I'll tell him something."

They laughed like children. Von Ertzum stole a glance at them and the perspiration broke out on his forehead.

Meanwhile Lohmann had invited the fat woman to

dance; Rosa left Kieselack to watch, for Lohmann danced well, and the fat woman was quite light on her feet. When he was tired of it he bowed to her courteously and returned to his seat without looking at Rosa. She followed him.

"I don't mind your dancing with other people. It's about all you're good for."

He shrugged, frowned with his accustomed manner-ism and more than his accustomed indifference and rose. They valsed together—slowly, dreamily, and voluptuously.

"Had enough?" he asked her at length and she awoke from her trance.

"I'm thirsty," she said, breathlessly. "Count, give me a drink or I'll faint."

"He doesn't look any too firm himself," said Lohmann. "Look at his open mouth."

Von Ertzum was panting as if he had been dancing with the girl all the time. He tipped up a bottle which shook in his hand and from which only a few drops poured out. On this he looked at Rosa in surprise and she laughed.

"Your old teacher had a good old thirst," explained the fat woman. Ertzum understood and went crimson. He seized the bottle by the neck as if about to use it as a weapon.

"Now, now!" cried Rosa and after measuring him with her eyes, she added, calmly: "My handkerchief has fallen under the table. Pick it up, please."

Ertzum bent down under the table and tried to find it, but his knees were shaking; he groped about and the girl saw him put it between his teeth and use his hands to help himself to crawl out again. But he stopped and stayed under the tablecloth, his eyes closed, intoxicated by the smell of cosmetics with which the room was full. The girl of whom he was dreaming night and day was standing there before his closed eyes, quite out of his reach—and he believed in her and would give his life for her! Because she was poor and he could not make her his as yet, she must jeopardise her purity and have to do with filthy people like Old Mud. It was a ghastly state of things!

Wondering at her power, she took the handkerchief from him and said softly:

"Good dog, then!"

"Fabulous!" commented Lohmann, and Kieselack, biting his nails, cast a glance from one comrade to the other.

"Don't forget the watchword—Loyalty to the Old School, my boys!" He winked at Rosa, for he himself had pulled it off already.

"Half-past ten, Ertzum," said Lohmann. "Your old man will be toddling home from the beershop; you'll have to be off to byse."

Kieselack had been whispering with Rosa and when the other two looked round, they found that he had already gone. They took their way to the gate of the town.

"I may as well see you home," said Lohmann." My people are at the Consul's ball. How is it we weren't invited? All the idiots who attended the same dancing class as I did are there."

Ertzum shook his head angrily.

"There's no one there like her! I was staying with all the Ertzum women last summer and lots of Püggelkrooks, Ahlefeldts and Katzenellenbogens——"

"And other old tabbies."

"But do you think there was one who had what she has?"

"What's that?"

"You know; she's something else too—like women of quite a different type—oh, you know!"

Ertzum said: "Oh, you know" this time because he was ashamed to use the word "soul."

"That handkerchief, too," put in Lohmann. "No Püggelkrook has a handkerchief like that."

"It dawned on Ertzum slowly that he was being laughed at. He suppressed the instinct that had led him to talk about these sacred things so openly.

"You mustn't think I'm a fool," he said. "I mean to show her that her want of birth is nothing to me and that I mean it when I say class is nothing and——"

"She's your superior, my boy."

Ertzum was rather surprised at this interruption and began to stammer:

"You wait and see! That swine, Old Mud, won't leave her dressing-room a second time alive!"

"I'm afraid he'll make it just as unpleasant for us as we shall for him."

"Let him try!"

" Sly old dog, isn't he? "

The thought was worrying them both but they spoke of it no more. They went along the streets where the people thronged in summer-time. Ertzum, his spirits rising out under the stars, began to have quite brilliant flights of fancy, now that they'd got away from those dusty streets and houses that were so trying to a country lad. For a country lad he was and love had made him revert to it; he was ridiculous when he stood up at school, stuttering and giving wrong answers, helpless in spite of his great bull neck, because the high-shouldered pedant on the rostrum cast that poisonous eye of his upon him. He had to be meek and tame there and all his muscular strength, feeling outraged, yearned for sword and flail, to cut a way to the woman he loved and throw her over his shoulder—to seize a bull by its horns. His brain worked as a peasant's works, after something he could grasp with his hands—after solid ground beneath all this silly classic learning, which took his breath away. He wanted to come to grips with the naked earth, the black soil that clings to a hunter's feet, and with the wind which beats about the face of a galloping horseman. He wanted stirrup-cups and the belling of coupled hounds, the steam rising from an autumn wood and a sweating horse. Some three years ago a country wench whom he had rescued from a stalwart farm-hand had tumbled him into a hayrick by way of thanks, and that girl had led the way to his adoration of Rosa. She had awakened him to thoughts of heaven—a crowd of lusty sounds

and smells. She had stirred the soul within him—
the real Ego. Therefore he paid her the compliment
of believing in her soul; he adored her.

The schoolfellows approached the house of Pastor
Thelander. It had two balconies, one on each floor,
and pillars with knotty creepers twining round them.

"Your pastor's back home," said Lohmann,
pointing to a light on the first floor. As they approached the house, it went out. Ertzum cast a
despairing look at the window on the second floor,
which was that of his own room. The books and
clothes up there smelt of school. The thought
of that classroom followed him day and night.
Angrily he leaped at the vines and began to climb,
halting at the first floor balcony to look up at his
own window once more. "Shan't have to do it
much longer," he whispered; then he started climbing
again, pushed his own window open with his foot
and disappeared inside.

"Pleasant dreams!" said Lohmann whimsically
and turned to go, taking no trouble to muffle his
footsteps. Pastor Thelander, who had purposely
put out his light so that he should not see, was not
the man to make trouble about the little evening
amusements of a Count von Ertzum, for whose board
he received four thousand marks a year. And Lohmann had only a few steps more to take to be with
Dora.

Dora was giving her first ball and at that very
moment would be laughing that crinoline laugh of
hers behind her feather fan. Judge Knust might or

might not be laughing with her, for Lieutenant von Gierschke might be having his chance and it might be that the judge had already received his sentence. Lohmann twisted his neck in his collar and pressed his teeth against his underlip, listening. He was in love with Dora Breetpoot, who was thirty and a married woman. He had been in love with her for the last three years, since he attended a dancing class that she held at her house. She had pinned an Order on to his breast—oh, only because she wanted to please his people; he knew that well enough. Since then he had caught glimpses of her through doors, at big receptions given by his people, to which, however, he was not invited. He had seen her going about with her various lovers—oh, yes! That door might open any moment, and he was standing there, torn with the pain of it! If his secret were discovered he would end things. He had an old gun at home; he used it to shoot rats.

He had quite a fatherly affection for her young son, a Fourth Form boy, to whom he gave his own old themes to copy. He loved that kid! Once, when he had saved young Breetpoot from a thrashing he had seen knowing smiles on the faces of the elder boys. He felt the muzzle of that gun at his breast already. But no, no one really knew; and he could go on living and suffering—the wild longings, the bitterness, the shy, proud contempt for the rest of the world that came so naturally to this youth of seventeen—and the verses he wrote to her at night on the back of an old dance programme.

And this girl Rosa expected him to fall in love with her, did she? Why, he was riddled through with passion already—for another! But it was, somehow, not easy to think of it all ironically. He wrote verses on her, too, of course—that sort of thing was usual with poets. If she thought it meant anything— she might look as hurt as she pleased, he'd only laugh, and of course that made her mad with him. Well, he couldn't help it. He certainly had no intention whatever of begging the singer at the Blue Angel to grant him her favours. There must be plenty of sailors and clerks in that room who would be glad enough to be made happy for the sum of some three to ten marks.

After all, perhaps he did feel a little flattered; why lie about it? There were times when he would have liked to see that girl at his feet; when he wanted her, just to humble her, of course, and make her feel that her caresses were, after all, a bit of a bore. But it would besmirch his own love and in the person of this thing—this Rosa Fröhlich—he would feel he was humbling Dora Breetpoot. Well, why not? But then—he would long to sink at Dora's feet and sob out his heart to her!

These thoughts were making his heart beat as he stood in the street, looking up at the Consul's house, watching the silhouettes of the guests passing across the blinds—waiting for that one shadow that he knew so well!

CHAPTER VI

THE next morning Ertzum, Lohmann and Kieselack showed white faces when they met in the noisy classroom. They felt much as a criminal might who knows that a report of his crime has been handed to the authorities, though those about him are unconscious of his danger. Their suspense lasted for some minutes. Kieselack had been listening at the door of the Headmaster's study and had heard Old Mud talking to him. He was not swaggering this morning, but whispered his forebodings behind his hand to Ertzum. Lohmann would willingly have changed places that morning with one of the poor in spirit, whom he usually despised.

Old Mud came hastily into the classroom and breathlessly opened his Ovid. He heard their recitation, starting with the head boy, Angst. He then took the boys whose names began with B, then those with C, and so on, but at E, he took a leap to the M's, and Ertzum gave a sigh of relief. Kieselack and Lohmann also cherished a hope that K and L would be passed over. When it came to translating he asked those three no questions, which oppressed them although, as usual, they had done no "prep." It gave them a feeling that they had been put beyond the pale and were now outside decent society. What was the old dog plotting? In the interval the three stood about together, linked by their shameful secret.

The three next hours, passed with other teachers, were a continual series of alarms. A step in the passage or a creak of the stairs; the Head was coming! But he did not come. The Greek lesson with Old Mud passed as the Latin had done; Kieselack had recovered his defiant humour and kept lifting his hand, though he really did not know the answers demanded. Old Mud consistently ignored him; noticing which he persisted the more in trying to call his attention, both with uplifted hand and a snap of his fingers. Lohmann gave up waiting for things to happen and under cover of the desk opened his copy of Gods in Exile. Ertzum, as usual, feeling a very small boy in the atmosphere of school hours, made a perspiring effort to keep up with the lesson and as usual was left hopelessly behind.

When closing time came they were certain that the porter would tell them to go before the Head, with his usual hateful smile. But no—he took his cap off to the three boys, and when they got outside they looked at one another with a triumph that they dared not openly express. Kieselack was the first to give it rein.

"There! Didn't I tell you he wouldn't dare?"

But Lohmann had lost his temper because he had let himself feel afraid.

"If he thinks he can lead us by the nose——"

"It may come yet," put in Ertzum, and added furiously, "if it does I know what I shall do!"

"Oh, of course," replied Lohmann. "You'd give

Old Mud a good thrashing, wouldn't you? Then you'd take Rosie in your arms and leap into the river."

"Oh, no, I shouldn't," denied Ertzum, highly surprised.

"You've gone and got a bit rattled, you two," said Kieselack. On this they separated, Lohmann remarking:

"I've no further interest in the Blue Angel, but I'm not going to be scared away. I shall go along there at once."

That evening he and Ertzum reached the house at almost the same time and waited for Kieselack. They always let him be the first to enter the dressing-room and start the talk, and indeed without him nothing of this would have happened, for they depended on him, on his smart impertinence. He had no money and they had to pay for him, Kieselack carefully refraining from comment, but it was a secret joy to him to give Rosa presents of flowers, wine and so on out of their money.

He came along at last, not hurrying himself, and they went in together. They heard from the landlord that their teacher was in the dressing-room and gazed at one another in confusion. This was annoying!

When Old Mud had returned home the night before he had lit his lamp and settled down to his writing-desk. The fire was still alight and the clock ticked loudly. He turned over the pages of his MS.

"Friendship and literature are the only things that are real and true," he said.

He felt that he had escaped from that actress woman, and the frivolities that attracted that boy Lohmann were a matter of indifference to him.

But when he awoke the next morning, he decided that things would not be in order unless he "caught" that boy Lohmann. He bent his mind once more to a consideration of the particles of Homer, but friendship and literature no longer enchained him. They would fail to do so, he thought with a sigh, so long as Lohmann was allowed to go and see that actress woman as often as he pleased.

One way to stop this, the actress woman herself had suggested; she had said: "But you must come along to-morrow, or your boys will be getting up to mischief." He blushed somewhat to find how well he remembered her words, for with them came to his mind her voice, her teasing look, her gay and charming face and those two slim little fingers with which she had tickled him under the chin. He glanced shyly at the door and then bent over his work with simulated industry, like a schoolboy who is trying to hide some naughtiness.

It was those three rascals who had peeped through the red curtain; of course it was. And if he tried to lay the matter before the Headmaster, then, seeing themselves on the verge of ruin, they would at once disclose what they had seen. In the list of Lohmann's delinquencies the wine stood at the top—the wine for which he had paid and which Old Mud had drunk. Perspiration broke out on his forehead at the thought. Those rascals would pretend that it was not he who had caught them, but they who had caught him. The thought of waging an even fiercer war than usual against those detested schoolboys filled him with self-confidence; he felt sure he could make things difficult for them, if not demolish their future careers entirely. With this passionate resolution he took his way to the school.

It was obvious that he could not report the three malefactors. As regards Lohmann there was that matter of the exercise-book; he would put artful questions in class, before witnesses, questions that would expose him. He was thinking them out already. But as he left behind him the gates of the town and neared the college other thoughts came to him; he saw a menacing future before him. No doubt the three wretches would stir up the class to rebellion, tell them all about the Blue Angel. What sort of a reception would he get? Revolution seemed about to break out. Panic seized the threatened tyrant, and he thought with dread of the street corners he would have to pass after school was over. When he entered the classroom he was the aggressor no longer. He was holding his hand, thinking to save himself if he preserved silence about the events of the preceding evening; he would ignore the three rascals, conceal their crime. He forced himself to self-control. He knew nothing of the suspense that the three culprits were enduring and they, in their turn, never suspected his feelings.

When school was over his courage came back, as did theirs. Lohmann should not have it all his own

way! He must be kept away from that actress
woman; that was a point of honour with Old Mud and
he owed it to his self-respect to bring it about. But
how? "You must come again to-morrow," she had
said. And there was no other way: when he realized
that he was startled, but his consternation had a
certain charm. He was so excited that he could eat
no supper and left home in haste, in spite of the remon-
strances of his housekeeper, hoping to be the first on
the field of battle—that is, in the actress's dressing-
room. Lohmann should not sit there, drinking wine!
He would not have it. Further than this he did not
consider.

When he slipped quickly into the Blue Angel he
did not at first perceive the coloured poster on the
door and looked round for it in great confusion. Oh,
there it was! Her name had not been taken out of
the programme as for a moment he had feared it
might be. She was to sing and be gay and look at
him with her teasing, provocative glances. This
thought gave him so much pleasure that it taught
him one thing; he had not come merely to keep Lohmann from sitting beside her; he wanted to sit with
her himself.

But he soon forgot this discovery.

The concert-room was still empty, almost dark
and terrifyingly large; the innumerable chairs and
tables stood huddled together like a flock of sheep.
The landlord was sitting with two other men by the
stove, playing cards by the light of a small lamp.

Old Mud did not wish to be seen and hugged the shadowy wall like a bat. As he was about to disappear into the dressing-room the landlord called after him in a voice that echoed through the empty room:

"'Evening, Professor. Glad to see you again."

"I—er—I came—er—Miss Fröhlich—er——"

"Go right in and wait; it's just on seven. I'll bring you some beer."

"Thanks," replied Old Mud. "I'm not in the habit of drinking but—I'll give a bigger order by and by."

He shut the door and felt his way into the dark dressing-room.

When he had succeeded in getting a light, he pushed corsets and stockings off a chair, sat at the table, which looked just as it had done the night before, took his papers from his pocket and began the same proceeding that he had used in class that day. He started correcting the work of the boys whose names began with A, B, C, but skipped quickly from E to M. But then he bethought himself, went through the papers again and scrawled a bad report against Ertzum's name. Kieselack and Lohmann each had their due attention. The room was quiet and he felt safe there; he let the spirit of revenge distort his face.

After a bit he heard the first guests coming into the concert-room and began to get impatient. The fat woman entered, wearing a large black hat with enormous bows.

"You again, Professor?" said she. "Anyone would think you'd spent the night here."

"My dear lady, I am here on business," he told her. But she threatened him with an arch finger.

"Oh, I know the sort of business you've come on!" She laid aside her boa and jacket. "But you must let me make myself tidy."

He stammered out something and turned his head away. She donned a greyish dressing-gown and came to tap him on the shoulder.

"I tell you I'm not a bit surprised to see you here again, Professor. That's the sort of thing we're used to with Rosie. Everyone who knows her loves her; it goes without saying. And she's such a dear girl ——"

"Yes, yes. Yes, yes. Quite so. Quite so. But not—er—not—er——"

"But such a good heart. That's the main thing, ain't it? That's what I always say——" She laid her hand on her own heart, under the grubby wrapper, her bosom heaving and her double chins wagging with emotion. "Why, she'd cut off her little finger to do a pal a good turn, she would. You see, her father was a male nurse and, whether you believe me or not, Rosie's always got a soft corner in her heart for elderly men. And ain't they the most in need of it? I've known her from a little tot, I have, and there's not much I can't tell you about her."

She sat at the table, hemming in Old Mud between her portly person and the back of his chair, and seemed to take complete possession of him.

"The girls go to the training school when they're
not yet sixteen and learn to be actresses, and it's from
an elderly man that they learn how to behave. And
that's everything, as even the tale of Adam and Eve
will tell you. When she first found out what the life
was like she came to me and howled her eyes out;
but I told her she'd just got to put up with it. But
she'd taken such a fancy to her old man that she
wouldn't look at any other. She pointed him out to
me in the streets and a fine old chap he was. But not
a patch on you, Professor." She tapped his cheek and
continued her story. "Not a patch on you, he wasn't.
He died soon after and what do you think Rosie did?
Bought his photograph! And framed it, too. A man
that knows something of life and how to be good to a
girl—that's the sort that's worth while, I always say."

"Really, my good woman——" began Old Mud.
Embarrassment made his smile particularly "poisonous." "It is obvious that a young man must be more
attractive——"

"Don't you believe it," interrupted she. "To
our Rosa, young men are *mud*." She gave him a
friendly shake as if to drive the truth of that unluckily
worded remark home to him and then she rose from the
table. "Can't stay chattin' with you any longer.
Time to get to work!" She sat down at the toilet-
table and rubbed grease over her face. "Now just
you turn your head away, if you please."

Old Mud obeyed; he heard the strains of the piano
and the sound suggested that the room was as yet
but half filled.

"As for those school kids of yours," she went on, a hare's foot between her teeth, "they can come yappin' and beggin' round her as much as they please, but they won't get no change out of our Rosie."

Old Mud could not resist the temptation to glance at the window. Behind the red curtain there was certainly the silhouette of a head.

From the concert room came a long "Hullo-hullo-hullo." Rosa Fröhlich was standing in the doorway and behind her came the fat singer, Kiepert.

"Glad to see you here again, Professor," he cried.

"Why, there you are!" was Rosa's greeting.

"I expect you're surprised——" he began.

"Not a bit. Just help me off with my coat, will you please?"

"——At my coming again so soon——" he tried to continue.

"Why?" She had raised her hands to her large red hat and was taking out the hatpins, smiling roguishly at him from under the brim.

"You said yourself that I must come again——" He wanted to make this clear.

"Well, and here you are." She sent the hat up into the air like a catherine wheel. "Isn't he an old dear, Gussie? She bent this time until her face was close to his. He looked like a child that is frightened because the fairy in the pantomime suddenly loses her wig. Seeing this she dropped her gay mood and sighed, drooping her head. "But you mustn't think I really expected you to come, you know. I said to Gussie—didn't I, Gussie?—he's a professor and I'm

just a poor ignorant girl. How could I possibly
entertain a man like him? That's what I said, isn't
it, Gussie?" The fat woman solemnly confirmed this
statement. "But of course you've only come for the
same old reason." She shrugged.

Kiepert was making inarticulate noises in the corner
to which he had retired to get ready. His wife
signalled to him to be quiet.

"But who could think you came on my account?
You haven't even helped me out of my coat. Of
course you've only come to make sausage meat of
those boys of yours again."

Blushing, Old Mud tried to explain again.

"In the first place—yes, yes—quite so—I must
confess—— Undoubtedly——" She bowed a meek
head. The fat woman got up from the toilet-table to
help her, having put on her own low-cut red blouse.
She was made up already, with the brilliant colour of
the previous evening.

"Why don't you help the poor girl out of her coat,
then?" she asked. "Is that the way you behave
when a lady asks a service of you?"

He began to tug at one of her sleeves, but the coat
did not come off and Rosa fell into his arms, which
added to his confusion.

"This is the way," explained the fat woman, showing him. Her husband stepped forward in his jersey.
A great roll of fat showed round his hips and he had a
wart on his neck. He held a cutting from a paper
before Old Mud's eyes.

"You must read this, dear boy. It beats the

band." Old Mud recognized the social-democratic
programme as set forth by the local paper. "Didn't
I tell you last night that all you board-school teachers
was going to have a rise?"

"But I'm not a board-school teacher," began Old
Mud, when Gussie snatched the paper from her
husband's hand.

"What's he want with any rise?" she said. "He's
in a good enough position as he is, isn't he? Get
along out of this, you blundering old donkey."

From the concert room whistles, stamping and
other noises, sounded above the thunder of the
piano. Keipert stood listening and evincing his
pleasure to think he had told the professor last night
how it would be. He then danced out into the
concert room where he was received with a round of
applause.

"Now we've got rid of him just help me to get Rosie
ready, Professor," said the fat woman.

"He's too modest," laughed Rosie.

"He must learn," said Gussie. "He ought to know
how a woman does up her things. Who knows if he
mayn't need to know some day?"

"If you really don't mind——" said Rosie and
slipped out of her frock. He noticed with a shock
that her underwear was a shimmering black, and also
that she wore no petticoat, but just a pair of wide
black knickers But she seemed to think nothing of
it; he felt as if the mysteries were being revealed to
him, but she seemed unconscious. He felt a sort of
pride, not without its pain.

In the concert room Kiepert's first number had gone well and he was giving an encore.

"He'd better turn the other way now hadn't he?" said Rosa.

"Nonsense; he's not a baby," protested the fat woman. But Old Mud had already turned away, and listened with a curious excitement to the rustling of falling garments. The fat woman handed something to him to hold, in a sort of haste.

"Take that," she said. He took it without knowing what it was. It was black, went into a mere nothing, and felt warm, with a soft, animal-like warmth. Suddenly he let it slip through his fingers, for he realized why it was warm. It was the black camiknickers. He picked it up again and stood still. Gussie and Rosa were exchanging some technical remarks about the make-up and dressing, and whilst they were still busy Kiepert was again at the end of his song.

"I must go," said Gussie. "You can help her, can't you?" And as Old Mud didn't reply she added sharply: "Deaf, ain't you?"

He turned round feeling as if he had been caught napping, like his own scholars when the lesson was too long. Patiently he held the corset ribbons, while Rosa smiled at him over her shoulder.

"What did you turn your back all that time for? I've been presentable for quite a long time." She was wearing an orange-coloured slip. "I only told you to turn round on Gussie's account. I didn't mind. I'd rather like to know what you think of my figure." He did not reply and she gave her head an impatient shake. "Oh, don't be silly. My God! Give me those laces. You've a lot to learn, old dear!" She laced herself in and as he stood there with his helpless hands idle before him, she added: "Aren't you going to be nice to me to-night?"

"Oh, yes," he stammered and with an effort he managed to tell her that he thought she looked very nice in that black garment.

"Old donkey, aren't you?" laughed she. The corset was properly laced now and Gussie was taking an encore like Kiepert. "My turn next," said Rosa, "and I haven't made up my face yet."

She sat down before the looking-glass, and became busy with pots and phials and coloured grease-paints.

He merely saw that her slim arms were being continually lifted, and before his bewildered eyes a many-coloured picture of lines and dabs, both rose and faintly yellow, began to take form. Each was succeeded by some other shade even before it seemed duly laid on. He had to keep taking up undreamed of things and handing them to her, and in spite of her feverish haste she found time to stamp when he gave her the wrong thing, or to thank him with a glance when he did right. It was undeniable that her eyes became more and more alluring. He could not fail to perceive that this was due to the sticks of grease-paint that he kept handing to her and which she was applying to her eyes: those little dabs of red, for instance, in the corners, the lines on the eyebrows, and that black stuff she put on the lashes themselves.

"Now I must make my mouth look a little smaller," said she.

And now he saw her face as it was yesterday—that bright face! This was the actress woman again, sitting before him. He had seen her come into being; a few moments had shown him the whole secret of this beauty, charm and art. He was both disillusioned and initiated, thinking at one and the same time: "Is that all?" and, "But it's wonderful!" His heart beat fast—and she was rubbing the bits of colour from her hands with a cloth.

Now she had to adjust the tiara of last night in her hair. The concert room was in an uproar. She pushed the door open a little with her shoulder and looked out, saying with a frown:

"Pretty noise, isn't it?"

But he had heard nothing.

"Well, I'm giving them serious stuff to-night, so I must have a long skirt. Hand me that green thing."

He had to feel about right and left among the feminine garments, his coat-tails flying. At last he found "the green thing" and there she stood like a fairy princess, with no waistbelt, except a garland of roses round her hips. She looked at him but he said nothing; the expression of his face contented her, however. She moved with dignity towards the door and then turned, for she remembered that she had not whitened her back, at which he now gazed.

"Don't need to show them too much though, do

we?" she said, with boundless contempt for "them."
Then she swept to the door and went through. He
sprang back for fear he should be seen. The door,
however, remained open and he heard the comments.

"My gawd! Green silk, eh? Long enough, ain't
it?" and a gross laugh.

The piano began to sob, while the bass fairly howled
with grief. He heard her begin to sing:

"The moon is full and all the stars are shining.
Look, dear, your lover's sailing on the sea.
His eyes are wet. For you his heart is pining——"

The notes seemed to fall like pearls over black
velvet, from the grief-laden soul of the singer.

"Piffle!" thought Old Mud, but the pathos of it
enveloped him. He peered through the crack and in
the lamplight saw the green folds of the singer's gown
slowly swaying. Her head was slightly tilted and he
could see the tiara on her reddish hair and part of her
rosily tinted cheek under the black eyebrow.

"Ain't she fine?" said a voice from one of the tables
near the platform. It belonged to a broad-shouldered
countryman in a blue stuff jacket. "I shan't think
much of my old woman when I get back home!"
Old Mud threw him an angry glance.

"All very well, my man," he thought. That she
should have to sing to gross creatures of that sort!
The man did not know the meaning of the word
"fine," and seemed to think it a great joke to speak
as if he had ceased to care for his wife!

The verse ended on a dying fall:

" So sails my boat, love, to thy hearts repining.
My heart is wae—and all the stars are shining!"

And then another of the audience laughed coarsely.
Furiously Old Mud sought for the offender among the
clustered heads, but in vain. The singer began the
second verse—"The mo-on is full"—she prolonged
the vowel—"fool"—and when she came to the refrain five or six began to laugh, one man in the centre
of the hall clucking like a negro. Old Mud discovered
that man; he *was* a negro! The filthy black affected
his neighbours and other faces began to crease into
grins, until Old Mud felt that he would like to tear
them limb from limb. He fidgeted from one foot to
the other, wrung with pain.

For the third time the singer announced that "The
moon is fool——"

"We're the fools," said someone distinctly and
with conviction. Some of the more decent expos-
tulated at the uproar that succeeded, but the shouting laughter of the negro overpowered their efforts.
Old Mud could see row upon row of open mouths,
black caverns with a yellow fang or two, or with
half moons of white ivory, stretching from one ear
to the other. Goatee beards wagged on their chins,
or half-grown bristles stood up on their lips. Old
Mud recognized the apprentice, his old pupil, among
them, the one who had grinned in his face the night
before; he was stretching his jaws wider than ever
now, laughing at Rosa Fröhlich. And, his rage making

his head swim, Old Mud felt once again the anguish of
the impotent tyrant. She was enduring what he had
to endure! He suffered with her, followed each
incident from the wings and felt as if he himself were
being pilloried! They failed to value her as they failed
to appreciate him! He had to cling to the doorpost
to prevent himself rushing out upon them, and with
threats and blows bringing that great roomful of
naughty school-boys to order.

He had found six or seven of his former boys in the
crowd. The room was sown with these rascals from
past scholastic terms. Fat Kiepert and his even
fatter wife went about among the people, drinking,
making themselves universally agreeable. He despised them. They were guttersnipes. She stood far
above them, on that platform with her green silk
dress and the diadem in her hair. But they would
have none of her.

"Get off! Shut up!" they bawled. And he could
do nothing to prevent it. It was terrible! He could
send his scholars out of the room, set them tasks as
penalties, force them to obey, drill their minds and
if they dared to disagree with him, decree: "Thou shalt
not think for thyself!" But he could not compel
them to admire what he thought worthy of admiration. This was the last stand—the last stronghold
of their disobedience, and his despotic instincts raged
in vain. He could scarcely endure it. He wanted
air—felt faint—writhed with the urge to right this
wrong, and with his own crooked fingers stand the
image of beauty once more in her rightful place.

That she could still seem so cheerful and throw them kisses amidst all that booing and hissing! It was astounding. She was great under adversity. Now she was turning away from the audience and saying something to the pianist, and now her professional smile gave place to a look of bitter contempt, one picture replacing the other as if on the screen. It seemed to him that she was prolonging the talk with the pianist as much as possible, to keep her back turned to them, and the wet white on her shoulders now had its chance. Then she turned quickly round to them again, the old bright smile on her lips, smoothed her green silk frock, switched up the orange petticoat and broke into that quavering ditty: "I'm such an innocent little thing!"

Her good humour was appreciated and they clapped and encored. When she came back into the dressing-room, slamming the door behind her, she turned to him panting.

"What do you think of that now? Nice, wasn't it?"

The trouble was over and everyone good-natured again. But against the wall near the entrance doors Lohmann was leaning with crossed arms, his face pale, thinking that his verses—his in spite of the laughter of these common folk—would go winged through the night air to the window of a bedroom—and that no one would hear them.

Fat Gussie and her Kiepert came back into the dressing-room; Rosa drooped her head and looked injured.

"Don't you tell me again I'm to sing that young fool's piffle!" she said, and though Old Mud heard the words he did not take any notice of them.

"You know you can never tell what'll go with an audience, dearie," replied Gussie. "It was that black chap as started it. If only he'd taken it into his head to do a weep instead of laughin' like a stuffed hyena!"

"Oh, what does it matter what muck of that sort do?" sighed Rosa, wearily. "If the professor would stand us a drink! Won't you offer us a drink, old dear?" And as before, she tapped his chin with two slim fingers.

"A bottle of wine," ordered Old Mud.

"Thanks, old dear; but why only one?"

Old Mud was not a connoisseur of wine lists and he looked about for help like a schoolboy whose ideas have run dry. Kiepert and his wife watched him expectantly.

"It begins with S," put in Fröhlich gaily.

"Schateau?" suggested the professor and winced at the inaccuracy. "Sham——" prompted she. But he was not prompt on the cue. "Don't know much, does he?" she laughed to the others. But his face lit up with triumph.

"Champagne!" he cried.

"That's got it!" And the fat couple also congratulated him on his brightness. Kiepert went off to order the wine and the landlord himself brought along the pail with two bottles protruding from it. Kiepert blew out his cheeks with an enchanted, "Oh-o!" and gaiety descended on the party in the dressing-room. As each glass was poured out, Old Mud thought with pleasure that this was *his* wine, and that Lohmann had nothing to do with it. Rosa herself made a similar comment.

"Those boys of yours never thought of offering us champagne." Her eyes flashed angrily. "I've done with them!" And as he still continued to look serene, she sighed.

"Chin-chin, dear boy!" cried Kiepert, lifting his glass. "Good hunting!" He looked from Old Mud to Rosa with a suggestive smile.

"Don't talk nonsense," said she, sharply.

His wife had to change for the next number, for their song was to follow the acrobatic dance, as before.

"The professor don't mind seein' me in me chemise. He's quite like an old friend, ain't he?" She put three chairs together and hung some clothes over the backs, undressing behind them. The screen was sufficiently high but insufficiently broad for her over-flowing form. Every moment another bit of her would heave in sight and be received by the others with hoots of merriment. Rosa laughed with her arms on the table and Old Mud was so carried away by her gaiety that he kept stretching out his neck to try and see a bit more of Gussie. She kept up a series of little shrieks on which he would retire, to begin the same game all over again.

But now Rosa rose and said with dignity:

"He wouldn't treat me like that! I'd kill myself first!" And she burst out laughing again.

The audience was impatient and the piano was

unable to keep them quiet. The fat couple had to hurry on and Rosa was left alone with Old Mud once more. He was again seized with embarrassment, and had nothing to say. The others could be heard singing. "That damned song again!" said she. "Piffle!" She turned to him. "Haven't you eyes in your head to-night, old dear? Haven't you noticed anything different?"

"Different? Here?" stammered he. "What?" He looked round.

"Oh, you'll never see! Wasn't there something on that toilet table last night? Each side of the glass, eh?"

"Of course. Two bunches of flowers."

"You didn't even notice it, you ungrateful man! And I put them in the fire on your account."

She sniffed and he leaned towards the stove, delighted. She had burnt Lohmann's flowers! Then suddenly he moved impatiently, for the thought came to him to replace Lohmann's flowers with two other bunches which he himself would bring her. He looked up to make sure that the red curtain did not hide a face and, impatient to measure himself with Lohmann, he turned to her.

"My dear—dear lady, you spoke to the boys last night?"

"Well, why did you go so early? Could I help it if the others came in after you'd gone? But I spoke my mind to them—especially to that chap."

"That's right. That's right. And to-night when they came in, you saw them, I suppose?"

"A lot of good that did me, didn't it?"

"My dear lady, you must have your flowers and champagne, but you shall receive them from *me*. It is not seemly to take things of that sort from schoolboys."

And flushing, animated, all his senses stimulated, he realized that she had been referring to a song written by Lohmann when she said she would not sing that piffle again. She meant that song about the full moon; Lohmann wrote it!

"You shall not only refuse to sing that piffle about the fool moon; you shall never again sing anything of Lohmann's."

"Then in that case," said she, smiling up at him, "will *you* write something for me?"

His joy was beyond bounds and he hastened to reassure her.

"We'll see what we can do!"

"That's right. And—there's a lot to do, isn't there? All sorts of things?" She held out her pouted lips. But he had not got to that point yet. He stared at her helplessly and suspicion shone in his eyes. "But what have you come for, then?" she asked impatiently.

"Those schoolboys mustn't——" he began.

"Well——" She nestled up to him. "I shall have to change in a minute and you can make yourself useful."

He did. The fat couple came back from their triumph very thirsty and only one of the bottles held about half a glass. Kiepert said he'd go and get some more and Old Mud told him to do so. Rosa had a glass quickly for it was her turn to sing again.

She had a great success. The champagne seemed sweeter and Old Mud became more and more cheerful. Kiepert walked to the platform for his next turn on his hands and had an unsurpassed reception, so he used that mode of progression for the rest of the evening. Rosa showed herself more and more temperamental every time she appeared and became more and more popular. Old Mud forgot that he need ever leave the place, but the last of the audience were already trailing out.

"We'll keep it up like this every night," said Rosie. "And on Sunday we'll beat the record."

But immediately after she suddenly broke out sobbing. Astonished, he saw, as through a sort of mist, how she buried her nose in her hands, leaning on the table, while the diadem fell out of her hair.

"It's all so bright outside—and so miserable within," she said sobbing. "In here, I mean," touching her breast." It's an a-a-arid desert!" She sobbed again and he tried painfully to think of the right thing to say. Kiepert came into the room and dragged him out of his chair, declaring that he was going to see him home, and as they went out of the door, he found the right thing to say. He turned and put out his hand, trying to touch her.

"I'll see you through," he said. A teacher could make a promise like that to a boy whom he happened to like, or at any rate, he could think it. Old Mud had never said it to anyone, or thought it of anyone before.

But she had dropped off to sleep.

CHAPTER VII

It was a quarter past eight and Old Mud had not yet arrived. His class, enjoying the unwonted freedom, were noisy to the point of deafening themselves and bursting their ear drums. They were all shouting:

"Mud! Mud! Where's Old Mud?"

Some of them thought he must be dead; others swore that he had turned his housekeeper "out of the room!" and so had had to go hungry. No doubt he had been run in. Lohmann, Ertzum and Kieselack, however, had no suggestion to make.

Unnoticed, Old Mud was striding towards the rostrum, and he slid into his chair with care, as if his bones were aching. Many of them had not noticed him come in and continued to yell:

"Mud! Mud! Where's Old Mud?"

But he did not seem to care whether he could "catch" them or not. He looked very white, waited patiently until they would let him speak and showed the changing moods of an invalid when pronouncing judgment on their work. One boy, whom he was wont to torment with zeal, he let run on with an entirely incorrect translation for fully ten minutes, while he fell with furious indignation on others at the first word. He was again ignoring Lohmann, Ertzum and Kieselack, and yet his thoughts were on them all the time. He was asking himself whether, when he took his somewhat erratic way home last night, they had not been standing at a corner when he was clinging on to the side of a house with both hands. He seemed to remember having fallen against them and said "Shcuse me!" to them. But his remembrance of that walk was not so clear as it might have been, and he really was not quite certain whether all that he thought happened belonged to the realm of fact. It was a great worry to him that he could not be clear about the matter. What did those three young rascals know? And what had happened yesterday after he himself had been helped out of that front door? Had they gone back to the Blue Angel? Had Lohmann gone back? It was true that Rosa had been crying her heart out and that she had gone to sleep. But had Lohmann awakened her again? He longed to ask, but he dared not.

The three boys did not take their eyes off him. Kieselack was amused, von Ertzum contemptuous, Lohmann saw the pitiful in what was happening; but all three were watching grimly. There was a terrible side to their understanding of the tyrant.

During the interval Lohmann leaned against the sunny wall of the quad, crossed his arms and listened again in his thoughts to the agony that his heart had poured into those verses which had been sung with such dire effect in that smoky concert-room. Ertzum came up as if casually and spoke in a careful whisper:

"Did you say she was lying asleep with her head on the table? It can't be true."

"I tell you she was snoring. He made her drunk."

"The damned scoundrel! I'll——"

But Ertzum did not finish his boast, for the yoke of the school was heavy on his neck and his own impotence seemed to him more shameful even than the doings of Old Mud. He was not worthy of Rosa!

Kieselack wormed his' way through the other boys until he reached his two friends. He was shaking with the sly humour of it all. "He's been making a night of it," he whispered behind his hand. "Old Mud's been on the razzle dazzle!" Then he added quickly: "Coming?"

The other two shrugged. They were expressing a certain contempt for themselves.

Old Mud looked on it as a duty, and it was one that grew daily more pleasurable, the more he saw of Rosa. So that Lohmann should not steal a march on him he was always the first to get to the Blue Angel. He put the toilet things in order, and looked out clean linen and stockings, putting anything that needed mending on a chair. Rosa did not come till later, for she was beginning to rely on Old Mud. He learned to be quite deft with his crooked fingers, loosening knots, pulling the bows more tightly, and taking out any pins or needles left in her clothes. When she made up, the play of her arms as she used the rose and yellow paints still held him enthralled. He learned to regard her face as a palette and knew the names of the paints and the uses of those little bottles and pots, the powders and creams; keeping quiet and ready when

they were being used. She noticed his improvement
and one evening, when sitting before the glass, she
leaned back in her chair and said:

"Now go ahead!"

He made her up so well that she did not need to dip a
finger in a single ointment. She was surprised at his
dexterity and wanted to know how he had managed
to learn so quickly. He flushed and stammered out
something, but her curiosity remained unsatisfied.

He rejoiced at the position he had gained in the
dressing-room. No fear of Lohmann ousting him
now! Would Lohmann have remembered that that
pink bolero was to go to the cleaner's? If that boy
had trained his memory on Homer, as he had!
Lohmann was suffering the consequences of idleness. Old Mud tiptoed about among the under-
garments lying on the floor and furniture like a great
black spider, waiting to snatch with his crooked
limbs. Under those grey, knuckly hands of his
rustled the soft and shimmering stuffs. Some of
them seemed to speak of the forms they enwrapped—
an arm, a leg—and he murmured:

"Yes, yes. Fine! Fine!"

Then he would steal to the door and listen to her
voice, sounding over the thunder of the piano,
watching the waving movements of her limbs as
seen through the smoke of the concert-room, and he
would turn his eyes to all those stolid forms, those
round heads like a great bed of tulips that gaped up
at her. He was proud of her and contemptuous of
the audience when it clapped or furious when it did

not. And the joy of it made a bond between them when she bent forward, bowing, offering the opening of her bosom to all those eyes. A pricking torment seized him. Now she was coming back amidst a storm of applause and it was his duty to throw her cloak about her shoulders and powder her neck.

So he came to know all her moods. Whether she leaned her shoulder against him tenderly or threw a powder-puff in his face, so that he was temporarily blinded, meant happiness for him, or misery. His eyes saw below the mere clothes of this woman; it was as if not only her garments and cosmetics came within his hands but also her very soul. She was now impatient and now friendly with him, and it lifted him beyond his accustomed self when she unconsciously relied upon their friendship. He was much less embarrassed when she scolded. She remembered from time to time to carry out a plan in her treatment of him although it greatly bored her; carrying out instructions that she had received and which she followed without conviction. So she would sometimes sit sentimentally, a little piece of needle-work in her hand, looking as if she were sitting at his feet; the expression that it was proper to put on when talking to a man who was "serious." But soon—and this was a relief to him, although he did not exactly know why—she would push him off his chair as if he had been a bundle of old clothes.

Once she slapped his face, but she quickly put her hand to her nose and said:

"You're greasy."

He reddened helplessly, but she went on quickly:
"The man paints his face! So that's how he
learned to do it so quickly! He taught himself on his
own face. Oh, you—Old Mud!" He looked furious;
"Yes, you are—Old Mud!" And she danced round
him. He broke into a laugh. She knew his nickname, had heard it from Lohmann and the others,
and apparently she had known the whole time. It
was a shock to him, but not a disagreeable one; on the
contrary, he was rather glad. He felt ashamed of
himself for being glad at hearing this girl call him by
that shameful name. But he was glad, all the same.
However, he hadn't much time to think it out, for
she sent him for some beer.

He merely ordered the beer and let the landlord
bring it through the concert-room; following him
like that was a precaution against the risk of someone else commandeering it. Once the proprietor had
hinted to Old Mud that he could carry his own beer,
but the offended dignity with which Old Mud received
the suggestion prevented his making it again.

"Chin-chin, Old Mud," said Rosa before drinking.
Then thoughtfully she added: "It's funny my calling
you that, isn't it? We have nothing in common,
really. How long have I known you? What a
thing habit is! But I must just say this—I wouldn't
shed a tear if I never saw Kiepert or Gussie again.
But with you, somehow—it's different." Her eyes
were dreamy and abstracted. Her voice was very
deep as she asked: "But what is it all for? What do
you *want* ?"

CHAPTER VIII

OLD Mud was not concerned with this thought and only one thing troubled him when he left Rosa late at night; his uncertainty about Kieselack, von Ertzum and Lohmann. The fear of their intruding on the forbidden brought him gradually to contemplate the extreme step and to throw aside all the accepted social barriers. Out there in the streets, on his way from the Blue Angel, he once heard their steps behind him. He trod softly, so that they should not hear, and at the corner of the street he listened, pouncing round at last, to their surprise. They started back, but he spoke cheerfully, though with his most "poisonous" glance:

"So I see you are pursuing your—er—artistic inclinations. Quite right, quite right. Come along and let us compare notes together; it will give me a chance to see how far your—er—studies in that direction have gone."

Then as they stared at one another, not knowing how to take this extraordinary candour from the tyrant, he added:

"My testimony might be useful to you the next time you—er—get into trouble." With this he walked on with Lohmann, leaving the other two to follow. Lohmann went with him most unwillingly, and without further preface Old Mud began to talk about his pupil's song of the "Fool Moon."

"'His eyes are wet. For you his heart is pining." said he. "Yet one would not think that love in the abstract should induce to weeping. But of course if you mean love in the sense of a personification of your own soul and the state of your own feelings, and not in the abstract—and are picturing yourself as a lover on an ethereal shore, why, that's another matter. But then your teacher may consider it his duty to the class in general and the Old School in particular, to inquire into the state of mind of a Fifth Form boy who—er—has had the—er—precocity to—er—develop such feelings."

Lohmann, startled and furious, felt as if Old Mud were mauling his very soul between his crooked fingers.

"It's poetic licence, sir, from beginning to end. Just a trifle—art for art's sake—you know the phrase. It has nothing to do with my personal feelings."

"Indeed? That's very interesting," said Old Mud drily. "Evidently, then, the—er—personal appeal of the song was due to the singer's art alone." The mention of her name caused him a thrill of pride, which he tried to cover, sheering away from that side of the subject and treating Lohmann to a lecture on the technique of romantic poetry, impressing on him the necessity for a close study of Homer. Lohmann protested that Homer was greatly overvalued as a poet. That episode of the dying hound in the "Odyssey," for instance, was to his mind handled

with far more effect by Zola in "La Joie de Vivre."
"I presume you know the book, sir," he added.
After this they discussed Heine and to Lohmann's
defence of that poet's philosophy of life Old Mud
shouted contemptuously, with all the fury of his
revengeful spirit at the back of his words:

"Nonsense! Absolute nonsense!"

They had reached the gates of the town and here
Old Mud's path really branched off from theirs, but
instead of following it, he called Kieselack to him.

"Go on ahead with your friend von Ertzum," he
said to Lohmann. He was most concerned with
Kieselack at the moment; the boy's family was of no
social importance, his father being an official at the
harbour and out all night. Kieselack said that he
lived with his grandmother and Old Mud suspected
that the old woman did not furnish any check to the
boy's nightly adventures. The door of the Blue
Angel remained upon so late——

Kieselack guessed what Old Mud was thinking and
did his best to reassure him.

"Grandmother has a heavy hand," he said.

Under Old Mud's watchful eye, von Ertzum had to
unclench his fists, but he whispered to Lohmann as
they walked along a few paces ahead.

"He'd better not carry things too far, I can tell
him. There is a limit!"

"I hope not yet," replied Lohmann. "I'm beginning to find the whole affair more and more amusing."

"I tell you what, Lohmann," said von Ertzum,
"it's pretty lonely here, not a light or a policeman

in sight. Suppose I turn round and give him a good hiding? You wouldn't interfere, of course. That girl—to think of her mixed up with that lump of filth! That innocent girl! I—I can't stand it."

He waxed the more emphatic as he felt his listener not in sympathy, but he did not care, for he felt ready for anything to-night. Lohmann, however, hesitated.

"Nice thing it would be if you happened to kill him. It would be somewhat difficult to explain away," said he at last. "It would rather tear things, wouldn't it? After all, there are things that we don't want known, aren't there?" He waited in some suspense for von Ertzum to throw in his face his own love for Dora Breetpoot, and felt his finger already on the trigger of that gun, which he had at hand to use if his secret should ever come to light. But his half confession had neither been heard nor understood. "Another thing is," he continued, "would you really do it? I don't think you would."

Von Ertzum made a wild gesture and Lohmann saw that his eyes were shot with red. He seized his friend by the arm.

"Now don't be a fool, Ertzum!" and continued sceptically, "the thing isn't really serious, you know. Look at the fellow! Is that the sort of chap it's worth while to murder? He's the type one just shrugs one's shoulders at. Do you really want to see headlines in the papers linking your name with Old Mud's? Altogether too compromising, my friend."

Ertzum's excitement gradually subsided, and

Lohmann felt a slight contempt for him when he saw how quickly he ceased to be dangerous.

"It was a fool thing to propose, and there's something else you should have done and haven't. You haven't got any money out of old Breetpoot, have you?"

"No, I haven't," replied Ertzum.

"There, you see! You said you were going to tell him all about it and that you were a man now and meant to do as you pleased; that you'd rather serve two years for your Rachel than see your beloved lost to you. You wanted your freedom, in short, for *her* sake. Now didn't you?"

"What would have been the good of going to old Breetpoot?" muttered his friend.

"What do you mean?"

"He wouldn't have given me any money, but would simply have tied the purse-strings tighter than ever. I should not have been allowed to see Rosa again." Lohmann had to admit that this was very probable.

"I can lend you three hundred marks," he said carelessly. "If you really want to bolt with the girl——"

"Thanks," said Ertzum between his teeth.

"You don't want the money! Oh, all right then!" Lohman laughed cynically. "I think you're right. It's as well to wait a bit before choosing a countess. And I don't expect she'd agree to anything else."

"I shouldn't offer her anything else," said von Ertzum, quickly. "But she won't. Oh, I didn't tell you. No one knows how wretched I've been since last Sunday. It's really funny to think that she treated me as if—and to think I could have been so mistaken!"

They said no more. Lohmann was restless; he felt himself humiliated, wounded in his love for Dora Breetpoot, because von Ertzum was suffering like this on account of that idiotic girl! Ertzum meant much to him—and perhaps she did, too.

"Well?" he said at last, wrinkling his forehead.

"Last Sunday, in the wood, I got her to myself for a moment without either you, Kieselack or Old Mud; it seemed such a good chance. I felt so sure she'd say yes."

"I see. You were confident and then she made a fool of you."

"Yes. When I think of it—how happy I was at first and then—you remember after we'd all had lunch in the wood, she and I were left alone; then you and Kieselack came back again. I had screwed up my courage, though at the last moment I felt awful! But she had always been so kind to me; quite different from the way she treated you. That's true, isn't it? I thought she was expecting me to propose: I had brought all my cash with me and had thought that we just would not go back to the town— see?—but slip through the wood to the railway station."

He stopped and Lohmann had to prompt him.

"She doesn't care for you, eh?"

"She said she hadn't known me long enough. Don't you think that was iust an excuse? She thought we'd be caught and as I'm not of age, get put in prison. She, I mean—for the abduction of a minor, you know."

Lohmann fought with his desire to laugh.

"If she can calculate so cold-bloodedly," he said gravely, "I am afraid she is not in love with you. At any rate she doesn't love you as you do her. You'd better be sure you really do care enough for her to—— Don't you rather feel that after her conduct on Sunday your future happiness is not so wrapped up in her as you thought it was?"

"Oh, no. I haven't had any such thought as that," replied Ertzum simply.

"Then I don't see what you're going to do," said Lohmann.

They had reached Pastor Thelander's house and Ertzum climbed up the creeper to the balcony. Old Mud was standing below, between Kieselack and Lohmann, watching him, and when Ertzum had gone in at his window the professor turned thoughtfully away. He was thinking that von Ertzum could climb down again whenever he liked. But he wasn't much afraid of von Ertzum; he despised him.

He took the other two back to the town and left Kieselack at his grandmother's. Then he went home with Lohmann, heard the door close behind him, saw a light spring up in his window above, and waited until it had been put out again. Even then he let a little more time pass, but nothing further happened.

Then at last he felt himself able to go home to bed.

CHAPTER IX

THERE was much curiosity about Old Mud, some of
the sailors taking him for the impresario who paid
the artists, but those who did not regard him as a
theatrical manager took him for Rosa's father.
Those who knew who he was sat listening to these
speculations with a grin.

That first evening they had spoken out, but he
was sure of himself and unmoved at that time. He
had too much to think of, as they dimly perceived.
They felt small in a way, though they had paid their
money to see the show. And he kept opening that
door for Miss Rosa of whom they all had a great
opinion. Against their will, they began to have some
sort of respect for Old Mud and their tendency to
think of him as a standing joke lessened every day.
They made up for it by whispering in the shops and
behind counters, and so the first rumours of this
change of habit on the part of the professor began to
circulate round the town. It was not believed; the
schoolboys declared that he'd locked up his housekeeper and each day had some fresh tale to account
for things. But there was no doubt that the whole
town was smiling at the joke.

An assistant teacher, under the patronage of the
oldest of the professors, who was himself half deaf,

visited the Blue Angel and saw the truth for himself, and the next morning the old man said a few words to Old Mud about the necessity for keeping up the dignity of their profession, but the assistant stood by with a sceptical smile. The other teachers present turned their heads away, some of them shrugging their shoulders. Old Mud was upset; he detected a want of faith in his omnipotence. His jaws worked and he broke out into angry ejaculations.

"Really, really! Upon my word—really! Kindly remember that this is a matter for myself alone to decide!" He turned his back on them, muttered a bit and eventually slipped away, but the remembrance embittered the whole day, for he had not found the decisive words to rebuke the interference. He should have told them that Miss Fröhlich was a person of more consequence than a mere assistant teacher, or even than that deaf old humbug himself—even than the Headmaster. She was unique and, like himself, far above the common herd who were equally impertinent in misjudging her and doubting him.

But these matters were too deeply rooted in the ideas of those people for Old Mud to be able to make much impression. He raged in the solitude of his own room, and shook his fists in the air.

On Sunday he went with Kiepert to a political meeting, of the Social Democrats of course. This was the outward sign of an inner resolve. The power of class—the class to which Lohmann belonged—now seemed to him a thing to be shattered. Until then Kiepert's enthusiasm had merely brought a disdainful smile to his lips; lips of the declared despot, prepared to overthrow the church, the sword, ignorance and immorality without troubling much about their point of view. But now he had decided to throw everything overboard, and to make common cause with the people against the upper classes and set going a general state of anarchy. In the gloom of the poorer quarters, cheek by jowl with the mansions of the privileged, he made his decision; and a hectic enthusiasm seized him. He banged on the table with his bony fists, crying:

"Let us be up and doing! I am not minded to bear this state of things with patience!"

It was a temporary intoxication and he afterwards regretted it, especially when he heard that while he was engaged with this new craze, the Fröhlich had spent a day away from the town. He thought with anguish of Lohmann, who was no longer attending the class! What infamy was responsible for his absence? Of course he had spent every moment of Old Mud's absence elsewhere with Rosa. He must have run to her and camped in her room. Old Mud determined to see that room and seek his absent scholar there!

The days were a jealous agony and in the classroom he fell on the Fifth Form boys with murderous zeal, while in the dressing-room he accused the fat Gussie of having an evil influence over Rosa. Gussie merely laughed and Rosa answered for herself:

"Think I'd want to go picnicking with your three schoolboys? They'd bore me stiff!"

He stared at her, and then, feeling that he could not handle her, he turned to Gussie again.

"Answer me! What have you been doing with this girl?"

"Ain't you a funny old thing, dearie?" replied she, quite unconcerned. Then she opened the door. "After all, I think we've had about enough of you," she said. "You ain't much to boast of, are you now?"

With that she made her exit and Old Mud flushed, while Rosa laughed.

"Still at it, old dear?" she asked when they were alone together. And that was all he could get from them.

Whenever he saw the fat couple his quarrelsome temper rose, and he treated them gruffly. The more he thought of Rosa, the more he felt the desire to protect her and the more apart from others he wished to keep her, so that at last it seemed to him as if the wardrobe of the fat couple had no right to be lying about on the chairs. He was contemptuous of their success with the audience and noisy good humour, and when Kiepert wanted to come into the dressing-room after an acrobatic turn he turned him out because he was perspiring, which was not seemly in the presence of a lady like Miss Fröhlich.

"Quite a bread-and-butter miss, isn't she?" remarked Kiepert, taking it with great good humour. His wife was somewhat offended, but she ended by laughing and giving Old Mud a friendly push. On this he angrily dusted his coat—and that did annoy her.

Rosa herself was tittering, but she could not but be flattered, and she found her own nerves on edge with that fat couple and their silly patriotic song. Old Mud regarded her as an *artist*. He naïvely roused her vanity and so brought her to his own point of view, looking down with contempt on the rest of the world; and this led her to look on him as her champion. He had the deepest disdain for the audience, as had she, though she worked hard to win their approval. He hated every single spectator who admired her. He hated the fat woman most of all because she was always coming into the dressing-room with tales of the impression Rosie had made.

"You don't mean to say the man dared——" he would cry. "That little Meyer, who never managed to pass his exam. and was a disgrace to the Old School!"

Rosie managed to hide beneath a smile the fact that she herself was rather taken with little Meyer. She wished she wasn't. She had a respect for authority, and the opinion of a man of Old Mud's standing meant something to her. It was the first time she had known anyone like that. The fat woman, who wanted to stand up for Meyer, found herself snubbed.

Another time she waved some flowers under Old Mud's nose.

"They came from the fat man, near the piano," she said.

"Nonsense, dearie. He ain't fat. He's the cigar

merchant from the market. Kiepert gets his smokes there," put in the fat woman.

"Well, what do you say to that?" she asked him. He replied at once that this old schoolboy was one of the worst of them all, and that he wasn't even any good at business, for he never sent in an account to his old professor without ending his name with the wrong letter. But the women did not think that mattered much; there was no doubt the tobacconist was a smart business man. Rosie, seeing that he was fuming, swung round to smell the roses.

"You've something against them all," the fat woman said. "What's it all about, eh? Can't you tell us?" And, as he stood, stricken dumb, she added: "I don't think they think much of *you*, you know."

"I'm sure they don't, Gussie," put in Rosie, and as Old Mud flushed red, she struck her knee and shouted with laughter.

"You shouldn't be so stand-offish," continued Gussie; "they may be a bit stupid compared to you, but they've got their good points. Don't you forget that either, Rosie. I've a reason for warnin' you, dearie." On this she got up to return to the platform and sing that eternal patriotic song with her husband. Rosa looked as if she were going to cry with annoyance.

"That woman!" she cried; then, more quietly: "She gets on my nerves and it's no good saying she doesn't. But you don't care, do you?" she added, bitterly.

And he felt that daily there had been growing up an obligation which it behoved him to fulfil; he had not the power to cast it aside.

All through the patriotic song, Rosa marched up and down the dressing-room, groaning.

"I tell you, if I hear that song again I shall go mad! Oh, how I hate that fat woman! How I hate her!" And the song was scarcely at an end before she ran out into the hall and screamed at the loudly applauding house:

"For everywhere upon the seas
A proud white mast is seen,
The German flag salute receives,
Of Ocean's kingdom queen!"

At first all were struck dumb, and then a tumult broke out, but in the end the novelty rather pleased them. Her audacity was greeted with cheers and she went back into the dressing-room delighted. But the fat woman was really furious this time.

"We two work ourselves to the bone to please the bloody fools and then you come and queer our business. If that isn't doing the dirty, I don't know what is."

Old Mud denied this, siding with the girl, taking the line that everything is fair in art. Art was what great artists made it, and Miss Fröhlich was a great artist. She had put the finishing touch to the others' performance.

"You may take it from me that——"

But Kiepert burst into the room, pushing in front of him a short, thick man with a band of red hair round his even redder face.

"My God, my girl, you're a stunner, you are! Never saw such an attractive piece in me life. I'm an old sea-dog, I am, and you must have a drink with me."

"This lady does not have drinks with anyone," interrupted Old Mud, angrily. "You are quite mistaken, my good man, and apparently you do not know that this is a private room."

"Funny dog, ain't he?" grinned the captain.

"Not at all," said Old Mud, stiffly. "I am sorry, but you can't come in here." But the fat couple thought this was going too far.

"Now, Professor," said Kiepert, blusteringly, "I can bring a friend in here if I like."

"I should think so, indeed," cried his wife. "He's nothing but a nuisance, and now he wants to send our friends away. Rosa, take the captain into the other room."

Old Mud went white. He shook with rage.

"Miss Fröhlich is not the type of woman you can offer a drink to, my man," he cried, in his most aggressive tones, and with his most "poisonous" glance. And before that glance she quailed and sighed.

"Better go," she said to the sea captain; "nothing doing!"

But Old Mud, his face flaming, sprang at the man in triumph.

"You hear, my man? Miss Fröhlich says you're to go. Out of the room with you!" He seized the captain by the collar and bundled him to the door and, strong as he was, the old seadog let the unexpected storm roll over him, giving himself a shake when Old Mud let him go, which was not until he was the other side of the door. He saw it slam behind him with a look of astonishment.

"How dare you?" Kiepert struck the table with his fist.

"How dare *you?*" retorted Old Mud with such fury that Kiepert drew back, afraid. "Remember this: Miss Fröhlich is under my protection, and I will not have her insulted. Remember that in future! Better make a note of it!"

Kiepert grumbled, but he was subdued and gradually subsided. Rosa looked at Old Mud and burst out laughing, ending with a very soft gurgle, mischievous and tender, as if she were amused both at him and at herself; but as if she were proud of him, too.

The fat woman got over her temper and laid her hand on his shoulder.

"Just listen to him," she said.

Old Mud wiped his forehead, his anger completely passed. The panic of the tyrant who might have provoked the rebels further by a burst of uncontrollable fury, had now seized him.

"Well, Kiepert's gone out and Rosie and I are here," Gussie put the facts of the case before him. "And the old captain's been turned out. He came

from Finland and he'd done awfully well, because
his ship has gone down and it was heavily insured.
You haven't insured *your* ship, dearie, have you?
No, your talents lie in another direction, don't they?
But you know you really must look at things all
round. What about Rosie, eh? The captain was a
man of substance and she liked him."

Old Mud stared at Rosa, upset.

"That's a lie," said she calmly.

"Why, you told me so yourself, Rosie."

"Liar!"

"Well, you won't deny that one of the professor's
schoolboys—that one with the black hair—made you
a proposal——"

At this Old Mud saw red and she had to silence
him.

"She's just telling the tale, old dear. It was the
red-haired one who wanted to marry me—the one
with the open mouth. He's a Count or something,
but what's that to me? I don't like him." She
smiled up at him like a child.

"P'raps I have made a mistake, dearie," said
Gussie; "but that don't affect the fact that you owe
me 270 marks for washing, and things, do it, Rosie?
Sorry, Professor, to speak of such a thing with you
about, but they say charity begins at home, don't
they now? Well, never mind about the money,
but you can't expect a young girl like that to get on
without love. It seems to me, Professor, if you don't
mind me saying so, as you've got no call to come and
upset things like this. You ain't offering her nothing!

I don't know whether I'm more angry or amused at you, I don't reely."

"If I don't complain there's no occasion for you to do so, Gussie," cried Rosa. But the fat woman tossed her head and left the room. She had said her say and made her exit with colours flying.

Rosa shrugged.

"She's silly, but she means well. Oh, never mind her! I guess you think we're both tarred with the same brush, and wish you'd never had anything to do with us."

But this was not at all what he was thinking as he sat there, staring at the floor.

"But if you want to know—I'm not at all that sort. I wouldn't do that sort of thing—the things she hints at—no, not even with you!" She smiled up at him mischievously and, after a moment, added: "No, that I wouldn't!" But she wasted her words, for he did not see that she was giving him a cue. He felt himself enmeshed and enveloped in a warm glow.

"Of course not," said he, and held out his hands to her. They were trembling and she let him take hers in his grasp. Her slim fingers, a trifle greasy, slipped softly between his bony knuckles. Her hair, her flowers, her painted face, all seemed to be swaying and swaying before his eyes like a catharine-wheel. He struggled for self-control.

"Of course you mustn't owe that woman money. I am determined——"

He broke off. Even at this moment that wretched

Lohmann boy was disturbing his thoughts; he had not been to school; was he hidden in her room?

"I—er—I will pay your rent——"

"That's not the question," said she softly; "that's a mere nothing. My rent's very little." Then she added: "It's upstairs, you know. Quite a nice room. Would you like to see it?"

She kept her eyes on the ground and looked as modest as custom prescribes a girl should look at her first proposal. And she was surprised to find that she felt no inclination to laugh, but that her heart was actually fluttering a little. She gave him a long look.

"Let's go up," she said. "Don't let those fools in the concert-room see us."

CHAPTER X

KIESELACK opened the door of the concert-room, put his little blue paw before his mouth and let out a low whistle. Lohmann and von Ertzum followed him.

"Gee!" cried Kieselack, dancing wildly across the hall to the very foot of the stairs. "Got as far as that, have they?"

"Got as far as what?" asked Lohmann languidly, although he knew very well what Kieselack meant, and was just as much excited.

"Gone up aloft, eh?" grinned Kieselack, twisting his mouth sideways. He slipped off his shoes and slipped up the wooden stairs, which creaked under his tread. The door was on the first low-ceilinged landing, as he knew well enough. He bent down to the keyhole. Then he turned and waved his hand, without taking his eye from the peephole. Lohmann shrugged and remained standing at the foot of the stairs with Ertzum, who was staring up at the door with wide-opened mouth.

"Well?" whispered Lohmann significantly.

"I—don't understand," whispered von Ertzum. "You surely don't think there's anything—going on? Kieselack would, of course, but——"

"Oh, of course," replied Lohmann, sympathetically. Kieselack signed to them again as he gazed in through the keyhole.

"I shall have to knock him down——" began Ertzum again.

"It would add a touch of excitement to the affair," drawled Lohmann. But von Ertzum was beyond understanding. His ideas of love had been stamped once and for all by the little incident of the girl who had tossed him into the hay after he had fought and overcome a young farm hand, some three years ago. This man here was a round-shouldered weakling. Rosa Fröhlich couldn't think he'd be afraid of a creature like that.

"She couldn't think I'd be afraid of him!" he said.

"Aren't you—just a little bit?" asked Lohmann, and von Ertzum, spurred on by the taunt, took the six steps in two strides.

"You shall see!" he cried. But Kieselack, who had left the keyhole, was doing a dance of triumph in his stockinged feet.

"What ho!" he crowed, his little eyes twinkling in his pasty white face. Ertzum was fiery red and panting and their glances met, each measuring the other. Ertzum's eyes demanded that he should confess it was not true, and Kieselack answered with a sly wink, which jerked a little. On that Ertzum became as pale as the other, and crumpled up as if under a heavy blow, shaking with the pain of it. He staggered down the six stairs again and Lohmann received him with folded arms, a look of contempt for the world and its ways on his handsome lips. Ertzum fell like a sack on to the lowest stair and hid his face in his hands.

"Lohmann, do you understand?" he said, after a
bit, quietly, in his deepest tones. "A girl I had
thought so—so pure. I believe that cur Kieselack
is lying. If so—God help him! I suppose he thinks
it a joke. A girl with—with a soul like hers!"

"Soul's a matter of inclination, nothing more.
She's behaving like a woman, that's all." Lohmann
smiled, feeling that he was throwing mud at Dora
Breetpoot too—Dora, the first of all women! And he
enjoyed it. "But Kieselack's at the keyhole again."
He made von Ertzum look against his will. "He's
making signs again. I say—let's go!"

He helped his friend to rise and dragged him to
the door. But once outside in the air, von Ertzum
would not leave the place; he leaned against the doorpost, in a heavy silence, glued to this house where
he had found disillusionment. Lohmann argued with
him in vain. He threatened to go and leave him;
and then Kieselack appeared.

"A pretty pair you are! What's up with you?
Old Mud's enjoying himself with his girl, and I've
given instructions that when they go back to the
concert-room they're to be received with rousing
honours! I've been laughing myself sick. They're
having a heavenly time! Come along! Let's have
a peep at them."

"Oh, you——" drawled Lohmann.

But Kieselack mistook him.

"You aren't afraid of Old Mud, are you? But
that's absurd. This is too serious a matter for him;
we shall be able to make what terms we like."

"The prospect does not charm me. Old Mud's below making terms with," pronounced Lohmann.

"Oh, don't be such a fish," begged Kieselack, eagerly. "I believe you're afraid!"

"He's right, let's go," cried Ertzum suddenly. A mad curiosity had seized him and he wanted to trample on this woman who had fallen from so high a pedestal. He wanted to cast a scornful glance at her seducer and see how they met his eyes.

"It's damned bad form," cried Lohmann. But he went with them.

In the dressing-room there was a clink of glasses; the landlord was uncorking the second bottle of champagne, and the fat couple were nodding with happy faces towards Rosa and Old Mud, who sat enthroned together at the head of the table.

The three boys walked round the table and stopped in front of Old Mud and his companion and wished them good evening, but only the Kieperts answered them and shook their hands. After this Ertzum repeated his good evening to the others, hoarsely. Rosa looked up surprised, and her voice quavered in a way he had never heard.

"Why, there you are. Look, dear, there are the three boys. Sit down and have a drink, boys." Her glance was so indifferent that it made von Ertzum tremble.

"Yes, yes. Quite so. Quite so. Sit down," said Old Mud, quite graciously for him. "Fill your glasses, you are my guests to-night."

He glanced towards Lohmann who had already taken a chair and was lighting a cigarette; Lohmann the dandy, whose well-cut clothes were a humiliation to ill-paid authority; Lohmann who was detestable in that he never used that nickname; Lohmann who was no boy with a pasty face and no fool, but with his irreproachable manners, his impersonal curiosity into the cause of his teacher's anger, was always deposing the tyrant. And he had sought to drag Rosa into the paths of immorality in which he himself indulged. But so far Old Mud's iron will had got the better of him. It was not he who had been admitted to Miss Rosa's room; Old Mud was now assured of that. He had carried out his first intention and the thought filled him with joy. He had put Lohmann and his two companions in their places, done the same for the old schoolboys there in the concert-room and the fifty thousand old boys in the town. He had snatched Rosa Fröhlich away from the whole lot of them, and he, and he alone, was the conqueror!

They found him markedly rejuvenated. With his cravat under his ear, his coat thrown open, and his sparse hair disordered, he was not the typical rip or drunkard by any means. He seemed somehow different. Rosa seemed softened, almost like a child, as she leaned tenderly towards him. To look at her gave them all a sense of their failure and his triumph. The three saw that at once and Kieselack began to bite his nails. Kiepert, who was not so sure about it, had forgotten his former displeasure and was drinking noisily with everyone. His fat wife was delighted at

the happy chance for Rosa and at the little festivity.
"Your pupils must be delighted too, Professor.
They think such a lot of you."

"I fancy they have somewhat lost their interest in
art," said Old Mud with his contemptuous smile.
"Here again, Kieselack? I wonder you can bear to
leave that old grandmother of yours so much. He
has an old grannie who thinks nothing of giving him
a good thrashing," he explained to Rosa, thinking
to make Kieselack seem a mere child to her. But
that youth did not think that age had much to do
with the way he had won the race for the Old School
in the Fröhlich stakes. He rubbed the seat of his
trousers and intoned in his high nasal voice:

"Grannie skins me alive when I lose my exercise-
book. Oh, it's gone under the table!" And he
slipped down beneath the table-cloth seized Rosa by
the leg, and whispered his conditions to her under
cover of the noise that the Kiepert pair set up. He
threatened otherwise to tell Old Mud.

"You little devil," cried she and kicked at him.

But Old Mud was talking to von Ertzum.

"My dear von Ertzum, you don't look any happier
here than you do in class. Wasn't it you who wanted
to marry Miss Rosa? I will take upon myself to
reply to your flattering proposal. She has, I believe,
set certain limits to your intimacy—but I need not
enlarge on that. Stand up!"

Von Ertzum stood up obediently. Then Rosa
laughed, and her laugh took from him the remainder
of his self-possession and left him helpless.

"Let us see whether you have profited by your repeated visits to the Blue Angel and that the claims of the Old School have not been allowed to suffer. Repeat the recitation for to-morrow!"

Ertzum's eyes rolled helplessly round the room. His forehead was wet and he felt the school yoke heavy on his shoulders. He dropped his head and mumbled:

> "'Should I not give thanks to Heaven
> Show a mien content and bright?
> When so many blessings given
> Prove that all He does is right!'"

Rosie now began to titter and Gussie beamed good-naturedly. Rosie, however, meant to wound Ertzum by laughing, but she dared not laugh aloud out of consideration for Old Mud, whose arm she pressed, gazing flatteringly at him and relishing his command over that red-headed gawky youth, who continued to repeat his hymn in a monotonous singsong:

> " 'Nowhere is a love more tender,
> Cherished in a truer heart——' "

But now the behaviour of the others became too marked. Kiepert had begun to appreciate the humour of the situation and he suddenly shouted with laughter, smiting his palm upon his knee.

"Oh, you naughty boy! What's this about hearts and love?" He winked at Old Mud, implying that this awkward youth, repeating hymns in the dressing-room at the Blue Angel knew a thing or two and brought the joke to a climax. He opened the door and pretended to play a Chorale, singing it himself. But Ertzum stopped. For one thing, he didn't know any more and for another, he was seized with a blind rage against that fat, laughing, singing creature. A mist swam before his eyes and he felt he should die if he could not lay his two hands on that man, knock him down and kneel on him. He turned, lifted his fists and—let fly.

Kiepert was out of breath with laughing and utterly unprepared, which put him at a disadvantage since Ertzum was absolutely in earnest and starving for a fight. They rolled from one corner to the other. In the midst of the tumult Ertzum heard Rosa give a little cry. He knew she was watching and took a deep breath, crushing his opponent's limbs against his own. He felt happy, for this was his right place; it was meet that he should be fighting while she looked on, as the farm girl had looked on before when he fought the cow herd.

Old Mud, paying very slight attention to the struggle, had turned to Lohmann.

"What's up with you, Lohmann? You sit there smoking a cigarette and yet you weren't in class to-day!"

"I could not manage to come, sir."

"But you've managed to come to the Blue Angel."

"That's different, sir. I had a headache this morning. The doctor forbade me to come and ordered a change of occupation."

"Indeed!" Old Mud snapped his jaws together, seeking the right answer. Then he had it.

"You sit there smoking," he repeated. "That certainly *is* a change of occupation for a schoolboy in the presence of his master." And as Lohmann merely looked at him with that strange curiosity from beneath his lowered lids, Old Mud rapped out:

"Throw that cigarette away!"

Lohmann did nothing for a moment and meanwhile Ertzum and Kiepert came tumbling up against the table so that Old Mud had enough to do to see to the safety of Rosa and of the glasses and bottles. When this was done, however, he returned to the charge.

"Well, sir?"

"This cigarette is in place here, sir," replied Lohmann. "The situation is rather unusual—for us both, sir."

Old Mud started at the veiled threat and cried with a quiver of anger:

"Throw that cigarette away, I say!"

"Sorry," shrugged Lohmann, "but——"

"You dare? You——"

Lohmann made a gesture of apology with his beautifully kept hand, and Old Mud sprang from his chair, mad at the opposition to his tyrannical rule.

"You'll put it away or I'll ruin your career. I'll smash you! I'll not allow——"

"Isn't that rather nonsense, sir?" shrugged Lohmann. "All that is past, isn't it? I am surprised you should so misunderstand the circumstances."

Old Mud foamed; his eyes were glowing like an

angry cat's. Great tendons stood up in his neck and slaver appeared at the corners of his mouth; he shook a menacing finger at the enemy; its yellow nail caught the light.

Rosa clung to him, startled out of the comfortable digestion of the delicacies they had been enjoying, and poured out a torrent of scolding words at Lohmann.

"Wouldn't it be wiser to soothe him down?" asked he.

Just then Ertzum and Kiepert fell over a couple of chairs and bounced into Old Mud and Rosa, upsetting them on to the table. From the comparatively quiet corner by the toilet table Kieselack started cheering. He was enjoying himself with Gussie.

When Old Mud and his beloved had picked themselves up, the quarrel started again.

"You'll not come here again!" she screamed at Lohmann.

"I will make a note of the fact, madame. I think you made another statement a few nights ago, equally agreeable to me."

And as she gulped at him, half out of her mind, her make-up running down her face, he was suddenly seized with a violent pleasure in the scene; the same pleasure that he always felt when vicious caresses humiliated his secret love.

However, this was momentary. Old Mud, in his anxious need to assert his power, began to threaten:

"If you do not throw away that cigarette at once, I will escort you to your father! At once, sir!"

Now it happened that many guests had been invited to the Lohmann home that evening and among them the Consul and his wife. Lohmann began to visualize Old Mud entering that drawing-room. The thought was the more distasteful to him because he had learned yesterday of a change in her condition. His mother had blurted it out, and it was the reason that he had not attended school that day. His head in his hands, he had sat all day in his room, in an agony at the thought of that child—perhaps Knust's, perhaps Gierschke's or perhaps even the Consul's.

"Come with me! I command you to come with me," cried Old Mud and Lohmann, with an impatient gesture, let the cigarette fall. On that Old Mud sank down in his seat again, pacified. "Ah! That's better! That's the right behaviour for a schoolboy who wishes to win his teacher's good opinion. And one must make excuses for you, Lohmann. *Mente captus*, eh? An unlucky love affair, eh?"

Lohmann dropped his hands; he was as white as a sheet and his black eyes glowed so that Rosie stared at him, astonished.

"Can't you soften her, my boy? You write verses, don't you?" Old Mud joked on with a "poisonous" levity.

"In honour of the Old School?" put in Rosa archly, for she knew the phrase through Kieselack's revelations.

"He knows! That wretch knows," said Lohmann to himself. "I'll go home, get out the gun and hold the muzzle against my heart. And Dora will be sitting downstairs at the piano. The little song she's singing—the sound of it will ascend as a voluntary to play out my life."

"You know those verses you wrote for me!" said Rosa, and her voice was soft and sighing. She wished he had given her more; she had always wanted more from him, as she now remembered, but she had found him grim and a trifle stupid. "How did the line run?

" 'And when you come to me next week——'

"You look as if you'd been knocked into the week after next!"

So she knew, too. Lohmann rose and turned to the door in despair and as he put his hand on the door-handle he heard Old Mud speaking again.

"Poor boy! Rosie didn't return your affection and decided to cut you, which is why I have said nothing about those outrageous verses. You won't be allowed to come here again, Lohmann, but you can go home now."

Lohmann started round again. Was that all Old Mud had meant?

"Yes, old dear," nodded Rosa. "He's spoken and what he says goes."

And the old fool was sitting there, overflowing with pride. His conquest was a girl of no attractions whatever; both were harmless, and neither of them guessed. The tragedy of those mistaken moments. He had been utterly mistaken and there was no need to shoot himself. He felt disillusioned, almost absurd, humiliated once again by the sheer comedy of the thing, but still alive—still at school to life.

"And now,von Ertzum," Old Mud was summing up, "you, too, must vacate the field. And since you have had the audacity to fight in the presence of your teacher you shall write out those pious verses which you had not properly committed to memory, six times."

Ertzum remained standing, confused, overwhelmed with the discovery that his joy in his own muscular prowess had only led to another disillusionment, that his victory over the acrobat had done him no good and that here there was only one conqueror—Old Mud. He looked despairingly at Rosa.

"Out of the room!" cried Old Mud.

Kieselack wanted to go too.

"Where are you off to without permission from your teacher? You will commit to memory forty lines of Vigil."

"Why?" demanded Kieselack mutinously.

"Because I say so!"

Kieselack cast a glance at him and lost all desire to contest the point. He held his tongue. The other two had gone.

Ertzum experienced a desire to reproach and despise Rosa.

"We must look on her as lost. I am beginning to get used to the thought already. I assure you it won't kill me, Lohmann. But what do you think of Old Mud? Did you ever see anything more shameless?"

Lohmann smiled bitterly; he understood; Ertzum had been beaten and so he was questioning the morality of it all, after the eternal custom of the vanquished. Lohmann dispised this sort of thing, though he, too, had taken a hard knock that day.

"It was stupid of us to go in and think we could make him feel embarrassed. We've been accessories before the fact for too long and have talked with him here so often. He played us up to make us look silly before Rosie. Does he think we're his only rivals?"

Ertzum stared at him, astonished.

"It's no good letting you keep your illusions, Ertzum. Be a man!"

In an almost inaudible voice, Ertzum assured him that Rosa was nothing to him now and asked no questions about her chastity. It was the thought of Old Mud that wounded his ethical sense.

"Oh, I don't agree," said Lohmann. "I'm beginning to find him interesting. Remember the circumstances and how everything was against him. He must have a remarkable power of concentration. I couldn't have brought it off. There must be a streak of the anarchist in him"

But this was beyond von Ertzum. He growled out something.

"Eh?" questioned Lohmann. "Oh, well—that scene in the dressing-room was a bit trying, but there was something great about it. Or, if you prefer it, it was eccentric to the point of genius. But there *was* a streak of genius in it."

Ertzum, however, could contain himself no longer. "Lohmann—is it true she wasn't—clean?"

"Well, anyway, she's pretty well sprinkled with mud now, isn't she? Surely that lets a light onto her past."

"And I thought her—virginal. It all seems like a dream now. You will laugh, Lohmann, but really I could put a bullet through my head."

"I'll laugh if you like."

"How shall I ever get over it? Does anyone ever get over a thing like that? I thought her so far above me that I—I scarcely dared to hope that I could win her. You remember how upset I was when she refused me. It wasn't pride; it was just agony at the disappointment. God knows, I had wondered if she would go with me. How could I reckon on it? She was so much too good for me. And now the dice have gone against me."

Lohmann cast a shrewd look at him. Ertzum must be in a bad way to talk of the dice going against him.

"I was in despair, I tell you. But that was nothing compared to to-day. Do you really understand how—how low she's fallen?"

"Fallen into the mud!"

"Just think! It can't be true. Or if it is—she is the lowest of women."

Lohmann gave it up. Ertzum was on the point of convincing himself that Rosa was still sitting on that nebulous throne. Apparently he wanted to believe it. Stupid as he was, he must know that he never had any real hope of Rosa Fröhlich, and the object of the self-deception was to prove that Old Mud had not reached up very far from his native puddle. The experience with the farm girl was of course at the back of it and this red-headed countryman was a hopeless dreamer, all to feed his own vanity, decided Lohmann.

"And when I ask myself why," continued Ertzum, "I can find no explanation. I offered her everything a man can offer. That she loved me I can honestly scarcely hope. She treated me no better than you! And why should she? But then—Old Mud! Can you believe it, man! Old Mud!"

"Women are unaccountable," said Lohmann, and sank into dreams. "I can't believe it. I think he must have deceived her—trapped her in some way. He will make her most unhappy." And the thought then came to him: "Perhaps—if he does——"

Kieselack now overtook them. He had been walking softly behind them for some little time.

"You look a bit blue," he cried cheerfully. "But cheer up. Old Mud paid her ten marks. I saw that through the keyhole."

"That's a lie, you swine!" cried Ertzum, and clenched his huge fist.

But Kieselack had expected this and had vanished in the distance.

CHAPTER XI

KIESELACK had been lying. Old Mud was far from the thought of offering Rosa money; not from either delicacy or meanness but simply, as Rosa divined, because it did not occur to him. She had to drop a good many hints before he remembered about her rent which he had promised to pay. He then spoke of getting a better lodging for her, but she lost her temper and demanded a place of her own. He was astonished.

"But you are used to living with the Kieperts——" He was seeking for firm ground in this unexpected upheaval; struggling to understand. "And suppose —suppose the Kieperts left the town?"

"And suppose I don't want to go with them? What then?" asked she. As he did not answer, she added archly: "Can't you guess? I should remain here, of course, old dear." She skipped about in triumph and a light broke upon him. He would never have thought of this for himself.

"You would stay here," he repeated several times, to get used to the idea. "Yes, yes. Quite so. Good! Good!" He was delighted. A few days later she employed all her wiles to instil in him the idea that he could not let her go on having her meals at the Blue Angel, but must pay for her at a good hotel. When he had grasped the suggestion he wanted to

have his own meals with her. This she refused and
he was disappointed, so she suggested that he should
pay, not only for her meals at this hotel, but also for
a room for her until she could get into a place of her
own. Every suggestion that tended to take her
from her environment and bind her closer to him
filled him with a childish pride. It was enough to
point out the possibility. He hurried on the uphol-
sterers, telling them it was for the well known actress,
Miss Rosa Fröhlich; he harried the furniture people
in the same way and threatened them with the lady's
disapproval. Everywhere he talked of her, undis-
turbed by glances of annoyance. He was continually
turning up, laden with parcels, continually thinking of
things that were, in his eyes, of the utmost importance,
things which it was necessary to talk over with her.
His pallid skin took on a tinge of colour under the
tonic of this pleasurable excitement. He slept well
at night and his days were happily busy.

His one trouble was that she would never go out
with him. He would have liked to take her round the
town and make her acquainted with his kingdom,
present his subjects, and protect her from noisy
roisterers. For Old Mud had no fear now of any
rebels; he would send them out of the room! But
she always had a rehearsal, or she was tired, or had
a headache, or the fat woman had put her out. On
this he would make a scene, expostulating with
Gussie, who would tell him that they hadn't set eyes
on Rosie the whole day. He could not understand
this. She smiled knowingly, and he returned to Rosa

in so worried a state that she had to invent another tale.

Her real motive was simply that she thought it too soon to be seen about with him. If she were seen in public by his side, there would be sure to be attempts to set him against her. She had not yet acquired sufficient influence over him for him to discredit all the tales that he might hear. She did not regard herself as a woman of immoral character, but everyone had something that it was as well not to let out. Nothing worth speaking about, of course, but if a man had serious intentions it was as well that he should not know. If only men were more reasonable, how much easier life would be! She could have tickled her Old Mud under the chin and told him all about it, but of course she just had to keep him in the dark. And the worst of it was he *would* misunderstand and get it into his head that she preferred to remain at home alone, and amuse herself without him. And God knew that wasn't the truth! She'd had enough of that sort of thing and was only too glad to enjoy a little rest with her funny old dear, who treated her as no one else had ever done and who really—she looked at him again and again—was not at all bad looking.

He had no idea of what she feared.

For the matter of that she need not have been afraid of what people might say. He was less influenceable than she thought, and as a matter of fact had met insinuations and put them aside without saying anything to her about them.

Thanks to Kieselack everyone knew of Old Mud's regrettable mode of life and some of the younger teachers, who had not yet made up their minds what line of conduct would be most advantageous to themselves, avoided him, so as not to have to speak to him. Richter, who had lifted his eyes to a daughter of a family far above that of a mere professor, greeted him with a mocking smile, but others avoided any intercourse with him. One of them spoke out before his class of an example which the boys must not allow themselves to follow; it was the same man who had made so much talk about Old Mud's son, spreading the tale of his immoral conduct. This, too, before the father's class.

When Old Mud now appeared in the courtyard of the school the master in charge would look the other way while the boys shouted:

"This place just stinks of mud!"

And the old professor in charge would stroll away as he approached, the shouting swelling in volume. Kieselack would then stand right in his path and slowly and insolently drawl:

"Stinking mud!"

He would shrink into himself, for he knew he could not "catch" the boy for it. He could never "catch" him again; he knew that very well. Nor von Ertzum, nor Lohmann either. He and the three boys were on a footing of mutual tolerance and he had no power to stop it when Lohmann took to staying away from class and gave as an excuse in his drawling, affected tones that he was busy. Nor did he dare to do much when Ertzum, impatient at his own long and fruitless efforts, snatched the extemporary exercise from his neighbour's hands and set out to copy it. He had to see Kieselack upsetting his school-fellows with wild remarks when they were being asked to answer questions; to let him talk noisily in class, leave the room without permission and even start a fight during the lesson. If he attempted to give way to anger and to order the culprit out of the room, then something even worse would be done. They would start making noises resembling the drawing of corks, shouts of "Chin-chin!" the smack of kisses and giggling and Old Mud had to stride to the door and call Kieselack back again. The other two would come with him unbidden, with expressions of contemptuous defiance.

He suffered terribly, but what was to be done? After all, they were the defeated; they had no share in Rosa Fröhlich. Lohmann was never in her room. Directly the door of the college closed behind him, Old Mud threw off his troubles and fastened his thoughts as to a rock on the image of his Rosa, whom he was to fetch, and on the bonbons which he had bought as a surprise for her. However, the Headmaster was not ignorant of the state of affairs in the Fifth Form and he asked Old Mud to come to his study where he spoke about the misconduct and want of discipline of the pupils. He did not wish to know the cause of this contagion, though he would have made inquiries in the case of a younger teacher. His esteemed colleague had grown grey in the service of the college and must decide things for himself, but without forgetting what was due to the Old School.

"Pericles the Athenian, sir," said Old Mud, "was, as we know, the lover of Aspasia."

But the Headmaster did not think that the precedent would quite do here.

"I should consider my life a failure," went on Old Mud, "if I had put the classic ideal before my students as a mere fairy-tale. To the humanist, the ethics of the lower classes seem a trifling superstition."

The Headmaster, who did not know all the facts of the case, let him go, and thought the matter over. In the end he decided to keep things to himself for fear of creating a scandal that would lower the prestige of the scholastic world in the eyes of the public.

His housekeeper, who had taken offence at Rosa's visits—gave notice with a quiet triumph against which his anger broke in vain, and a servant from the Blue Angel took her place. She looked a scarecrow and received the butcher's boy, the chimney-sweep, the gas man and the whole street in her kitchen. A dressmaker of pallid complexion whom he often went to see on Rosa's account had behaved with cold propriety until one day when he was settling a bigger bill than usual, when she suddenly spoke up. He ought to hear what people were saying about him! It was a shame! At his age—and so on. Without answering, he put the change in his pocket and went out, but then he turned and put his head through the half closed door.

"I gather from what you have thought this a

suitable moment to say, madame, that you are afraid
your candour may affect your pecuniary interests.
You need not fear! You will continue to work for
Miss Fröhlich." With this he left the house.

One Sunday morning, when he was using the back
of a page from his MS. on the particles of Homer to
make a rough draft of a letter to Rosa, there came a
knock at his door, and in stepped the shoemaker
Rindfleisch in his black tail coat and top hat. He
bowed awkwardly and with considerable embarrassment.

"Good morning, sir. May I venture to ask you a
question?"

"Yes, yes. Yes, yes," said Old Mud.

"I have been thinking it over and I don't find it
easy. But God's will be done!"

"Well, well, my good man, what is it?"

"I really can't believe such a thing of you, sir.
People are all talking about it and I thought to myself
—the professor himself must know best. But a
good Christian finds it difficult to believe; indeed and
indeed he does."

"Quite so, quite so. Then don't believe it," said
Old Mud in tones of finality, to close the interview.
But Rindfleisch kept turning his top hat round in his
hand, his eyes fixed on the ground.

"But I feel that it is laid upon me to remind you,
sir, that Our Lord does not approve——"

"What doesn't He approve of?" asked Old Mud,
smiling poisonously. "Of Miss Fröhlich, do you
mean?"

The shoemaker breathed heavily and oppressively. His flaccid, ponderous cheeks began to shake.

"I ventured to tell you once before, sir, that Our Lord only approves of—of that sort of thing when——"

"When He wants more angels for Heaven? I know. I'll see what I can do in the matter."

Without attempting to hide his amusement he edged the pious shoemaker to the door.

But though he was living in the clouds, dreadful things began to happen.

A keeper complained that the wood had been damaged and one Sunday when things were at their worst he had found a party of young people there. After much fruitless inquiry, he appeared on Monday morning walking with the Headmaster across the school hall. He stood waiting through prayers, and while the Head read a chapter from the Bible and the boys sang a hymn, he took careful note of the whole assembly from the Headmaster's dais. He kept wiping his forehead with the back of his hand and did not seem any too comfortable. Then he came down from the dais and followed the Headmaster down the whole rank of pupils, looking very much a fish out of water. He did not raise his eyes until he reached von Ertzum, who trod on his foot and received an apologetic bow in return.

As there seemed no hope of discovering the culprit when the whole school was assembled, the Headmaster made another attempt. He read yet another chapter from the Bible and said that he hoped the guilty boy would be moved to confess and would feel that it was his duty to come to the Headmaster's study and point out his companions in wickedness, giving himself and them up to justice. If he made a voluntary confession, he himself would not only escape punishment but would receive a monetary reward. This brought morning prayers to an end.

Three days later it happened that Old Mud, trying to give a lecture on Titus Livius to his noisy, mutinous class, lost his temper and shouted from the rostrum:

"Lohmann, kindly keep your private reading for another time and place. Kieselack, you've been whistling down that key long enough. Von Ertzum, you can leave your rubbish at home! I shall not order you three boys out of the room, for that is far too small a punishment for such depravity. No, I will put you in your right place—among thieves and vagabonds. You shall no longer associate with decent boys; your moments with us are now numbered!"

On this Lohmann rose and demanded an explanation, but Old Mud's deep tones rang with such bitter hatred, his manner was so triumphant that he bore all down before him, and Lohmann sat down again with a shrug.

In the next interval he, von Ertzum and Kieselack were called to the Headmaster's study and when they came back they stated, with apparent indifference, that it was about the affair in the wood. However, they found themselves sent to Coventry by the other boys.

"Who'd have thought it?" piped Kieselack, but

the other two exchanged glances and then turned their backs on him.

The next morning the three, excused from school, went to the wood with an escort and were confronted with the scene of their misdeeds. The keeper recognized them and the progress of the inquiry necessitated other schoolless days, but at length they were brought before the magistrate and from the benches reserved for the public Old Mud's poisonous smile was turned upon them. In the court also were Consul Breetpoot and Lohmann's father and the Counsel for the Prosecution bowed deferentially to these magnates. He deplored the folly of Lohmann and his friends in not confessing earlier, as then this painful publicity could have been avoided. Naturally everyone had supposed that the culprit was some lawless young rascal of the type of Kieselack.

When the case commenced the magistrate asked the three accused whether they admitted their guilt, and Kieselack at once began to deny it. But he had confessed the whole affair to the Headmaster and when questioned had admitted the whole thing. The Headmaster stated this fact on oath.

"It's a lie!" cried Kieselack.

"The Headmaster has stated the fact on oath."

"He's told a dirty lie," repeated Kieselack.

He had thrown aside all caution, for he was furiously annoyed that he had not only not received the promised reward for his confession, but had been brought up before the magistrate like this. His faith in mankind was shattered!

Lohmann and von Ertzum both pleaded guilty.

"It wasn't me," piped Kieselack.

"It was us," said Lohmann, painfully," ashamed of his schoolfellow.

"Excuse me, but I alone was to blame," said von Ertzum.

"Excuse *me*," said Lohmann quietly but firmly. "My share in the wretched business cannot be denied."

"I alone was to blame," repeated von Ertzum. "I tell you I was the only one concerned."

"That is not true," replied Lohmann, but the other cried:

"It is true. You had gone some time before. I was sitting there with——"

"With whom?" asked the magistrate.

"With no one—I mean——" Von Ertzum flushed painfully.

"With Kieselack I suppose," put in Lohmann.

The magistrate thought it better to divide the guilt between them than for the son of Consul Lohmann and the ward of Consul Breetpoot to shoulder it all. He read von Ertzum a lecture on the seriousness of his offence.

"This is really a scandal," he said, and von Ertzum replied stolidly:

"Yes, your Honour."

The magistrate then commanded him and Lohmann to name their companion.

"You were evidently having a pleasant time. Tell us, please, whom you had escorted to that place."

But the accused remained silent and through the

whole inquiry stood firm in their resolution not to compromise anyone else. Their counsel made the most of this noble silence. Even Kieselack had held his tongue, but no one gave him any credit for it. Moreover he was only biding his time.

"Then there was really no one with you?" they were asked once again.

"No one," declared von Ertzum, and Lohmann said the same.

"Oh, yes there was," piped Kieselack, with the virtuous triumph of the good little schoolboy who knows his lesson. "Rosa Fröhlich the actress was with us." And as all hung on his words: "It was her fault we did all that damage."

"That's a lie," said Ertzum furiously.

"It is a complete lie," confirmed Lohmann.

"It's true," shrieked Kieselack. "Ask the professor. He knows her better than we do." He turned and grinned at the bench where the public was sitting. "You saw her that Sunday, didn't you, sir? She had been lunching with us in the wood."

Everyone turned to stare at Old Mud, whose jaws were working furiously.

"Was the lady with you?" asked the Prosecuting Counsel of the other two boys, in a tone of purely human curiosity. They shrugged, but Old Mud shouted, beside himself:

"This is the end of you, you rascals! You aren't fit to live!"

"Who is the lady," asked the magistrate as a matter of form, for everyone there knew about her₄ and Old Mud. "Perhaps Dr. Mud will kindly give us a few particulars."

But Old Mud merely replied that she was an actress. On this the authorities decided that she must be summoned to appear, that they might decide how far her influence was responsible for the affair. The decision taken, the process server went forth to perform his task.

Meanwhile the young barrister who was defending Ertzum and Lohmann was expressing his opinion upon Professor Mud, who, in his opinion, must take the responsibility for the general, mental and moral development of the three accused, his pupils, and the court agreed. The Prosecuting Counsel, who was afraid of disclosures harmful to the son of Consul Lohmann and the ward of Consul Breetpoot, tried in vain to protest.

When Old Mud stepped into the witness box there was general laughter. He was greatly excited, shaking with rage and damp with perspiration.

"There can be no doubt whatever," he began, "that Miss Fröhlich had nothing to do either with the act of destruction nor with the whole affair." He was asked to take the oath and then he wanted to repeat his statement, but they interrupted him again. They only wanted his testimony as regarded the three boys. On this he began to shout and wave his arms, and his voice sank to its deepest notes as if he found himself confronted by a blank wall and saw no way out.

"Those boys are the wickedest rascals! Look at them! The very scum of the earth! They are not

content with defying the authority of their teacher
themselves, but they lead others to revolt. Thanks
to them, the Fifth Form has become a miniature hell.
They have upset everything either through revolu-
tionary machinations, attempted deceptions or other
evil deeds, and deserve the fate that awaits them here.
This indeed is the place to which I always believed
they were steering——" And he turned with a cry
of triumphant revenge to the three traducers of Rosa
Fröhlich.

"I say it to your face, Lohmann——"

He then began to arraign each in turn before the
court and onlookers. Lohmann's love songs, von
Ertzum's nightly escapes from home by way of
Pastor Thelander's balcony, Kieselack's constant
presence in a locality forbidden to the schoolboys—
he poured it out, trembling with the force of his
hatred. He spat out the facts relating to Ertzum's
unhappy uncle, to the purse-proud Lohmann family
and the drunken harbour-master—Kieselack's father.

The court listened to this fantastic eloquence with
painful embarrassment, the Public Prosecutor throwing sympathetic glances at the two Consuls. The
young barrister defending the boys listened scorn-
fully and appeased the impatience of the other
spectators. Old Mud made merry and let his anger
have full play, until at last he was informed that the
court was now sufficiently informed with regard to
his relations with his scholars. But he continued to
spit out his venom, without hearing.

"How long will these modern Catalines continue

to burden the earth? They now dare to assert that Miss Fröhlich has been the partner of their orgies! It was the one thing lacking that they should try to attack the honour of a woman!"

But the laughter that broke out on this brought him to a halt, for his words had not expressed what in his inmost heart he knew to be the truth. He felt sure that on that fateful Sunday Rosa had been to the wood, since she had not been under his own eye. More than this; a glance at circumstances to which he had attached little importance before left him speechless. She had always refused to go about with him. What did all those excuses to be left alone at home really hide? Lohmann?

He stared at Lohmann again and called out that these overbearing aristocrats must be pulled down! But the magistrate ordered him to stand down and then Rosa Fröhlich was called to the witness-box. Her appearance created a sensation and the magistrate threatened to clear the court. Order was secured once more, for she made a good impression. She was gowned in grey with modest elegance, her hair was beautifully dressed; she wore a hat of no great size with an ostrich feather and had not put too much rouge on her cheeks. One girl was heard saying to her mother how pretty she was.

She took her place modestly and the magistrate made her a slight bow. To the question of the Public Prosecutor she replied with a smile that of course she had been one of the party. Kieselack's Counsel then thought to play his trump card.

"May I ask you to take note of the fact, your Honour, that my client was the only one of the three accused who spoke the truth?"

But no one was interested in Kieselack.

The other boys' Counsel took the line that obviously the instigator of the mischief had been this young lady and that the boys had acted out of mistaken gallantry. Kieselack's barrister seized the chance to rub in the fact that what he must call the unsympathetic attitude adopted towards his client should really have been directed to the class of corruption exemplified by this young person.

"I don't know what all this fuss about the wood is," stated the witness cheerfully, "but as for the corruption this gentleman is talking about I only know that on the Sunday afternoon in question one of the young gentlemen made me a formal offer of marriage and that I refused him."

There was laughing and shaking of heads at this and she shrugged, but refrained from looking at either of the three youths. But von Ertzum, very red in the face, spoke up.

"What she says is true!"

"Of course it is," she put in, "but you understand what I mean when I say that though we were always good friends there was never anything but a bit of fun between me and the three boys." This was said for Old Mud's benefit and she accompanied it with a glance in his direction, but he did not lift his head.

"Do you mean to state on oath that your behaviour

with the three accused never passed the bounds of morality?" asked the prosecutor sternly.

"Well, it depends what you mean by never," she said and made up her mind to open the old dear's eyes by way of a statement in court. It was becoming a matter of intricate diplomacy to keep in mind and unentangled all the tarradiddles she had to tell. "Perhaps not exactly within the bounds, but as much as makes no difference."

"What do you mean by that exactly?" asked the Prosecutor.

"Well—that one," she pointed to Kieselack, who with the eyes of the whole court upon him, squinted down his nose. He was feeling more and more injured at the treatment he was receiving.

"She's lying," he said mechanically.

But the court paid no attention to him. Lohmann, who was furious at Rosa's open allusion to von Ertzum's proposal, seized the chance to speak, using the tone of a man of the world telling a good story.

"The lady seems to have had her choice. She belonged to Kieselack, as I hear now for the first time, and we all know of another who took her fancy. To be a countess as well would have been asking too much of life! And although I have never presumed to beg for her favour, she has voluntarily declared that I shall be the last whom she will ever love."

"That's right," said Rosa, fervently hoping that her old dear would pick up a bit of heart at hearing this. There was loud laughter in court; even the magistrate had to blow his nose with a trumpet-like intonation and place one hand on his rotund belly. The prosecuting Counsel protruded his lips, the defending one twisted his sceptically and Ertzum whispered to Lohmann:

"Kieselack! You heard? That finishes it. For me she is finished."

"We're well out of it, anyway. But poor Old Mud!"

"Now don't contradict," whispered Ertzum quickly, "if I take the matter on my own shoulders. I must get out of this hole."

The magistrate, speaking in his fatherly tones, was telling the witness to stand down, but instead she took her seat among the spectators, for she did not know how her old dear was going to take his little dose of medicine.

He had left the court-room during that burst of laughter, hastening as if dams had broken, clouds burst and volcanoes erupted. His whole world had come tumbling about his ears—for she was a harlot! Lohmann and those others that he thought he had ousted—she didn't care what she did, so long as he wasn't there to see! She had no decency; anyone could share her! She confessed to Kieselack though she still denied it as regards Lohmann, but then he could no longer believe her. And he was utterly surprised; that she should prove untrustworthy! Until to-day—until this terrible moment—she had seemed his other self; and now she had torn herself from his heart. He could see that inner wound

bleeding, and could not understand it. Since he
had had no intimate relations with others he had never
been deceived before, and now he suffered like a
child—as his own pupil Ertzum had suffered with
regard to this same woman. He suffered uncouthly,
with bewilderment.

He went home. At the first word his servant
spoke, he broke into a rage and chased her out of
the house. Then he flew into his room, locked the
door, threw himself on to the sofa and groaned.
Utterly ashamed, he pulled himself together and took
out his MS. on the particles of Homer. He leaned
on his desk, that desk which for thirty years past
had been pushing up his right shoulder out of its
place. But sheet after sheet had drafts of letters to
Rosa—others notes of some favourable criticism
concerning her. There was no more paper; he had
thoughtlessly spoilt it all. He saw even his work
undermined by her, his thoughts absorbed by her,
his whole life come to an end through her. The
discovery sent him back to the sofa.

Night had fallen and from the darkness her bright,
whimsical, teasing face looked out at him; he turned his
eyes from it with anguish. For he felt it the index
to every shame. She belonged to—everyone. He
hid his face in his hand—the blood had rushed to
his cheeks. This late-blooming sensuality—
moving like a slow corruption through his dried-up
body, changing the whole current of his life and
driving him to hysterical extremes—was now tortur-
ing him with remembered pictures. He saw her

in her little room at the Blue Angel—watched her
alluring hands—those hands that had first beckoned
him to love. That teasing glance—provocative.
But glance and hands were beckoning now to another
—to Lohmann. He watched the whole thing
happen—saw her dancing—and he sobbed—he
sobbed!

CHAPTER XII

HE went about his work, thanks to a fundamental habit of regularity, although he foresaw that one day soon he would be taking his last walk to the school. The other teachers had tacitly agreed to ignore him; in the masters' room they all sheltered behind newspapers, or hurried from the table, looking into the corners of the room as soon as he appeared with his exercises to correct. Lohmann, von Ertzum and Kieselack were all missing from his class. The pupils remaining he despised and let them answer much as they pleased. Often he would sentence one of them to half a day's detention, but then he would forget about it and the school attendant was not told to see the sentence carried out.

In the streets he crept about, seeing no one, hearing neither insults nor sympathy, and was unaware when the cab-drivers stopped their horses to point him out to strangers as a celebrity in the town. Wherever he went the trial was being talked of, but for the townsfolk he was the accused, and his appearance before the " beak " excited both pity and anger. Older men, his former pupils, who cherished amused recollections of him, gilded with the glow of youth, would look after him and shake their heads.

"What's happened to the old fellow?   It's a pity there should be all this talk."

"But is he the sort to teach youngsters?   And then his outburst against capitalists and family! Before the court, if you please!"

"Who hasn't had his little adventures in his time?   But of course a teacher sits in a glass-house. There'll be talk about this for a long while to come, and I know from Breetpoot that they aren't going to keep him at the school.   He can get along out of this with his lady friend."

"She's a nice piece of goods."

"She is!"

On this the talkers would laugh, with a knowing glance of the eye.

"How on earth did Old Mud come to fall for her?"

"Haven't I always told you?   Give a dog a bad name—and he's in the mud this time all right."

Others remembered his son, who had once been seen in the market-place with a woman of no character. They quoted the apple that never falls far from the tree, and decided as had old Hübbenett, that this backsliding of the father's might have been foreseen. They had always wanted to hear of something really despicable and furtive in connection with Old Mud and declared that they were not at all surprised at what they had heard.

"Ought to have been shot out years ago," said the cigar merchant Meyer, leaning against his shop door; his accounts had always ended with a "d" crossed out.   When Old Mud slunk past the Café Central

the proprietor said to the waiter tidying up the
room:

"Must get rid of all that mud.":

Yet there were discontented people who hailed his
emancipation with joy; they had rejoiced in his
outbreak against the privileged classes and debates
were held on the subject of his speech at meetings,
at which they wanted him to speak. In their
proclamations they said: "Hats off to this man!"

But he left their invitations unanswered, and their
delegates he dismissed through his locked door. He
sat there brooding over Rosa with mingled hate,
longing and ferocity, thinking how he could force her
to leave the town—go as far from it as possible. He
remembered that when they first came together he
had forbidden this. If only she had opposed his wish
then! Now she would leave a cloud of scandal and
trouble behind her, and he could think of nothing he
desired more, in his impotent and tragic resentment,
than that she should pass her life in some dim and
distant corner—imprisoned. While daylight lasted
he shunned the streets in which he might meet her,
and only at night did he slink out, at an hour when
under the hanging eaves no other teachers might be
hidden, their heads set with grinning teeth. Then
only—bitter, nervous, tortured by desire—he made a
wide circle round her hotel.

Once a man approached him from its dark corner
and gave him greeting; it was Lohmann. Old Mud
started back and fought for breath. Then, tottering,
he stretched out his hands to seize the boy, who turned

away with a courteous inclination. When he was
once more firm on his feet, he started foaming.

"So you dare to come before me again, do you,
you rascal? And right by her lodging! You've been
up to your shameful games again!"

"I assure you, sir," answered Lohmann gently,
"that you are mistaken. You are entirely mistaken
where I am concerned."

"Then what are you doing here, you damned
kna ve?"

"I am sorry I cannot tell you, except that it in no
wise concerns you, sir."

"I'll knock you down—I'll——" His eyes shone
like those of a maddened cat. "You shall be expelled
from school, sir!"

"I should be glad if it would give you any satisfaction," replied Lohmann, not with satire, but with
compassion; then he turned and disappeared, followed
by the curses that Old Mud poured out upon him.

Lohmann had no longer any desire to hurt the old
man, for when he heard everyone crying out against
him he now felt ashamed. He was sorry for him, this
poor old fellow who still spoke of having him expelled
when really his own dismissal had been decided on. He
felt not only compassion, but a sort of sympathy for
this man who breathed enmity and defiance against
everyone, alone against the world. He was interested in this anarchist trembling on the brink of
ruin.

Old Mud's constant suspicion of Lohmann with regard to Rosa was most pitiful; it was full of a tragic

irony, when one compared the suspicion with the real purpose of Lohmann's presence there that night. Dora Breetpoot had been delivered of a child that night and Lohmann's undeclared love for her had hung solicitously over her bed of sickness. His heart on fire with this fruitless, humble devotion, yearned after the tiny mite, who might owe its existence to Knust or von Gierschke, or even to Breetpoot himself. He had been walking past the house and had pressed a kiss upon the closed front door.

A few days later their various destinies had changed. Lohmann, who did not wish it, was to remain at the school until he went to England; his family was too important for any question to arise of his expulsion. Kieselack's absence had nothing to do with his behaviour in the wood; rather to the impropriety of his behaviour before the court, but most of all to his relations with Rosa Fröhlich and her own testimony to them, as this was considered too profligate for a Fifth Form boy. Von Ertzum left of his own accord. Old Mud was dismissed.

He had the right to continue teaching until Autumn, but he brought it to an end, then and there, with the full approval of the authorities. On one of his first free afternoons, as he sat on the sofa with nothing to do—no plans of any kind—Pastor Quittjens came to see him. He had watched while this man fell deeper and deeper into sin, but now that he was disgraced, the pastor felt it was time to show Christian feeling. He therefore called and smoked a cigar like any other man, trying to bring comfort in this tragic case, so lonely, seeing enemies even in the best of mankind. Something must be done about it. If Old Mud would at least take up his accustomed work! Idleness would leave him a hopeless prey to bitter thoughts. Perhaps that was putting it too strongly; the pastor was sure that all would yet be well. We must look on the best side of things; he could take up politics, join a club, learn to play some game—skittles, now! The mental condition was everything and this seemed to the pastor to presage evil. Old Mud should repent of his sins before God and man and bring them to an end.

Old Mud scarcely answered; this sort of thing did not interest him. He could not look on skittles as a substitute for Rosa Fröhlich. The pastor became more emphatic; he pitied the scholars whose young lives might have been poisoned by such an example. Not only the boys of the Fifth Form, but all of them; and not only those attending the college, but outside its walls, all the former students. In short, the entire town. They must all—the pastor let his cigar go out—feel that the instructor of their youth had sown a doubt among them and that was the way that a man's faith became infirm. Old Mud had a great deal on his conscience. That boy Kieselack had already got into trouble, and Old Mud could not deny that he was responsible for the errors of that child. Nor was this the only scandal which the downfall of a man like Old Mud from Faith and Morals would have to answer for——

Old Mud was bereft of words. This was the first

he had heard of Kieselack's downfall and he burned with joy at the thought of having been instrumental in it. That his example could be dangerous to others and sow evil in the town he had not realized and the thought opened up a prospect of revenge that excited him. Those red flecks appeared in his face and his fingers started plucking at his coat—his breath came short and laboured, stirring the sparse hairs on his lip.

The pastor misunderstood and said that he had known Old Mud would see the matter in its proper light; naturally, he had brought the greatest inconvenience on himself and others and the *faux pas* was obvious. Old Mud asked him if he had heard anything about Miss Fröhlich. But of course! Naturally, after her open confession before the court, Old Mud's eyes had been opened. Love makes us blind, as everyone knows.

The pastor relit his cigar. Besides, Old Mud had only to remember his own days as a student and the things one got up to in Berlin. One was no innocent— hm—to be mistaken about a woman of that sort. They were not worth jeopardising one's interests and those of others for. Yes, when one remembered the little adventures that came one's way in Berlin——

Pastor Quittjens smiled knowingly and prepared to exchange confidences, but Old Mud had been getting more and more impatient and he now interrupted him. What had all this to do with Miss Fröhlich? The pastor was offended and started stammering—on which Old Mud jumped up from the sofa and went stamping up and down, foaming and cursing, the saliva from his mouth spraying over Quittjens.

"You have insulted Miss Fröhlich, who is under my protection. Out of the room with you! Out of my house!"

The pastor was so startled that he jerked his chair right back, but Old Mud hastened to the door and opened it. He then turned on his guest, shaking with rage, and Quittjens seized his chair and circled out of the door with it in his hand. Old Mud slammed the door upon him.

He paced up and down the room for a long time after, admitting to himself that but a short time before he too had had hard thoughts of her. But that did not give that pastor fellow the right to insult her! She was miles above his head. She was superior to them all—unique and holy in the sight of men. It was a good thing that at last he could see things clearly again. She was his affair! And those who did not leave her alone would have to answer for it to him. He was seized again by his tyrannical rage and he had to give it vent as once before when the audience at the Blue Angel had laughed at her. Laughed at her, when he himself had made her up! Failed to appreciate the performance in which he had had a hand! It was not a frivolous matter, like that picnic party in the wood and it had given him much pain, but that was between him and her. He would go to her, he could not stay away any longer.

He seized his hat and then—he hesitated. She

had betrayed him—cheated him. Moreover she had pointed the way that had led to the undoing of his pupil Kieselack. Well, was she not justified? But suppose she had led others, too—to ruin?

He stopped with drooping head, that red cloud mounting up his cheeks. His lust for revenge warred with his jealousy until he could hardly bear it, but at last revenge won. She was justified.

He began to dream of the boys whom she should have brought to ruin. What a shame that the cigar merchant, Meyer, was no longer at the school; and that young apprentice, who grinned instead of saluting him; and everyone else in the town. She should have ruined the lot of them! They had all driven him out of the place with shame and contumely; and that was the only sort of ruin that he could picture. A form of downfall of quite a different sort, driving one out of school, did not come within his conception.

When he knocked at her door she herself appeared, dressed to go out.

"There you are! I was just coming to see you. Of course you won't believe it but may I die if it isn't true."

"I do believe it," said he. And it was the truth.

When he did not appear she had said to herself: "Oh, very well!" And by dint of not paying her rent and selling bit by bit the furniture he had given her, had managed to finance herself while looking for a new engagement, for the Kieperts had gone off elsewhere. She had the friendliest feeling for her

old dear, God knew, but one couldn't live on air and
if he didn't believe her he could do the other thing.
She had a philosophy of her own. It was much easier
to make a man believe you when there was something
to conceal than when you were innocent. Moreover,
one really couldn't be bothered by a man who made
such a fuss about a little thing like that visit to the
wood and wanted to pretend that she would demean
herself with anyone and everyone! That sort of
thing wouldn't do for her! But of course, when one
made a mistake one said so and that was all about it.
In the street a man might run after one for half an
hour before he risked touching one's arm and drawing
one aside. And then as like as not he would change
his mind and pretend he didn't mean it. Old Mud
hadn't understood, and as soon as he did—of course,
he was off. Oh, well——

But as time went on and she was bored and had no
money, she decided that it was too silly to leave things
like that. Of course the old dear was ashamed to
make the first advance and was waiting for her to
hold up her little finger. Well, why not? He was
a silly old thing—a regular scream. She remembered
how he had turned the captain out of the dressing-
room, and then done the same to Kiepert, and she
laughed. But then she remembered those staring,
dreamy eyes with which the old dear used to look at
her. He was jealous, that's what it was; and the
thought made her feel proud. No doubt he was
sitting and thinking putrid things about her, and he
wouldn't be able to eat a bit of lunch. That was

dreadful and she couldn't have it, really.   And it was
not only self-interest, but pity and a trifle of pride
too that was sending her to him.

"It's quite a time since I saw you," said she shyly,
but with a touch of mischief.

"There were reasons," said Old Mud.   "I was—er
—busy."

"Oh?   What with?"

"With my retirement from the staff of the college."

"I see.   You mean that as a reproach to me."

"You were justified.   That boy Kieselack has been
sent away and his career is gone for good."

"The little beast.   I'm glad."

"It is to be hoped that the same fate may overtake
many of the others."

"How are we to bring that about?" she smiled up
at him.   He went red and there was a pause, while
she took him in and made him sit down.   She then
slid on to his knee, hid her face on his shoulder and
asked with playful humility:

"Not cross with me, are you, old dear?   What I
told the court—that really was all; it was indeed.   I
nearly said by God it is, but that wouldn't help,
would it?   But you can believe me, indeed you can."

"Yes, yes, quite so," he said and feeling that he
must bring her nearer to him by an elucidation of the
past, he added: "I have always been inclined to think
that conventional morality was merely a form of
stupidity.   The great Humanists had no doubt about
it.   It is, of course, a protection for those who, not

having any such standard, would exercise no self-control. Therefore one should inculcate it firmly with the ordinary rank and file, but I have never denied that there are other orders of—er—intellect which—er—are widely different from the average Philistine. Yes, yes—quite so."

"You mean that?" she said, astonished. "You're not getting at me?"

"I myself," he continued, "have lived strictly by rule, not because I was convinced of the value of such bigotry but—er—because—well, because I had no desire to—er—do otherwise."

He was trying to intoxicate himself with the sound of his own words, but he stuttered and went red, feeling the shameful weakness of it all, and so he brought his little speech to an end. She wondered at what she heard, and felt flattered that he gave her best, as she put it. But he had more to add.

"I—er—have never felt that I could tie you to my own way of life——" But at this she broke in with a kiss, so that he could scarcely continue—"yes yes. But it has not prevented——"

"Prevented what, old dear?"

"My feeling considerable pain that you—er—in short, it has hurt me very much. For I did not think you one who—er—who would easily—er——" She was looking serious and thoughtful and he finished hastily and lamely: "Yes, yes. Quite so, quite so." The storm of recollection overcame him and he cried:

"One thing I could never forgive you. You must never see him again. That Lohmann!" He was

all wrought up, perspiring, and she did not understand for she knew nothing of the tormenting picture
that once more had sprung before his eyes—that
picture of Lohmann with her!

"You've always been dotty about that boy," she
said. "You wanted to make sausage meat of him
didn't you, old dear? And so you shall. I don't
care for the fellow, I can tell you. I wish I could
make you believe it, but I can't. It's enough to
make me cry my eyes out." She really meant this,
for she wanted to think that she was entirely cold
with regard to Lohmann, because she was afraid it
was not so; and because Old Mud, the silly old dear,
was such a bore about it and she didn't see how
otherwise they were ever to have the peaceful life
her soul yearned for.

But he wouldn't have understood what she was
crying for and she didn't want to tangle things up
still more, so she forewent the pleasure of a good
cry.

And now indeed they started having a good time.
They went about everywhere together and she was
established in a comfortable way. She sat almost
every evening in her box at the theatre in a smart
frock and Old Mud at her side endured with fortitude
all the amused and scornful looks that were cast
upon him. The Summer Theatre had opened now,
and one could sit in the garden amidst well-off people,
eating salmon sandwiches and enjoying oneself as
one had never done before. She took no further
pains to keep him from others, for the worst was over

and he had openly assumed the position of her
protector regardless of the universal contempt.

At first she found it rather dull; whatever she
seemed outwardly, to herself she admitted that she
had got him on her hands. Then she shrugged her
shoulders. "Men are like that," she thought. But
gradually she saw that he was right and that it was
meet and proper for a girl like her to be looked after.
He kept repeating to her how wonderful she was and
of how little consequence other people were compared
to her until she at last began to take herself seriously.
No one had ever taken her seriously before and so
of course she had not thought of it. She was grateful
to him for teaching her her true worth. She felt
that she, in her turn, ought to cherish this man who
had set her on so high a pedestal. She did more;
she forced herself to care for him.

Suddenly she declared that she wanted to learn
Latin and he complied at once with her wish. She
let him talk, answered all wrong, or failed to hear
and poured out questions on her own part. At the
third lesson she sought for information.

"Which is the most difficult, Latin or Greek?"

"Greek."

"Then I'll learn Greek."

"Why?" asked he, delighted.

"That's why, old dear." She kissed him; it
seemed a parody of love, and yet she meant it. He
had roused her ambition and to do him honour she
would learn Greek instead of Latin because it was
more difficult. The very desire was a declaration

of love—the indication of a love she wished to feel. And she found it hard enough to love her old dear. Even Greek was not more difficult than that. As if she wanted to make him her very own she was always stroking that wooden face of his with her slim fingers —the working jaws, the rucks from which his eyes peered out, with their poisonous look for all others, but for her full of a childish worship. She felt sorry for him and that made for tenderness; the comic affection of his caresses and the laborious learnedness of his talk, these things moved her, and she was constantly reminding herself of the respect that was due to him. But further than this she could not manage to go.

To make up for this she really did do her best with the Greek. Those red flecks rose on his cheeks and he dwelt with enthusiasm on the particles. When he opened his Homer and read out to her for the first time Μὲν – – – δέγϋν—when those loved syllables fell for the first time from those equally loved lips of hers, his heart swelled. He had to lay the book aside and gather her in his arms. His breath came haltingly and he took that small white, but still somewhat greasy hand and declared that he could not part from her again even for an hour. They must get married.

At first her lips trembled as if she were on the brink of tears and then she smiled, leaned her cheek against his shoulder and gently swayed rocking with pure joy. Her delight would not be suppressed; she pulled him from his chair and valsed him round.

"I shall be Mrs. Mud! Oh, I shall die with

laughing. Mrs. Mud—no, I mean Mut. Sorry, old dear." She began to play the part of a grand lady, letting herself drop languidly into a chair. She chatted away delightedly for a moment and then she decided that her new furniture was not good enough now; most of it could be sold. She must come along to his house and see how it could be done up. Then off she went again with more chatter, but at last she calmed down and fell into thought.

"Just think!" she said, wonderingly.

When he asked if she would like to get married as soon as possible she only smiled, her thoughts still absorbed. Nor did she seem her usual self for the next few days, but kept going into a brown study and then indignantly denying it. She went out and was impatient if he wanted to go with her. He was worried and began to suspect some painful secret and one day he saw her leaving a cheap lodging-house. They walked on together for a bit in silence and then she said darkly:

"Things aren't always what they seem, old dear."

This added to his uneasiness, but she would not explain.

On a day soon after this he was going along with a worried mind through the empty noon-tide streets, when a child dressed all in white ran up to him and cried in baby tones:

"Come along home, daddy!"

He stopped, astonished, looking down at the little hand in its white glove that the child was reaching up to him.

"Come along home, daddy," repeated the little girl.

"What's this? Where do you live?" asked Old Mud.

"There!" the child pointed and Old Mud turned round. At the corner of the street stood Rosa, smiling, her hand held out. She made a gesture as if apologizing—pleading.

He worked his jaws, for he understood. Then, without further words, he slipped his hand into the child's.

CHAPTER XIII

THE family was visiting the neighbouring watering-place. They put up at the hotel and rented one of the wooden huts on the shore. Rosa was dressed in white—summer frock, hat and shoes—and looked charming with a white veil floating from the soft hat, holding her little girl, also in white, by the hand. Even Old Mud had on a white flannel suit, and along the promenade and dunes, from all the wooden huts, opera glasses were trained on him, while someone from their town told strangers all about him.

When the child was playing on the sand she had to be careful not to lose any of her playthings or some good-looking young man would at once bring it back, not to Mimi but to Rosie. Then the stranger would bow and introduce himself and so it came to pass that soon the family were sitting and drinking coffee in their little bathing hut with two Hamburg merchants, a young Brazilian and a manufacturer from Saxony. With these new friends they went boating and everyone was seasick except Old Mud. He and Rosa laughed at the other men. Mimi received chocolates and sweets every day, and presents of boats and spades and rubber dolls. Everyone was good-tempered and cheerful and they went for donkey rides, Old Mud with his feet out of the stirrups,

clinging to the animal's mane. They galloped past
the bandstand to the strains of music and kept it
up until the concert commenced. Rosa shrieked,
the child enjoyed herself hugely and remarks were
made at all the other tables.

When a Berlin banker arrived with a Hungarian
dancer, Old Mud wanted to push "those people" from
their accustomed seats, was always complaining of the
table d'hôte, demanded that the band played certain
pieces—the conductor had met Rosa before in a
professional capacity—set fireworks going with his
own hand and started strife, amusement and annoyance.

Old Mud was a riddle to those who shared his
company for the sake of his wife. He laid down the
law, wore his smart clothes awkwardly, and seemed
to have no serious occupation other than an amusing
habit of continual complaint; he seemed like a lost
dog. But when one began to flirt with his wife an
ironic glance would appear in his eye and when he
admired a bracelet that one had given her, one could
not resist the feeling that one had been caught out.
And even after one thought one had attained one's
end—after a walk in the dusk with the wife along the
sea-front while the husband was kept busy with a
game of bowls—there would be that disquieting smile
on his face when one shook hands and said good
night, so that one wondered whether, after all, one
was not wasting one's time.

And that was what happened, for Old Mud was
much too cunning to forbid his wife to see other men,

but when he was alone with her he would mock the Hamburgers' way of talking, shrug at the Brazilian, who always sent coins spinning across the water instead of pebbles, and mimicked the feudal manner of the man from Leipzig when lighting a cigar or opening a bottle. This would set Rosa off laughing, although she was not in agreement with him in thus making fun of her friends. Moreover he always said the same old thing—that the Greeks did not behave like that. Never mind! She loved a good laugh and his obstinacy and majestic refusal to think any man good enough for her worked their own result. She was beginning to acquire a certain personal dignity through always being in association with that strong will of his. When the Brazilian got her alone behind a breakwater by the sea and, kneeling, seized her hands, she said in a tone of conviction, as if she were really awake at last to his intentions:

"So you're a rotter too!"

She had been flattered that this young fellow, who was staying with a family from their town, should leave his friends to gypsy along with her, and spend his money on her, but he was just a rotter, for Old Mud had said so.

He never asked any questions after she had been on one of these excursions and showed no annoyance even if she were a little too easy in her manners, or when her summer frocks were a trifle too provocative. On the contrary, her admirers would be kept waiting while Old Mud helped her to dress and make up, just as he used to do at the Blue Angel.

"They'll be getting impatient," he would say with his mocking smile. "Yes, yes. The piano must keep them quiet." Or it would be, "Suppose you put your head through the door with your makeup half on, they'd shout Hullo, hullo, hullo again, wouldn't they?"

There was a lively incident before they left the seaside. At the station they were waiting for the train and the Brazilian was seizing the chance to speak a few words in Rosie's ear, when an old fellow called Vermöhlen, to whose family the young fellow belonged, sneaked up and laid a hand on Rosa's handbag. It had been given to her by the Brazilian and Old Mud had to hurry up and protect his wife, while the young fellow, red with embarrassment, denied his relationship with Vermöhlen. But the old man excitedly informed Old Mud that the Brazilian was his nephew and had been spending far too much money in their society. He had refused to give the boy any more, though unfortunately his wife had been weak enough to do so, but it was old Vermöhlen's money and he objected.

To this Old Mud replied calmly that it was certainly much the same thing whether the money belonged to the husband or the wife, but that such details of the family affairs of the Vermöhlens were no concern of his and that they should lose the train if they did not hurry. His own fingers closed firmly on the handbag as he pushed his wife into the carriage and then he lifted his hat to each of the men in turn, though old Vermöhlen was threatening with raised stick.

Rosa was very upset at the affair and feared the consequences, but he reassured her. He explained that old Vermöhlen's sons had been among his former pupils and that he had never managed to "catch" them. Vermöhlen was related to nearly everyone in the town. Rosie calmed down and showed the jewels in the clasp to her little girl, telling her they should be hers some day, while Old Mud openly rejoiced that he had "caught" a Vermöhlen at last. Gradually it dawned on him that here was a way to punish unruly scholars without turning them out of the room or even getting them expelled. There were other forms of disgrace and ruin besides those connected with school discipline. New ways, that he had not thought of before.

Back in the town their old life began again. It was monotonous. Rosa lay about in a dressing-gown until evening, when they always dined at a restaurant and then went on to the theatre. He tried to amuse her by teaching her Greek, but she was not interested now. One evening when a comedy was being performed she recognized an old friend in one of the actresses.

"Why, that's Hedwig Pielemann. Fancy her appearing here! She's a rotten actress." She then poured out a lot of stories about her former friend. "She must come and see us," she added.

The Pielemann came and to give her friend an idea of her importance Rosie insisted on inviting her to lunch and supper, and now there would be two women lying about on the sofas instead of one, smoking and

reminding one another of former experiences. Old
Mud saw uneasily that they were both bored and felt
it his duty to do something in the matter, but he
could not think what, worried as he was with secret
cares. Whenever there was a ring at the door he
would slip out and open it himself. The girls noticed
that he never let the servant go to the front door.

"Either he's got some surprise for me, or he's
deceiving me," said Rosa. "He's a queer old sport
is my old dear."

One day a letter arrived from their Hamburg
friends. They were going on a pleasure trip to the
Spanish coast and then on to Tunis and wanted Old
Mud and his wife to go too.

"What a joy!" cried Rosie. "Of course we'll go
and you must come too, Pielemann. You can take
a vacation, can't you? We'll get so brown and
sunburned, but we shall have to take our own sheets.
I'll wear that tiara of mine. I haven't worn it since
I left the stage."

The Pielemann was perfectly agreeable and Old
Mud's consent was not asked, although they expressed
surprise that he did not show more pleasure at the
idea. He said nothing until the Pielemann had gone
and then he had to speak out. He had no more
money.

"It's not possible! A professor must have money!"
cried she.

He smiled with some embarrassment. He had had
some 30,000 marks saved up, but they had all gone
in furnishing, frocks and amusements. Their spend-

ings were not at all within the limits of his pension,
but far overran it. He was always receiving bills,
which he took in himself at the door, from restaurant-
keepers, dressmakers and tradesmen of all sorts. He
told her with bitter humiliation of the tricks he had
to get up to to avoid having the brokers in. It
could not be put off much longer.

She was horrified and remorseful. She had never
given the matter a thought. But now of course she
understood and those two fellows could go off on their
own. They'd make do with soup for lunch to-day,
and sausage for supper and she would go on learning
Greek, since that didn't cost anything. He was
touched and assured her that—er—yes, yes, quite so
—he knew his duty and she must have everything
she wanted.

"Untold gold, eh, old dear?" said she. Then she
sat down to write the news to the Pielemann as of
course this made a difference in their plans. The
Pielemann solved the difficulty. Old Mud must
take pupils.

"Well, they're not very partial to the old dear
here," admitted his wife.

"I'll get my friend to do something," said the Pielemann in the proud tone of a benefactor.

"Lorenz the wine merchant? That won't do. He
used to be a pupil of the old dear's who said he
wouldn't have him come to the house, though he
didn't mind you. If I went to him behind his back,
it would put Lorenz wise and he'd just sell us up."

"You don't understand," said the Pielemann. "I

should tell him what I expected him to do! 'Take it or leave it, Lorenz,' I should say. 'You know what you've got to do if you don't want to lose me.'"

Old Mud was accordingly told that Lorenz the wine merchant wanted to learn Greek because he bought Greek wines, and Old Mud was to give him lessons. He was very upset at the news but he did not refuse. He commented with his ironical smile at this late blossoming of the Tree of Knowledge in his former pupil and of the many occasions on which Lorenz had called him by his nickname without his being able to "catch" him.

"Still, all is not yet lost," he thought and added:

"You remember when we were married, my dear, the tumult that broke out on the harbour and how they ran after our carriage——"

"Well, why shouldn't they?" said Rosa hastily, annoyed at this reminiscence being brought forward in the Pielemann's hearing.

"That rascal who stood in front of the registrar's office and shouted out indecencies—er—yes, yes— and threw stones which dirtied your white frock? Quite so, quite so. But it is undeniable that besides the boys who were shouting out my opprobrious nickname Lorenz on that occasion earned for himself undying infamy."

"Then I'll jolly well tell him so," declared the Pielemann.

"I was not able to 'catch' him," continued Old

Mud sadly. "I had no proof. And now he is to learn Greek. There are so many I've never been able to catch. I wish they'd all come for Greek lessons."

Lorenz arrived and was treated with mildness, but every time he made a mistake or brought a bad exercise Old Mud called in Rosa and involved her in the interview. She must display her prowess to Lorenz, but after this the talk passed to mundane matters. Lorenz had come along at first with his tongue in his cheek, but he changed his tone when he saw how gracefully she fitted into this new environment of hers; he found that she was better dressed than his own wife, who made a fuss every time she saw "that actress woman" at the theatre. He decided that a dash of make-up and a little lively talk, a bit of Bohemia, gave spice to family life. That old blighter! Old Mud! One needn't bother to go to the club or anywhere else now. And instead of the rôle of patron, Lorenz found himself their debtor.

He begged for permission to bring along a bottle or two of wine, and with this he also brought a pasty so that a trifling refreshment might enliven the Greek lesson. When anything else was wanted Old Mud went out to fetch it. He went first after a corkscrew and then, when the wine had been freely sampled and Lorenz was getting gay, after a good many other things.

When this state of things showed a tendency to recur, Rosa ventured to hint that it would be livelier

if the class were bigger. Lorenz was all for privacy,
but Old Mud agreed with his wife and Lorenz had to
invite his friends. The Pielemann brought a member
or two of her cast and there were dishes, fruits and so
on to have ready. The hostess herself poured out
tea. Champagne was called for and Old Mud would
remark with his ironical smile:

"You know, of course, that I no longer hold my
old position at the college; we will not inquire whether
justly or unjustly—no, no, quite so."

They let him make his speech and enjoyed themselves, putting up a little pool to pay for the champagne. Often he would go himself and fetch it, and
he would be seen coming back along the streets with
the bottles in a basket, trying to hide the basket
as he used to try to hide the pail at the Blue
Angel.

When they had all reached a certain degree of merriment Rosa would yield to entreaty and sing them her
old songs; and when she was sufficiently drunk she
would add the one about the "fool moon," but at this
Old Mud would interfere and send them all off home.
They were surprised at this and began to expostulate
and exchange impertinences, but when they saw
him angry and not inclined to put up with it, they
apologized and Rosa softly begged him to forgive her,
though she had no idea what she was being forgiven
for.

They were all young people and most of them had
been among the audience at the Blue Angel, and so
long as there were not too many of them they were

content enough to be on friendly terms with Old Mud,
having their fun behind his back and feeling something of the submission of schoolboys when they
had to pay for their joke. Then their number increased and individuals were transformed into silent
spectators. The personal feeling was at an end. It
was as if Old Mud had transported the former troop
of artists to a smaller room, where the audience
could . talk to the actresses more conveniently
and comfortably and where the doors were open
later so that one need not leave until one felt
inclined.

Once when there were not so many present Lorenz
proposed baccarat and Old Mud showed some curiosity
to learn the game; and when he had grasped its rules,
took the bank. He won. So soon as this happened he
gave up the bank and as originator of the party,
Lorenz felt himself obliged to put a little life into it.
He took from his pocket book a number of hundred
mark notes and many of those present were soon
declaring that they hadn't another penny. The bank
won once more and Rosa slipped behind her husband
to whisper:

"You see? Why did you give up the bank, old
dear?"

"That hat at eighty marks is now yours, my dear,"
he replied. "I can also pay the restaurant keeper,
Zebbelin—enough to stop his mouth, anyway. I think
that is sufficient." He watched Lorenz winning
equably enough and then it happened that Lorenz
begon to lose. On this Old Mud felt himself stirred

with a wave of excited triumph. When the wine
merchant was cleared out and was looking with some
chagrin into his empty notebook Old Mud said softly:
    "I think our Greek lesson has lasted long enough
for to-day, Lorenz."

Rumours were soon spreading through the town
that Old Mud was holding regular orgies at his house.
The employees at the bank, the members of the club
and all the shopkeepers heard exaggerated accounts
from various unmarried men and echoes of these
sifted through to their families, the women whispering
among themselves and wanting to know more. What
was that cancan which Old Mud danced? Their
husbands thought it better not to enlighten them
and of course they then imagined that it was a case
of unheard of profligacy. And ridiculous tales had
quite a vogue in the town. Dark stories circulated
among the young girls in the place and they would
talk it over for hours, with round-eyed curiosity.
They had heard too that women appeared in that
dreadful house with nothing on at all! "How
terrible!" But they thought it rather fun, all the
same.

Lorenz brought along some officers who bought the
wine for their mess from him, and among them was
Lieutenant von Gierschke. Judge Knust had been
one of the first to present himself; he and young
Richter, the assistant teacher, were rivals for Rosa's
favours. Richter was now engaged to be married to the
girl of good family, but he was a poor fiancé. He was
susceptible, pleasure-loving, and lost his head pretty

quickly. Led away by Lorenz' example he lost at
play at Old Mud's place more than his month's
salary in one evening, made foolish bets and in the
heat of his passion for his hostess forgot all decency.
In the masters' room there fell on him for this
a shadow of the shame that attached to Old Mud
himself.

Old Mud's own affairs were good or bad as the luck
of the game decided. Now Rosie would have a
chinchilla coat, and her bright face would look
piquantly from the greyish fur. Another time Old
Mud would have to stay in bed and pretend to be
ill when the guests arrived, for not a single restaurant
keeper would send him any food. A day or two after
he went to see them and pointed out that if they
forced things to a catastrophe they wouldn't get a
penny, and they saw the justice of this and gave him
longer credit. Then again he would win and pay
up.

Rosa herself seldom punted but when she did she
did not rise from the table until she had lost everything. One evening, however, her luck was so
fabulously good that her antagonist, Lorenz, had to
withdraw. He was as white as a sheet and left the
house muttering curses. She sat there as delighted
as a child, her hands full of coins and paper. They
all began to show her a certain respect and begged
her to count her winnings, which came to more
than twelve thousand marks. Then she said she
wanted to go to bed and when she was left alone with
Old Mud, her eyes glowed feverishly.

"Got a little nest egg for Mimi now, old dear. Talk about mascots! Here's a little bit of all right for the child."

But in the early morning their house was besieged by creditors demanding their money. As Rosa wanted that nest egg for her daughter she'd have died rather than part with it, but they wrung it from her. The rumour went round that Lorenz was going to send in his bill for wine and Old Mud went to find out. When he came back he was white and shaken and could not get out a word.

"He's going bankrupt. Lorenz is filing his petition," he said, snapping his jaws, when at last he could manage to speak.

"I don't care," said Rosie, curled up on the ottoman, her hands between her knees.

"He's a bankrupt—Lorenz—my pupil," repeated Old Mud. "He's down and he won't rise again! His career is—quite so—is ruined." He said the words softly as if he were terrified at his own joy.

"Oh, what's it matter? They've taken Mimi's nest egg," she said, unhappily.

"He's caught now," muttered Old Mud. "I've done it at last. I've caught him. And now he'll go to his well-deserved punishment."

She looked round at him as if she thought him crazy. His hands were trembling as he kept repeating:

"He's down—he's caught! He's ruined!"

Gradually his curious behaviour absorbed her attention and ousted the thought of her own cares.

She sat staring at him, shocked at this passionate hatred, startled at the realization of how near akin it was to madness. She shuddered—but there was sweetness in the shudder, for she felt more bound than ever to her old dear through this—this violent —this dangerous thing.

CHAPTER XIV

SOME of the pupils still at the school were among Old Mud's guests and one of them, a tall fair youth, lost considerable sums. At the end of the season on an early spring evening, Old Mud saw Hübbenett appear at his door—the teacher who had always been his enemy, who had said spiteful things about his son and spoken of himself to his own class by that nickname. Now here he stood, very stiff and upright, and Old Mud smiled that ironic smile of his. He had been expecting his late colleague, for Hübbenett's son it was who played for such high stakes and he must know that all was not right in his home. Hübbenett shouted at his unhappy son and ordered him to follow him home at once. The boy sat overwhelmed. Looking at nobody, his father declared that he meant to have inquiries made into the circumstances and how it was that adventurers were allowed to carry on like this, laying traps for weak young men; robbing their fathers and using filthy means to scatter their mud.

One officer hurried out of the house and another guest, very perturbed, faced the overwrought teacher and pointed out to him how unwise it would be to make a public scandal of it. Did he really think that what went on in that house was immoral? Why not stop and see for himself? Did he not recognize the gentleman over there by the green table? That was Consul Breetpoot and that man frowning at Hübbenett was the well-known barrister, Flad. Did Hübbenett really think it would be wise to cause trouble that would involve gentlemen like these?

Hübbenett did not; that was very plain. He spluttered a bit, but his voice was less loud; then he went away, and no one thought any more about him. Old Mud, however, glowing with triumph, hurried after his late colleague and offered him a drink and as the other declined with a virtuous shrug, he called after him that he would always be glad to see both the father and the son.

Then holiday time came again and this time a gay crowd followed Old Mud and his wife to the little watering place, where Old Mud had rented a furnished villa. On the humble hired sofas Rosa laid beautiful Japanese silk covers and a roulette wheel was placed on the table. From the glasses with the legend "Greetings from the Seaside" upon them they drank champagne, and after they had gambled the night through with boisterous gaiety they would go down to the beach to see the sunrise and on Sunday breakfasted to the strains of the morning service in the church. Some nights they spent away from home. Thanks to the number of her friends, the café and restaurant on the beach were open to Rosa whenever she pleased, even long after closing time.

She was insatiable and drove the crowd of her

admirers day and night in any direction she pleased, as if throwing a stick for dogs to fetch, and awarding this or the other a coveted bone. And Old Mud watched it all with his ironical smile, rubbing his hands with delight. She demanded some sort of test from every one of them. One—a fat, rosy-cheeked man called Jakobi—she insisted should swim out to the sandbank directly after dinner. A six-course dinner too!

"Oh, it would kill me," he protested, honestly frightened, but she replied quickly:

"Then you must be a weakling. Mustn't he, old dear?"

"A weakling, yes, yes, a weakling," agreed Old Mud. "Yet Jakobi used to be something of an athlete when at school and climbed over the wall and in at a window on our floor where I was teaching with a bottle of goat's milk. It was days before the smell of it was got out of the room. He ought to be able to swim."

After this, amidst roars of laughter, the young man decided to try and make the attempt. Everyone collected on the beach to see him come out of his bathing hut, and bets were freely made upon him. How fat he was and how rosy! But when he was only halfway he had to be pulled into the boat that was accompanying him and he was brought to land unconscious. Bringing him back to life became the subject of more wagers and some, who had lost on their first bet, wanted to make up for it by betting either that he would be round very quickly, or that he would die. But the women took it in bad part and there was some hysteria. When a quarter of an hour went by and he had still not come round, they all fell silent and many went away. But Old Mud stayed.

He looked into the white, still face of his old pupil and remembered how often he had seen it mutinous and scornful. But there he lay and there they all lay—all defeated. There was nothing more to fight; no one to discipline. And the thought oppressed him a trifle. His triumphal path seemed to shake beneath him; his head swam with the very height of the mountain that his madness had reared.

But Jakobi opened his eyes——

The two men from Hamburg, the Brazilian and the Leipziger had much to say about this incident, partly out of personal pique, for they found that they no longer counted, and they could not understand what had been happening. Instead of the always good-tempered girl of the preceding year they now found a Rosa who had all the audacious despotism of an acknowledged beauty and who was courted by everyone as if she really were one. And yet she was not, by any means; her friends of last year found the very idea of such a thing quite laughable. And yet each day they succumbed a little more to the spell; the very first day the Brazilian wanted to get back on to the old footing, but he found he had to languish from afar.

The nearest to the goal were Judge Knust and the

teacher, Richter, for they had the most to offer. One was the most run-after bachelor in the town and the other was engaged to be married. Rosa was unable to chose between them for a long time. Knust was the more desirable, but the ensnaring of Richter would bring more renown. His fiancée was a sort of rival, for she alone wore frocks that in any way compared with Rosa's.

From Knust she demanded that he should box the ears of the first man whose name she happened to mention on the following Wednesday. He smirked and said that he wasn't going to be such a fool, on which she declared that in that case she had done with him and that anyone who wished to win her regard must do everything she asked. Richter was the man for her; that engagement must be broken. One afternoon when the band was playing he was seen to be riding a donkey with Rosa. He was sitting on the same saddle and clasping her with intoxicated fervour. They galloped right along the row of coffee drinkers and his fiancée was among them.

Directly after dinner Rosa rose and told Richter and Old Mud, who were one on each side of her, that she felt tired and was going to bed early. She was escorted to her home by a procession carrying gay paper lanterns and some of the men sang a serenade under her balcony. When silence fell again Old Mud, who was half undressed, called out to his wife, thinking she was on the balcony. But no. He looked for her everywhere, calling and calling; he

wanted to have a good laugh with her over the doings
of his late colleague Richter; that young man's career
was threatened with ruin!   But his rejoicing evapor-
ated before those empty rooms, and a strange oppres-
sion seized him.   Still—he knew her moods—she
had probably gone down to the sea.   He sat down
by the child's little iron bedstead and chased the
flies from her face.

Yet another good man turned into a fool by his
Rosa!   Receiving just a little moonshine illusion for
his bracelets and silver toys.   Old Mud went off to
bed.   But in his innermost consciousness—depths
that he preferred to leave unexplored—he knew that
Rosa had a companion and that that companion
was Richter.   And that Richter had not been made a
fool of.

He tossed and turned till midnight; then he jumped
up and dressed again, saying that he must wake the
servant and send people out with lanterns to find his
Rosa, for some accident must have happened.   He
seized a candle and started for the servant's room,
but as he reached the stairs he woke from his self-
deception, put out the light that it might not betray
him and went sadly back to bed.   The moon shone
wanly on Rosie's empty pillow and he had to keep
looking and looking, his breath coming faster.   Then
he crumpled up and began to whimper, but his own
voice startled him and he sank under the bedclothes.
Then he decided that he must take it like a man,
dressed himself again and thought out the reception
he would give her.   He would say: "Had a little

walk? That's right; it happened that I wasn't sleepy either and I've only just come in." He rehearsed this speech for a whole hour, striding up and down his room. Then he heard a sound at the front door and wildly tore off his clothes and jumped into bed He listened, his eyes shut, to her muffled movements, to the soft rustle of her garments as she cast them off, to the careful way in which she got into bed—to a soft sigh—and at last to her light snoring, so familiar and so dear.

In the morning they both pretended to be asleep. She decided to be the first to yawn and when he turned towards her, he found her suffering— on the point of tears. She pressed against his shoulder.

"Oh, if you only knew, old dear! We can't always help ourselves," she sobbed.

"Yes, yes. Quite so. Quite so," said he consolingly, but she cried the more to think how kind he was in accepting such a poor excuse.

They remained indoors all day and Rosa, languid and abstracted, sat with eyes that dreamed of sweet remembrance—large wide-opened eyes from which he turned away ashamed. In the evening one of their friends came along to ask her if she had heard the news. But how could she, since she had not been out?

"Richter's engagement has been broken off."

She sprang up and looked at her husband.

"He's done for," said her informant. "Compromised to the ears. You know the influence her family have and you may take it for certain that they'll get him kicked out of the college. They won't have him in the town, for it would be a perpetual humiliation for her. He's done for."

She saw her husband flush and go pale again, and sway from one foot to the other, link his fingers and pull them loose again; she saw him sniff the air as if he were savouring the sweetness of those words, inhaling their delight. He rejoiced and quailed at the same time, for this time he had to pay for his triumph and her uneasy conscience read in his face the price he knew that he had had to pay.

He left the room and she found some excuse to escape from her guests.

"You're glad?" she said, hiding her anxiety. "But it's mean to rejoice at another person's misfortune."

He sat on the balcony, one hand grasping the rail, and peered between the bushes at the sea, as if he were gazing at an infinite horizon which he could only reach by passing over an abyss. She sensed something of his thoughts and now it was she who played the part of the consoler.

"There is nothing to worry about, old dear. The man is down—that's certain."

But she had to sigh, for she had but to think back a few hours to realize how ungrateful she was to poor Richter. How had it happened? He was a poor sort of fool, but if it hadn't been for Knust she wouldn't have thought of it. She had been so put out! Well, let's forget it! It was quite another thing with the old dear; he made one feel quite a prostitute. Look at him, sitting there!

"Us two!" said she and reached out her hand. He took it, but he said:

"One thing is certain; that when one thinks to touch the mountain top, one must reckon with its unfathomable gorges."

CHAPTER XV

WHEN they went back to the town they found their circle awaiting them.

"Here's an end to boredom, thank goodness," said the young men in the clubs.

On the day after their return they held their first reception and the whole town was talking about it— who would be there—what they would eat—what sort of new frocks the Fröhlich had. Married men, on coming home, would bring news of something that had happened at the harbour or unexpected business turning up, and vanish again as quickly as possible.

Many kept away, either through moral conviction or a cool temperament, or from motives of economy. These people yawned among the empty seats at the casino; they would be angry and then overwhelmed as they saw their number continually diminishing and the staunch found themselves unjustly treated. The theatre was so badly supported that its very existence was threatened. There was no good variety entertainment. The five or six ladies of the demi-monde who used to be patronized by the better class were so well known that everyone was tired of them and the pleasure they had to offer paled before the thought of Old Mud and his attractive wife. In this old world town where there was no escape from the boredom of family life except that offered by a crude sort of vice, there was a rush for that house near the gates where one could gamble and drink and meet women who were not of the streets and yet were not quite ladies; where the hostess, wife of the old professor, sang piquant songs, danced magnificently and when one went the right way about it, was ready for other things—this amazing villa near the gates of the town was draped in a fabulous shimmer, the silvery, quivering air of a fairy palace. To think of it! Not an evening passed without talk of this house where Old Mud lived with his wife. An acquaintance was seen to slip round the corner, a clock would strike and one would say:

"There's something going on down there, of course." Then one would go to bed tired, without knowing why one was tired, and would say to oneself:

"They're having a good time down there."

There were men in the town, though not many, who, like Consul Lohmann, had passed their youth in another country, and were as much at home in Hamburg as here, and went to Paris and London and who had not the slightest curiosity about the receptions given by the dismissed schoolmaster and his young wife. But well-off citizens, who had for thirty years, perhaps, trotted through those five streets plying their trade in fish and butter, saw an unhoped for and most enjoyable return for their money. Here was indeed a reward for their pains, and they now enjoyed what they had always longed for. Others who had known bigger towns once upon a time and were somewhat bored, like Consul Breetpoot, decided to make the most of the chance and found there unrivalled entertainment. Others, again, came in sentimental remembrance of the ladies whose loves had graced their younger days; as for instance the magistrate who had sat on that case about the wood, and Pastor Quittjens. For even he went there, just like any other man. Smaller tradesmen came there too, like the restaurant keeper and the cigar merchant, flattered to find themselves among their betters, which was not possible in any other environment. Naturally they were in the majority and set the tone.

That tone was not polished and in that sense only was it bad. All those people were there in the expectation of unusual and somewhat ambiguous pleasures and of an unaccustomed environment, where love would not be unrepresented and one would certainly not be bored. The mere fact of a woman being there meant something. If she were not as honest as any respectable woman in her own family, then she must be—the other sort. There was no medium. One might start by behaving well, yet soon, after some drinks, a touch of looseness would creep into one's speech, and one would call things by their true names, "dear" the ladies and begin to get quarrelsome. This sort of thing was destructive to ceremonious manners towards the fair sex and they accepted familiarity with pleasure. The Pielemann was unrecognizable; she let herself be dragged out of the room in which she had been shut in with one of the guests and came back with the lively troop to the gaming table without turning a hair. Rosa felt that the Pielemann would hardly have been equal to that the season before!

She herself observed formalities to a certain extent. It had to be admitted that she might find it difficult to choose—Consul Breetpoot possibly, and perhaps Knust. One knew nothing for certain where she was concerned; nothing ever happened at her home. She managed things with all the circumspection of a properly married woman; with thick veils, closed cabs, rendezvous in the country. This observance of etiquette heightened her prestige and no one would have thought of classing her with the other women. This was due to the fact that no one knew who was her protector or how much he would stand. It seemed obvious that Old Mud would not tolerate much. He had been known, in the midst of the most friendly gathering, to fall on a man who had made a remark about his wife behind his back. Old Mud had fumed and foamed and would listen to no explanations and in the end had had a stand up fight with the man, a great fat fellow, and hurried him out of the front door; and he had never been allowed to come again. He had been a man who played high and what he had said of Rosa had been the most harmless thing that could be said of her— of all the things that might have been said! Therefore one knew Old Mud's point of view with regard to his wife and took heed.

After all, Old Mud was a man of one idea. He rubbed his hands if anyone except himself broke the bank and greed-besotted, envious and irresolute faces showed about him. He accepted the presence of a drunkard with great good nature, met every empty wish with piercing scorn and found the climax of enjoyment when he heard of another's dishonour. One young man of good family was convicted of cheating and Old Mud insisted on his remaining. A chorus of virtuous protests arose and some of those present left the place, but two or three evenings later they came back again and with his "poisonous" smile Old Mud made up a party for them at the table where the same young fellow was sitting.

Another incident was more dramatic. A packet of banknotes that one of the players had laid down beside him was found to be missing and he raised an outcry, demanding that all doors should be locked and those present searched. The crowd started quarrelling and abusing one another, threatened to thrash the man, and within five minutes suspicion had turned on everyone there. Old Mud's voice rang out in its deepest tones and dominated the turmoil. He asked those whom he considered should be searched to agree, leaving it to him. Their curiosity aroused, and feeling that suspicion was now attaching to everyone, they shouted "Yes." He then turned his head this way and that and picked out

Lieutenant von Gierschke, the boy Kieselack and Consul Breetpoot.

"Breetpoot? *Breetpoot?*" cried they all.

Yes, Breetpoot. He stood to it without explaining. And von Gierschke? An officer? That had nothing to do with it in Old Mud's opinion. The lieutenant, fuming, asked him to consider what he did.

"The general opinion is against you and will remove your sword. That gone your honour would also be lost and you would have nothing but a pistol left with which, however—yes, yes—you might shoot yourself. Still, it would be more cheerful to let yourself be searched."

With this choice before him, von Gierschke agreed to the search. Old Mud had not the slightest suspicion of him; he merely wished to trample the man's pride in the mud. Moreover during this Kieselack had slipped to the window, wishing to throw the banknotes away and had been taken in the act. Consul Breetpoot was now demanding satisfaction of Old Mud, who, however, spoke one name in his ear— inaudible to anyone else—just a name. And Breetpoot's anger dropped. He came again within a few days and sat there without a word; Von Gierschke let a week pass but Kieselack came once more and gambled just once more. And then his grandmother appeared before the board of assessment, where Kieselack had a small job, and stated that he had robbed her, which gave an excuse for his arrest, for they would not have dared to give him in charge for the theft at the card table. Kieselack was now done for and Old Mud hugged the joy of it to himself alone.

His enjoyment was drily malicious. In the tumult caused by a bankruptcy, a disgrace, a crime, Old Mud would make his appearance, knock-kneed and unperturbed, an old schoolmaster whose class was misbehaving and who, from behind his glasses, was making a note of certain names, with the intention of reporting them for punishment later. They had dared to defy his authority; well, now they might crack their ribs and break their necks in their own way. The tyrant had turned anarchist. And he seemed proud of his new state and had a liking for his own appearance since he had so remarkably rejuvenated. Twenty times an evening he would bring out his pocket mirror; he kept it in a little case with the inscription *bellet*.

Often in the midst of the mighty turmoil he would think of former evenings. He had been insulted at the Café Central and had slunk home. From one corner of the street his nickname had been flung at him like a pellet of dirt. One night only had he ever wanted anything of these people—then he had wanted to know who that actress woman, Rosa Fröhlich, was and where she was to be found, in order —this was most important—to prevent three boys from succumbing to evil ways and above all Lohmann, the worst of them all. No one had answered his question; he had met with nothing but grins and not a hat had been lifted to him. He had had to run from that alley where the children's voices shouted his name with a force to break one's eardrum. He had not confronted any other of the rebels, but had slipped by the lighted shops; the houses where fifty thousand former rebellious schoolboys were hidden he had slunk past with a nervous dread at the top of his head that from an upper window his name would be shouted out accompanied by a pailful of dirty water. At the end of the most silent of the streets, by the Home for Indigent Gentlewomen, he had shaken off the nervous fear, the despairing dread—and had felt the bat circle round his head. Yet even here he had expected to hear that nickname.

That nickname! Now he called himself by it; he set it on his own head like a crown. One man who had lost heavily he had clapped on the shoulder and cried:

"Yes, yes; quite so, quite so. Don't forget I'm Old Mud."

His nights now! How different they were. His house was the best lit in the town and the best known and filled with the most brilliant guests. What anguish, greed and servility, what frantic appetite for self-destruction circled round him! All burnt offerings to him! All were eager to kindle fires in his honour. What brought them here was the emptiness of their own heads, their silly ignorance, their idiotic curiosity, their hardly veiled lusts, their avarice, passions, vanities, and a hundred quickened desires. Was it not his creditors who sent their relations and friends here in the hope that he would make money enough to pay his debts? Was it not

women who coveted luxuries who sent their husbands
that they might have their share of the money that
was flying about? Others came themselves. Under
the masks, in carnival time, respectable women
might be seen taking their pleasure. One had
noticed suspicious faces, keeping an eye on their
wives. Young girls whispered secretly about how
late mother had come home—"from that house near
the gate." They hummed softly fragments of the
songs sung by the Fröhlich. Those songs hummed
through the town—in secret.

Before the summer came, three women of respectable reputation and two young girls went off, as they
said, to a holiday resort where spring came early.
Three fresh bankruptcies followed. The cigar merchant Meyer forged some bills of exchange and hanged
himself. As for Consul Breetpoot, there were
whispers——

And this depravity which no one could stop because too many were involved was all due to Old
Mud—this ruin was his triumph. That secret obsession of his—that obsession which betrayed itself
merely by a poisonous glint of his green eyes, a pallid
grin—it had undermined a town and compelled it to
villein service.

He was strong. He should have been happy.

CHAPTER XVI

IT would have been better if he had been stronger; if in a crisis of his life which centred in hate, he had not given himself up to Rosa Fröhlich. She represented the reverse side of that passion of his; she must have everything, as the others must lose everything. She deserved his protection the more because all the others deserved to come to grief, for upon her this enemy of mankind had lavished the whole tenderness of his heart. This was not well for him; he saw that himself. He told himself that she should have been nothing but an instrument to "catch" his scholars, and lay them low, but instead of that she stood too near himself, high and holy in the sight of man, and he was forced to love her and to suffer in that love which reared its head against the service of his hate. His love was dedicated to her service, and for her he would have committed crime, for his love was entirely human. Therefore it brought weakness in its train.

It happened that one day, when she returned home, she found him shut in his room and not visible. She spoke to him through the door, her voice sympathetically low, but he would not even eat. She warned him anxiously that he would make himself ill, and decided with a sigh that she must wait for the mood to pass over. He had evidently been looking through her drawers again and had probably found that letter. He would fall into a fit of madness, as she knew, whenever she came home with her clothes crumpled, and would hide himself, seized with the shame of it, in any corner, out of sight. It was exasperating, really it was! One couldn't take things so seriously! Life was too full of troubles. Wasn't she his wife? She couldn't help things. She thought of that morning when she had sent her little daughter Mimi to the old dear—he'd been a brick and one did feel grateful. If she did have a bit of fun with a man or two, it was a nuisance having to tell a lot of lies to get a chance to slip away for a bit—especially as he really knew all about it. Yet she was grateful to him for playing his part in the comedy since her now daily lapses meant so much to him still. But it did make a performance of Life! Funny that he never seemed to get accustomed to it.

It seemed to matter so much more to him than it did to her. Sometimes he would seem to slip right off the rails, as if he wanted to kill all conscience in himself and her. He would say, as if he could not keep it in:

"Let me suggest that fellow Vermöhlen. Turn your eyes—yes, yes—quite so—on young Vermöhlen."

What did he mean by that, pray? One didn't dare to ask him. And when he made such a fuss about Consul Breetpoot! She shrugged her shoulders.

Old Mud, whom she did not understand, was torn to pieces by his obsession. His love which he must daily wound to feed his hate, fired that hate to a veritable fever. Hate and love worked upon one another, dangerously inflammable. He was haunted by the delectable vision of mankind at his feet, begging for mercy; of the town, shattered and laid waste; one mass of gold and blood running molten to grey, burnt out ashes. But then he would be seized with the thought of Rosa loved by others, and the vision of her in their arms suffocated him. And they all showed the face of Lohmann! The worst, most hated, most deserving of hate was always— Lohmann! The boy he had never been able to "catch" and who had now left the town.

Yet in the midst of it all his heart would yearn with sympathy for himself and for her. He would tell her consolingly that it was now time to withdraw and leave the place, and enjoy the fruits of her—her earnings.

"How much do you think it amounts to?" asked she, shrugging. "You're thinking of what we make but you forget what our creditors have taken. They distrained on our furniture, didn't they? And we couldn't raise a bean on what they've left us. You're pretty badly mistaken if you think we could, old dear. Those sofa cushions are ours and that picture frame, but that's about all."

She was in pessimistic mood, overwrought from the exhausting chase after men, had quite forgotten the amusing side of her life and was taking it out on anyone who happened to be near her. He took her mood seriously.

"It is my duty to consider your comfort. I am afraid I have not given it sufficient thought. You must forgive me," he said, but she was not listening. She rose and began pacing about, clasping her hands.

"You don't seem to realize that I took up this damned life to please you and help you to get your revenge on these rotters. If it weren't for Mimi! But I must think of Mimi. Please God she'll be a different sort of woman to her mother!"

Then she would bring down the child in her little white nightgown, and on that would follow a burst of tears. Old Mud, drooping with distress, would go out, leaving her to go to bed. But when the guests began to arrive she was always up again and in the wildest spirits, and made up to him for it all. She was gentle and friendly and whispered little nothings to him so that they might all see how much he was to her still. She laughed with him about those whom he most despised, flattered him until he thought that nothing serious had happened after all. For an hour or two he almost believed that his domestic troubles were imaginary. He did not really think so; but he put aside any thoughts that would stand in the way of that belief, so overwhelmingly ecstatic was the reaction from his former agony.

One bright spring day, the first cheerful day after many of these crises, he and Rosa went walking through the town and he soothed his distressed soul with the thought that after all she was his—the best and only woman in the world! But she, having laid aside her intention of really growing to love him with her ambition to learn Greek, fed her sense of self-righteousness with the thought of her honest friendliness towards her husband. They were both laughing at Dröge, the shopkeeper at the corner of the street who, when he saw them pass, rushed out of his shop door with clenched fists, shouting insults after them. The greengrocer woman was equally upset at sight of them and had told Dröge she had a mind to empty her bucket of dirty water over that Old Mud. But such things no longer troubled them. They owed money right and left but the tradesman who, instead of bolstering their credit, had shaken it would have had the most to regret. By cheating their creditors, she felt she was saving money for her child and he was willing to acquiesce in the dishonesty for her sake. Whenever the broker came he came in vain, for they pretended that neither her frocks nor anything else had been paid for and so did not belong to them, and they raised a storm of complaint, anger and despair. How could they have been expected to foresee a thing like this? How could she be expected to keep accounts? His obsession was always too concerned with the ruin of others to take heed for his own interests, and from the evil they wrought sprang their own undoing. Hemmed in, cheating and cheated, they hugged to themselves the hope of some unbelievable run of luck at the tables and of the death of their creditors. They felt the ground heaving under their feet and sowed as much disgrace about them as they could.

They met the furniture dealer on their walk and he

declared that they had been selling furniture they had not paid for and threatened them with arrest. Old Mud smiled his ironical smile and Rosa answered at greater length:

"Don't you worry. There's nothing to make a song about."

The clank of a sword made her start, but she quickly turned away.

"Look there!" cried a voice and she did not hear what further the furniture man had to say, for she stood for a moment and then went on in some confusion, and not until they had gone some distance did she realize that Old Mud had not spoken a word. Her conscience pricked her and she began to talk feverishly to make him forget what he had seen, and he suddenly pretended to be in the best of spirits and took her into the confectioner's shop. While he was giving his order at the counter she went into the inner room. She heard a knock at the shutter and tried to see through, for she knew it was Ertzum and Lohmann.

Old Mud remained upset all day and moved in and out between the guests that night making remarks of a wild, drily ironical kind.

"My name's Mud, you know," he would say. "All we really own in this place is a sofa cushion and the frame round that picture there. Funny? Yes, yes. Quite so!"

When she went to bed that night he followed her into the room.

"That boy Breetpoot will shortly be found to have done credit to the Old School," he told her.

"Really?" she replied. "I don't believe it, old
dear. His credit's been bolstered up again."

"Yes, yes—but the really important thing is—to
find out where the bolstering came from."

"Well?"

He came closer to her with a smile that seemed to
strip bare the soul.

"I've found out. His cashier gave him away.
He's been dipping into the Ertzum trust money."
He saw that she was dumb with surprise and added:
"Well? Aren't they all alike? That's the second
of the three. That boy Kieselack was sent to prison;
the Ertzum boy will now find out he's ruined; and
then there will only be one of them left." But she
could not meet his eyes.

"Who do you mean?" she said, confusedly.

"There's still a third to be caught. He must and
shall be caught."

"Oh," said she, her glance wavering. Then,
suddenly: "That's the boy you're always down on,
isn't it? The one I'm not to speak to even in the
street? How about it?"

He sank his head on his breast, fighting for
breath.

"Yes, yes—I hadn't forgotten," he said on his
deepest note. "And yet—that boy *must* be caught.
He *must*."

"What's the matter with you?" she shrugged.
"You're feverish. Go to bed, old dear, and sweat it
out of yourself. You're always working yourself up;
it's bad for the digestion, old dear. You know—I

feel there's something going to happen. Something—pretty bad."

But he was not listening.

"But you—*you* mustn't catch him," he was muttering, over and over again.

He spoke with a note of fierce entreaty which she had never heard from him before and which affected her painfully, filling her with alarm—as might a soft knock on the door in the darkness of the night.

CHAPTER XVII

NEXT morning she gave much thought to what she had better do, and when she had decided she went out. She used her pocket mirror at every shop window and had already taken two and a half hours over her dressing. Her pulses were beating with suspense and she came to a stop before the bookseller's, a thing she had never done before. Her head was bent over the volumes in the window and she felt a light breath tickle the back of her neck, as a voice spoke behind her.

"So we meet again, my dear?"

As she turned, she made up her mind to display a languid pleasure at the meeting.

"Mr. Lohmann? Have you come back again?"

"If it does not displease you, pretty lady."

"Why should it? But where's your friend?"

"You mean Count Ertzum? Oh, he's got affairs of his own to see to. But shall we walk on, eh?"

"What does he get up to as a rule?"

"He's in the army, but he's on leave now."

"Oh? And is he the same nice boy he used to be?"

But as she failed to upset his equanimity, however much she talked of his friend, she had the feeling that he was laughing at her. It was a feeling she always used to have about Lohmann in those Blue Angel days, but never with anyone else. It was very warm and he asked her to come into the confectioner's, but she curtly refused.

"Go by yourself. I must get along."

"We've been standing at this corner rather a time, my dear. The eyes of the town will be upon us." He pushed open the door of the shop and she sighed and rustled past him. On the way to the inner room he was a step behind her and remarked how her slim figure was shown off to advantage by her frock and how well dressed her hair was; how really well cut her things were and how she had improved. He ordered chocolate.

"You have become quite a famous personage, I hear."

"S'pose so," she replied, and changed the subject. "What about you? What have you been doing and where are you living now?"

He answered willingly enough that he had been for some time in Brussels and then to England to learn something of business from a friend of his father's.

"Had a fine time, haven't you?" she commented.

"Fair!" was his contemptuous reply, that well-known frown appearing on his forehead. She watched him with covert interest. He was dressed in black and his face was somewhat sallow and had grown thinner; he was clean-shaven and kept his eyelids down over his eyes except when something roused him. She felt she must make him look at her and also she wanted to see if he still wore that lovelock that used to droop over his eyes.

"Aren't you going to take your hat off?" she said.

"But of course! Sorry." He took off his hat and she saw that his hair was still as thick as ever and that the rebellious lock was brushed back over his head. And now at last he turned his eyes upon her fully. "You weren't such a stickler for etiquette at the Blue Angel, were you? How you've changed. We've all changed, haven't we? And yet it's only two years ago."

He turned his eyes away again and was so obviously thinking of something else that she dared not speak for a bit, although his manner was annoying her. But then perhaps he did not mean it.

Lohmann was really thinking of Dora Breetpoot, whom he had found greatly changed, or at least unlike the picture he had carried of her in his heart. He had loved, as he thought, a *grande dame* and she had been the greatest lady in the town. She had met an English duchess once in Switzerland and had preserved that memory with ritual fidelity. She played the duchess in that little town, for that the English aristocrat is the finest in the world no one could deny. But afterwards, when travelling in the south of Germany, a cavalry captain from Prague had made love to her and then the Austrian aristocracy contested the first place with the English. How Lohmann could have let himself be enthralled by that sort of thing was now incredible to him; yes, it was astounding! And to think it was only two years ago. Now he had come back to the town, he found that she had shrunk into an indiarubber doll and the house even was not half so large as it had seemed.

Its mistress was provincial, that was all. Of course she still had that creole head of hers, but it spoke the dialect of the district! Her frock? Last year's and not put on properly. Worse still, she had tried to make up and done it badly. His reception, as if he must be thrilled to see her, the pretentious pose—so irritating! But why had he not felt it irritating before? Certainly he had hardly exchanged a word with her; she had taken no notice of him. He was a schoolboy then, but now he was grown up and attempts were made to add him to the circle of admirers. He felt bitter to the core. He thought of his old gun which had always lain ready to his hand, waiting in case his secret be discovered. He took a certain melancholy pride to-day in the thought of that boyish passion, which had lasted so long, in spite of humiliation and contempt, even nausea, at the back of his consciousness. Yes, in spite of Knust and von Gierschke and the others, the crowded court of the desirable woman. That night when he had kissed the door of her house! It was something to feel like that and he was the better and richer for it. Yet he had always been bored, and he was now. That woman had given him the best thing he had had in his life, though she had been entirely unconscious. And now when he had nothing to give her, she was trying to attract him. He always valued things for what came of them—the love of women for the sake of the bitter loneliness that followed, and the happiness of a longing that brought a choke to one's throat. He could not endure that little empty

headed provincial snob! She left no merciful shadow
to brood over that first love of his. Everything she
did irritated him, even the signs of decay in her
environment, though not in her person. He knew of
Breetpoot's pending misfortunes; what a wealth of
tenderness that would have awakened in him once!
Now he could only see the mean shifts she made to
hide things and felt ashamed that she should pretend
and lie in that way to cover her poverty. He was
distressed when he saw her; distressed and humiliated,
when he realized what his present feelings were.
What life did to one! She had sunk and when he
left her he felt with painful justice that he was escaping
from his past and that a door was closing on a love
that had vanished with his boyhood.

This had happened on the morning after his return.
He had then met Ertzum and both had seen Old Mud
in the street, but in so small a place that sort of
meeting could never be long delayed. Though he had
been back so short a time, Lohmann had heard plenty
of gossip about him and Old Mud's doings had
appealed to his love for the study of eccentric character. He declared that Old Mud had fulfilled all he
had prophesied two years before, and perhaps more.
But even more striking seemed to him the change
in Rosa, from the singer of serio-comics at the Blue
Angel to a chic *demi-mondaine*. For that he could
see at a glance, but when he came to study her the
stamp of the small town became visible. And how
hats were doffed when the couple passed! How
servile everyone was if she so much as wafted a whiff

of her perfume across their path! Evidently some magic hypnotism had taken place between her and her audience, the town. She had played the rôle of an acknowledged beauty and had been spoken of as such until she herself had come to believe it. Something of the sort must have happened with Dora Breetpoot and her pretensions to being a woman of the world. Lohmann found a provocative irony in it as he now sat talking to the Fröhlich. He remembered the time when he had written verses on them both, when he, in revenge for his hopeless love, had wanted to besmirch Dora and with her image in his heart savour the taste of murky vice in the caresses of another. Vice? But now he no longer loved there seemed no vice in it. No bitterness in his heart towards Dora came to the aid of Rosa. He would feel nothing if he passed the Breetpoots' house with her. He would merely be escorting a *chic* woman of the half-world through the town.

But he would not take Ertzum with him. As soon as Ertzum saw the girl he began to rattle that sword of his with embarrassment and his voice was hoarse. Ertzum might again develop a serious passion for her. The past was the present with Ertzum—so Lohmann, sitting in the empty shop this morning, took nothing from his glass, which he did not empty, except the misty aftertaste of the moods of long ago.

"Would you like some cognac in that chocolate?" he asked. "It's a good mixture." Then he added: "The things they say about you, my dear!"

"What things?" asked she, attentive at once.

"Why, it seems that you and Old Mud between you have set the whole town talking, causing all sorts of mischief, so they say."

"Oh, that sort of thing? Oh, well, they will talk. But people like to come and see us; we do see that they have a good time—if I may say so much of myself as hostess."

"I've heard that—and that no one can quite make out Old Mud. They think he needs the money he makes at gambling to live on. I don't. You and I, my dear, know him better."

She was somewhat embarrassed and sat silent.

"He is a tyrant and would rather be ruined than suffer a diminution of his power. An insult—and he hears them still at night through the purple hangings of his bed and in his dreams, of that I'm sure—it brings flecks of blue to his face and it takes a bath of blood to wash them off. He has a patent in rights divine and would have invented them if it hadn't been done already. No one could approach him even with the utmost self-effacement but what he would cry that he hated that rebel! He is a misanthrope in grain. That any lungs should dare to inhale or expel breath without his permission fills him with resentment—strains his nerves to snapping. A contradiction, or even contrary circumstances—such as that affair of the wood and all that came from it, which fed his obsession—and the tyrant, in panic fury, calls on the mob to set fire to the palace, and lets loose anarchy."

She sat with open mouth; which pleased him. It

was his habit to entertain ladies of this kind so that they could do nothing but stare. He would then smile his ambiguous smile. He merely meant to set forth an abstract possibility and not to relate the life story of Old Mud, whom he still saw from the perspective of the school rostrum. He could not think of really vital things happening to the man who had dictated that malicious theme on Schiller's *Maid of Orleans*.

"I have the greatest sympathy with your husband," he continued with a smile and again enjoyed her bewilderment. "Your domesticity is famous, you know."

"Oh, we're quite a comfortable couple," she said. "But you know"—she leaned towards him—"we haven't any too much for so much entertaining. Why, you could stand on their heads sometimes— its quite funny. Now if *you'd* come along, I'd sing that silly song of yours. I don't as a rule because its a bit too highbrow."

"I quite agree."

"You will come along then?"

"You flatter me. Do you know, you seem to me the only person here whom I find interesting."

"Is that so?" cried she, pleased, but not surprised.

"Your dress alone; that reseda green frock is quite the latest and that black hat is chosen marvellously. If I may make a criticism—those point lace collars are not worn this year."

"Aren't they?" she edged closer. "Then the rogue told me a lie. A good thing I haven't paid for it." She flushed, and added hastily: "I'll pay, of course, but I won't wear it. But never mind that now." She was happy to agree with him, to humble herself before him. His attack on Old Mud increased her admiration for him to overflowing. And he was an authority on dress! And how well he talked!

"How cramped you must feel in this little town! a woman like you. A Semiramis—— You conquer them all, don't you? They fall before you!" And as she seemed scarcely to follow, he added: "I mean you can have any man you like and get what you want out of him, eh?"

"Oh, that's exaggerating. I have had luck here, though. That's true." She stopped to drink but there was something she wanted him to know. "If you think that I want to leave this town—no! But you needn't think—" she looked into his eyes— "that I'd sit here drinking chocolate with every man."

"Only me? That so?" He leaned back and frowned, and she found that she could only see his eyelids again. "But I was to be the last man with you, wasn't that it? I seem to remember something of the sort. Didn't you promise me that—throw it in my face, my dear? Then—" he opened his eyes and stared at her, shamelessly—"are the others getting tired?"

She was not offended, only a little frightened.

"You do get funny ideas about people, don't you? Tired? Why, look at Breetpoot. He was going to give me the earth and now it seems he's run through

Ertzum's money." She realized too late what she
had said and sat staring into her cup.

"Hard lines," replied he, drily. He turned away
and there was a short silence. Then at last she
bethought her that a sob might help.

"It wasn't my fault. He did beg so—like a child,
the old rip. That's what he is—an old rip! You
wouldn't believe what I went through with him.
And speaking as if butter wouldn't melt in his mouth."

Lohmann was already regretting that he had seemed
to give a moral twist to this entertaining comedy.

"I must come to your soirées," he now said.

"I have invited you already," she cried happily,
"and I am set on your coming. Oh, but then—I
forgot. Oh, bother!" She twisted about, fidgetting
with her hands. "The old dear said he wouldn't
have it and he made fuss enough last time, God
knows! So you understand——"

"Absolutely, my dear."

"Oh, don't take any notice of the old fool. Come
when there's no one else there. This afternoon at
five. That suit?" And she rustled with every sign
of haste through the door.

Lohmann did not quite know how it had all come
about or why he should feel so cheerful. He suspected
hidden dangers; Ertzum had once been brought near
ruin by this Venus with the cynical, slangy tongue.
And he loved her still; he might at least have had
some happiness for his money. Lohmann went to
the rendezvous quite coolly; he was going instead of
his friend, who had deserved to go by virtue of his

long distress. How impossible it would have been two years ago. He remembered how Old Mud— himself on the verge of dismissal but still thundering that he would have him expelled—had roused his pity, and sincere pity too, not offensive. And now he was going to see his wife. What life makes of us! thought he, Byronically proud.

He heard a noisy discussion within the house when the embarrassed servant opened the door to him, and found Rosa, very excited, talking to a man with a bit of paper in his hand—a dirty, perspiring creature.

"What's the matter?" he asked. "I thought so. How much? All that noise about fifty marks!"

"But I've had to come fifty times, sir," cried the creditor. "Once for each mark."

Lohmann paid and sent him away.

"Don't be offended at my interference, my dear," he said somewhat stiffly, for he felt in a false position. He had no wish to seem to be paying for the coming performance; certainly not so small a sum as fifty marks. That touched his pride. "But as I have begun—I have been told that you are somewhat in difficulties——"

She wound her fingers in and out painfully, turned her head this way and that in the stiff collar of her teagown. The thousand little worries connected with tradespeople, lovers and moneylenders rushed into her mind—and there, in his pocketbook, was a thick roll of banknotes.

"How much do you want?" asked he quietly, and then with native caution; "I'll go as far as I can."

But she had fought her fight. She would not be bought by Lohmann. No, not by him!

"No, it's not true. I don't want anything," she said.

"Oh, well—perhaps I might have felt too flattered ——" He thought of Dora Breetpoot. Now that *she* wanted money *she* might be selling herself—who knew? But to allow Rosa a chance of changing her mind he left his pocketbook lying open on the table.

"Now let's talk," said she, but with a side glance added: "Nice fat pocket-book you've got there." And as he said nothing: "We shall see you with rings on your fingers next."

"I don't care to buy women," he explained, indifferent whether she understood or not. "It's a humiliating thing to do. Besides it isn't necessary. They are works of art, for which, God knows, I'd make any sacrifice. But can one call such things one's own? One sees a picture in a shop and dreams of it. Then one returns, perhaps, and buys it. But what does one buy? One can dream without paying, and the fulfilment of a dream is never worth buying." He turned from that pocketbook morosely—but almost at once he took a lighter tone. "I mean I've had about enough for to-day."

She was awed by his Byronic manner, but also a little inclined to tease.

"You'll pay for your dinner by and bye, I suppose?"

"Can't we talk of something else?" He frowned and stared at her again with that shamelessly naked stare. "Am I to buy you? You?" He shrugged, as answering the unanswerable. "That sort of physical love is repulsive."

She was baffled, but then the funny side of it struck her and she said: "Listen to the old thing!"

"One must keep oneself above that sort of thing," he continued. "Ride away, like Parsifal. I believe I am going into the cavalry, by the bye, and I'm going to learn to *ride*; when I say ride I mean the *haute école*, of course. Why, except for circus folk, I don't suppose there are a hundred people in Germany who can really *ride*." On this she laughed quite openly.

"Be a circus rider, old thing—then we'd be fellow pros. That would be fine." Then she sighed: "You remember the Blue Angel? Those days were the best." But she had interrupted him.

"Oh, perhaps," he said. "Yes, no doubt."

"We had many a good laugh and didn't have to bother about all these silly people. When I remember how we used to dance together, just you and me— but then Old Mud came along and you had to go out of the red window. You know he's still awfully fierce about you." She laughed with some embarrassment. "He wants to make sausage meat of you."

She was listening to any sound at the door and looked at Lohmann reproachfully because he was leaving everything to her. All right, then she'd start. She had set her heart on Lohmann, partly because he alone was forbidden. That of course was not to be endured. Moreover a trifle of desire still survived from that past time of which she now thought with a sigh, thanks to Old Mud's jealous suspicions and his terrifying hate, and to that past Lohmann belonged. His distinction and exaggeratedly superior air had changed the old inclination to a dizzier feeling. Then —it was dangerous, for the air about her here was charged with catastrophe, and this was in itself an allurement.

"Those lovely verses you used to write," she said. "I suppose you don't do that any more. You know —that song about the full moon which I sang once when the audience laughed so cruelly?"

She leaned dreamily over the arm of her chair, laid her right hand on her breast and sang softly:

"The moon is full and all the stars are shining——"

She sang the whole verse and was thinking the whole time that it was the only song she was forbidden to sing; Old Mud's face was before her eyes. It was terrible, but she thought of him as rather comic, made up, the case with the pocket-mirror in his hand.

"My heart is wae and all the stars are laughing."

Lohmann, unpleasantly affected, sought to stop her, but she went straight on with the second verse:

"The moon is fool——"

The door was thrown open and Old Mud strode into the room. Rosa screamed and flew into the corner, behind Lohmann. Old Mud was speechless with rage and she remembered that he had looked just like that when he had heard her sing the song before. He had the same horrible eyes as yesterday! " Oh, why won't he take camomile tea," thought she in an agony of fear.

He was thinking that all was at an end. His whole work, his whole labour of righteous annihilation, was in vain, for here sat the boy Lohmann with this actress woman. He had thrown everyone else at her, had striven that one after the other should fall down before her and now his worst fears had come to pass through her, his fears for her with Lohmann, the wickedest of them all. The one of all others his hate would most gladly have shattered What was left to him? Here was an end of this actress woman, this Rosa Fröhlich, and also of Old Mud. He must condemn her to death—and with her, himself.

He said nothing—but suddenly sprang at her throat, gurgling as if he himself were being strangled. For one second she fought for breath and during that second she managed to scream, but Old Mud seized her again. Then a heavy hand fell on his shoulder. Lohmann had hesitated to interfere, for he felt there was no part for him in this scene; it seemed to him a dream. These things didn't happen! To him it seemed as if Old Mud were something out of a book; this was too obvious—too palpable—to be real. He had worked out an interesting theory of his old teacher's motives, but he had not visualised his soul; he had scarcely divined the fundamental force, that erupting volcano that brought about its own destruction.

Old Mud turned to him and Rosa fled screaming to the next room, where she locked herself in. For one moment her husband stared as if spellbound; then he pulled himself up and began striding round Lohmann, who had retreated to the table and taken up his pocket-book. He thought of the interpretation that might be put on it. How ghastly the man looked! Something between a spider and a cat, with madness in his eyes, into which the drops of sweat were running, while foam flecked those working jaws. It was no pleasant position to have to dodge those clutching arms! What was he saying? It was indistinguishable.

"Rascal—to dare—catch you—catch you at last —— Out of the room! Out of the room with you!"

With that he snatched the pocket-book from Lohmann and stood staring at it.

Lohmann stood there horrified; for this would end in a crime. Old Mud, the professed anarchist, would end in crime. An anarchist was morally eccentric and a confessed extremist, and crime was the climax to human passions and desires. Old Mud had tried to strangle his wife and now he had stolen that pocket-book; such was the view taken by this commentator on the play—this spectator deprived of his right to smile. Lohmann's soul had never been tempered by any such incredible experience before, and when the word "crime" rose to his mind, he responded conventionally with "police." This was no unusual case, he tried to think, but he said to himself: "This must stop," and with the thought he left the room. He walked firmly to the door of the next room and rattled the handle for he had heard Rosa lock herself in, but it was his duty to convince himself that she would not fall into the hands of her murderous husband while he was away. Assured of this he left the house.

An hour went by; and then an ever increasing crowd came surging round the street corner. The town was rejoicing at Old Mud's downfall. At last! The weight of their own misdemeanours fell from them since he would soon be gone. They threw a backward glance on the ruin wrought and felt that it was high time. Why had they waited so long?

A brewer's dray, half filled with barrels, was drawn up across the street, but the cab had to pass; for in it were the police. The greengrocer woman from the corner ran beside it and Dröge the shopkeeper snatched up the rubber hose.

Before Old Mud's house the crowd jostled and swayed until at last he appeared between the police officers. That actress woman, Rosa Fröhlich, wild and dishevelled, crying and shaken with remorse and with the disgrace of it, was clinging to him, hanging from his neck, and had to be dislodged. She had been arrested too, which Lohmann had not foreseen. Old Mud himself lifted her into the closed cab, which was quite dark inside, the shutters being up, and then he stopped to stare brokenly at the howling crowd. One fellow in a leather apron, the drayman, stretched out his pasty face and shouted:

"Mud! Mud! Old Mud!"

Old Mud swung quickly round when he heard the

name that was no crown of victory now but once again—what it used to be—a filthy insult. He recognized Kieselack and shook his fist, his jaws working, his neck outstretched, and a stream of water from Dröge's hosepipe went straight into his mouth. He spat it out, was pushed from behind, stumbled over the step and fell headfirst on to the cushions beside that actress woman—into the darkness.

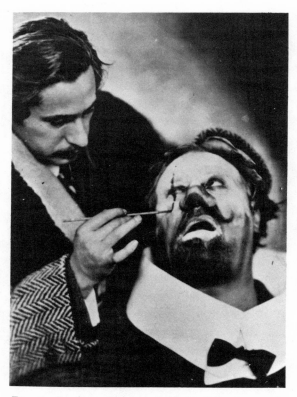

Director Josef von Sternberg helps Emil Jannings with his clown makeup for the final sequences of the film. Sternberg said of his star that "his forte was to portray the zenith of personal misfortune. . . . To be humiliated was for him ecstasy."

The novel's Rosa Frölich was rebatized Lola-Lola by Sternberg, who in his search for the perfect actress for the role one evening at the theater "noticed a woman on the stage whose face promised everything. This was Marlene Dietrich."

During a backstage visit, the stern Professor Rath is delighted when Lola-Lola playfully sprays him with face powder. Though hardly unknown at the time, after the release of *The Blue Angel* Marlene Dietrich became an international star.

Sternberg denies that he "discovered" Dietrich. "I am a teacher who took a beautiful woman, instructed her, presented her carefully, edited her charms, disguised her imperfections and led her to crystallize a pictorial aphrodisiac."

Having "saved" Lola-Lola from the unwelcome attentions of a sea captain, Professor Rath pays for the champagne ordered by the latter and is suitably rewarded as Guste (Rosa Valetti), wife of the theatrical manager looks on.

Having awakened in Lola-Lola's bed the next morning, Professor Rath enjoys the charms of breakfast with a beautiful woman. The scene has a domestic atmosphere that contrasts with the opening sequences that show Rath dining alone.

News of the professor's scandalous liaison spreads through the small town and undermines his ability to maintain classroom discipline. His announcement that he intends to marry the cabaret singer results in his dismissal.

„Der blaue Engel"

An entertainment at the wedding festivities during which Kiepert (Kurt Gerron) magically plucks an egg from under the professor's nose inspires the clown act of the final sequences during the time of Rath's greatest humiliation.

„Der blaue Engel"

Professor Rath (Emil Jannings) circulates through the audience selling the feather-clad photos of Lola-Lola. In the hands of his former students, these same photos had so scandalized Rath that he had paid an indignant visit to The Blue Angel.

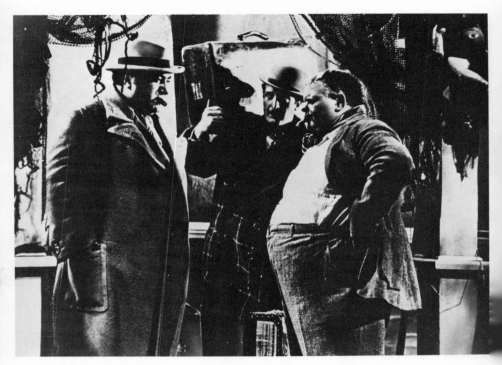

Kiepert (Kurt Gerron) discusses his troupe's engagement with The Blue Angel proprietor (Karl Huszar-Puffy) as Mazeppa (Hans Albers) looks on. Mazeppa immediately pays court to Lola-Lola, who does little to discourage him.

Professor Rath (Emil Jannings) is told by Kiepert (Kurt Gerron) that he must perform at The Blue Angel, as Lola-Lola (Marlene Dietrich) reads the telegram announcing the troupe's engagement. Rath initially refuses to agree.

The proprietor (Karl Huszar-Puffy) and Gusti (Rosa Valetti) attempt to calm Rath after he has spotted Lola-Lola and Mazeppa embracing in the wings of The Blue Angel stage.

Josef von Sternberg instructs Emil Jannings and Kurt Gerron before the filming of the dramatic scene in which Professor Rath acknowledges his humiliation and defeat with a desperate crowing that recalls the happier wedding scene.

Dietrich's costumes on this and the following page were the work of a talented Hungarian named Varady, "whose erotic designs were to add so much to the film." Sternberg's conception of Lola-Lola was inspired by drawings of Félicien Rops, a 19th-century Belgian artist.

JOSEF
VON STERNBERG

THE
BLUE ANGEL

*(Film continuity translated
from the German)*

INTRODUCTION

A long while ago, though it seems but yesterday, a steamer no longer in service carried me to a country no longer undivided. This is written in haste, for I am impatient with the past except that 'The memory of past troubles is pleasant.'

Words cannot describe an image in motion, words cannot describe an image. Today *The Blue Angel* is used to describe night clubs, air squadrons and re-makes; before I gave that title to a film it had no existence. An expired passport helps to fix the date. I was dropped at Le Havre on the twelfth of August, 1929, for what was hardly to prove an enjoyable escape from a stint of two years in a Hollywood film factory. I had just finished my first sound film, an indifferent work featuring an actor whose temporary fame was sustained by a so-called silent film called *Underworld*. The entire cast was inferior, all of them unable even to echo my instructions. There was some good warbling in the death row where most of the action took place, but I looked forward with pleasure to making a sound film in Germany. I was not aware, of course, that Europe had only the most primitive method of adding sound to a quite elaborate camerawork which would cause me a lot of trouble. Incidentally, the silent films had never been silent — a piano tinkled, an organ moaned or an orchestra thundered out music that rarely helped the silent film.

This German venture had a curious beginning. I had received a flattering cable from Emil Jannings asking me to guide him in his first sound film, adding that he had the choice of every director on earth but that he preferred me. This touched me deeply, as I had told him in plain language that I would not do another film with him were he the last remaining actor on earth. Once before I had directed him in *The Last Command*, an opus which required him to portray an extra who was called upon to play the part of a commanding general of Russia, a post he had actually had. It was an interesting anatomical survey of the brutality ram-

257

pant in a motion picture studio. His behaviour interfered with everything I planned. I was slated to do the next film with him, another story by me, *The Street Of Sin*, but I refused and gave the story to Mauritz Stiller. Jannings was impossible to handle, details are in my book. But two years had passed and bygones were bygones, or at least they should have been.

So on a pleasant day in August, I arrived at the Zoo Station in Berlin, to be greeted by a group containing Emil Jannings, Eric Pommer and Karl Vollmoeller. Emil vowed he would be different this time, as indeed he was. Eric Pommer was to be my producer and he was considered an able one. Karl Vollmoeller was a poet and at the time my best friend. Jannings was the one I was to direct. A director's function, if he is to function, is difficult to describe. It embraces a skill in all the arts, though this in itself means little. Every step and every moment is filled with imponderables. ' Trifles light as air ' must be ready to become substantial. An audience of one, he controls the camera according to his vision, uses light, shadow and space as his mind dictates, dominates the tempo and content of sound, controls the sets, chooses and edits the actors, decides their appearance and make-up, arranges the scenes in rhythmic progression, eliminates and adds moments that have no meaning to those who stand in attendance, and is solely responsible for every frame of his film. Aside from that he is chief of his crew of workmen, often numbering hundreds though it were better if he managed the giant task of harnessing the cumbersome machine by himself alone. That was my task and this I intended to do. In addition to that I wrote the manuscript on which the theme was based. Now I don't mean to infer that all this permitted me to behave like an angel. Far from it, but my word was law, I was boss, my behaviour was known and this is why I had been called.

After a few friendly exchanges, I asked what the plans were and I was told that the film I was to do was *Rasputin*. I shook my head, this failed to interest me and I suggested that I return to the States. This caused vociferous objections, they would look around for some other idea that would provoke my interest, and I settled down comfortably in a hotel which is now razed and is a pile of rubble behind the ugly wall that divides Berlin.

Among the many subjects and story ideas that were brought to me in the following weeks one caught my fancy. A story by Heinrich Mann, *Professor Unrath*, published in 1905, the locale Lübeck and as any reader of the original can see, a teacher falling in love and marrying a cabaret singer by name of Rosa Fröhlich with child, resigning his position and then using his wife to obtain a footing which enabled him to make a gambling establishment that was to settle his score with society. In conveying the substance of Mann's story to me Jannings was superb, his eyes sparkled, and I began to analyze the ingredients that were to form the basis for *The Blue Angel*.

It took little time for me to make up my mind. Rosa Fröhlich would be Lola-Lola, deprive her of her child, give the pupils intriguing photographs of her, make her heartless and immoral, invent details that are not in the book, and best of all change the role of the teacher to show the downfall of an enamoured man *à la* Human Bondage. None of the distinctive features that fill the film are indicated in the story by Mann. Also not wishing to outrage the author, I asked to see Heinrich Mann. I then told him what changes I contemplated. Mann agreed, saying that he wished he had thought of my ending, and stated that he had no objections to any cinematic devices that might further the story. That was my only contact with the author.

I then gave the go-ahead to the studio and asked for their most able writer to take down my ideas and was given a Herr Robert Liebmann. Next, my immediate concern was the musician, Friedrich Holländer, whom I chose to write songs to fit my plans, a man who had accompanied one of the females proposed by the studio. My next step was to find a designer for the daring costumes I contemplated for the female lead. After rejecting many, I found a talented Hungarian by name of Varady, whose erotic designs were to add so much to the film. His name is absent from the credits of *The Blue Angel*, while many others mentioned are non-contributors. Among those who are mentioned are Karl Vollmoeller and Carl Zuckmayer. Both men were called in to

259

lend their name to the manuscript because it was feared that Germany could not afford the authoring of a German work by a non-German. As a matter of fact, Vollmoeller has denied any authorship, while Zuckmayer in his writings persists in saying that he contributed. He is a brilliant author, but his contributions in *The Blue Angel* are not worth mentioning. However, everyone connected with the film, including the janitor and the night watchman, took pride in the association.

Then after a few cursory glances at the German encyclopaedia, which revealed an uninteresting statistical summary of Lübeck, I started to look around for some woman that could match the ideal creature that I sought. In my book which deals with the problem of directing I mention that the figure looked for was designed by Félicien Rops, a Belgian artist (1833-1897). She was not to be found among the numerous charmers that were paraded in front of me. And I don't mind telling you that many of the women were extremely appealing. But they lacked *das Ewig-Weibliche*. Then on an idle evening I visited a play which contained two actors already chosen, and I noticed a woman on the stage whose face promised everything. This was Marlene Dietrich. I am credited with her discovery. This is not so. I am not an archeologist who finds some buried bones with a pelvis that indicates a female. I am a teacher who took a beautiful woman, instructed her, presented her carefully, edited her charms, disguised her imperfections and led her to crystallize a pictorial aphrodisiac. She was a perfect medium, who with intelligence absorbed my direction, and despite her own misgivings responded to my conception of a female archetype. The balance of the players did as they were told.

But not so Jannings. Curiously enough, in the many books written about and by Emil Jannings, my name is mentioned only once, and incidentally. But that is scarcely the whole story. He was a magnificently bulky man who had the many characters he had portrayed firmly embedded in his person, and had a powerful array of demons everpresent in his make-up. Fat and ungainly, with a complete memory for his own tricks, shifty like a pellet of quicksilver, agile in his repertoire of misbehaviour, he was the perfect actor. His forte was to portray the zenith of personal misfortune; his limpid eyes brimming with misery, he could picture debasement in the most abject terms. To be humiliated was for him ecstasy. Shrewdly aware of his own pranks, powerful as he was as a box-office figure, he would always choose the most formidable directors to restrain and guide him. Aside from his objections to my choice of Dietrich, he opposed me every step of the way. This cannot be seen in the film, even I cannot see it. He gives a competent performance and there is no trace of any obstruction and the untold blocks he laid down to his interpretation and that of the others. As *The Blue Angel* recedes into time, he becomes more and more effective. And that he ended his days as senator of culture for the Nazis (to me he boasted that his mother was a Jewess) will be forgotten long before the perishable celluloid crumbles into ashes.

The set designer, Otto Hunte, endeared himself to me by building a town clock with effective rotating figures; Holländer played the piano and constructed melodies that were irresistable; the cameramen, Rittau and Schneeberger, were fine, and the producer, Eric Pommer, behaved just like a producer should, endorsing my work and visiting the stage only once. The workmen assigned to me were competent. One of them brought his eleven-year-old daughter to watch the scenes and when I objected, saying that she would be corrupted, he remarked '*Ach, die ist ja schon so verdorben!* ' (But she is already so corrupt!) And the actors concerned me little when in front of the camera, but as I had taken on the task of being their father for the length of the film, I had to deal with all their problems at home. In one case the young wife of the old sea captain threatened to divorce her husband during the film and when I suggested that she wait until the film was terminated, she screamed that she could no longer put up with her husband whistling when he opened his eyes in bed. This he did, he told me, to assure himself that he was still alive. *Nous dansons sur un volcan.* The filming began sometime in November and finished sometime in December. The year was 1929, Germany was undivided, although the real Germany, its schools and other places pictured in the film were not German and reality failed to interest me.

Film actors, as all students of film history know, are nothing more than glorified marionettes. But unlike a real puppet-master, the director of a film does not manipulate strings on expressionless puppets. For him the dolls are extraordinary personalities who are prone to move every muscle of face and figure to demonstrate every awkward emotion. And when the strings are manoeuvred to present acceptable masks, there is dismay and rebellion. What to reveal and what to conceal is the function of the director. There are standards that go back to the beginning of time. Should anyone ask how to direct a film it would place me in an unenviable position. *Ignotum per ignotius.* It is not possible to give a lucid explanation of the fluid that has to transfer itself to the actors. An alertness and awareness of every moment is essential. The homogeneity of the entire work is constantly at stake. This can only be accomplished by the eye of the camera and by the dangling microphone. Actors are called to the stages to work but a short time. They are costumed, made up, rushed in front of the camera, pose for the adjustment of lights, used but little, and are dismissed. One guides actors in the short time alloted for instruction somehow, by producing perhaps a trance, a sort of mesmerism otherwise unknown, by blotting out their traits and substituting a behaviour alien to them, by gesture and mimicry, by the drama of light and shade, by foiling every obstruction, by movement and angle of the camera, by constant alertness to voice and cadence, and most important of all — by inspecting oneself.

This self-inspection is indeed difficult. At any moment during the working weeks the entire mechanics can take a misleading tangent. The director has no privacy. The stages are littered with many dozens and at times hundreds of others who attack the film-maker with problems and questions that make concentration impossible. Though all are apparently sympathetic, few care anything about directorial labour. And a stream of language from the director is essential. The crew follows orders, but the actor is not part of the crew. Language is hardly the best way to convey ideas and meanings to them. Words trigger wrong ideas, actors retain only words that have a meaning to them. Even when you ' speak to a fool according to his folly ' the reactions stimulated by words are faulty. One says No many times before Yes is heard. And how does one explain abstraction and resonance.

And finally, when the actor is no longer present, thousands of feet of film are inspected that can no longer be corrected. Now comes the task of putting tempo and rhythm in what presently glides through a machine that lacks emotion. Disconnected strips of celluloid float by and haunt with their inadequacies. Wince all you like, but that does not alter a single frame. The director is now alone. Cohesion is now made with scissors and cement. To put life into lifeless material is now the task. The harlequinade of making a film is not made easy.

This is an authorised translation of the film continuity in *The Blue Angel*. It was photographed in Berlin during the late winter of 1929. No comprehensive scenario was ever made. Most of the film was improvised on the stages. Its creation, including all difficulties, are mentioned in my book, *Fun in a Chinese Laundry*, published in England by Secker & Warburg in 1966, and in the United States by Macmillan Company in 1965. Very little of the dialogue was in English, and consisted mostly of Berlin slang. Dietrich and Jannings spoke English with each other, in the English version. Both the German and the English version were photographed, one after the other. Little stress was placed on the dialogue, though it is best when understood. As this was the first sound film to be made in Germany, the recording conditions were primitive and dubbing and mixing tracks were not possible.

JOSEF VON STERNBERG

263

CREDITS:

Directed by	Josef von Sternberg, after a free adaptation of the novel *Professor Unrath,* by Heinrich Mann
Produced by	Erich Pommer
Lyrics and dialogue	Robert Liebmann
Music	Friedrich Holländer
Photography	Günther Rittau, Hans Schneeberger
Sound effects	Fritz Thiery
Décor	Otto Hunte, Emil Hasler
English lyrics	Sam Winston
Courtesy credits	Carl Zuckmayer and Karl Vollmoeller

CAST:

Professor Immanuel Rath | Emil Jannings
Lola-Lola | Marlene Dietrich
Kiepert | Kurt Gerron
Guste, his wife | Rosa Valetti
Mazeppa | Hans Albers
The clown | Reinhold Bernt
The headmaster | Eduard von Winterstein
Angst | Rolf Müller
Lohmann | Roland Verno
Ertzum | Karl Bollhaus
Goldstaub | Robert Klein-Lörk
The proprietor | Karl Huszar-Puffy
The Captain | Wilhelm Diegelmann
The policeman | Gerhard Bienert
Rath's maid | Ilse Fürstenberg
The caretaker | Hans Roth

First shown in Germany | 31st March, 1930
Process | Black and white
Screen | 1.33/1
Length | 2,920 metres

The music is played by | The Weintraubs Syncopators
Songs | ' Ich bin die fesche Lola '
| ' Kinder, heut' Abend such' ich
| mich was aus '
| ' Ich bin von Kopf bis Fuss auf
| Liebe eingestellt '
| ' Nimm dich in Acht vor blonden
| Frauen '
Music by | Friedrich Holländer
Words by | Robert Liebmann

THE BLUE ANGEL

The screen remains dark for several seconds as music is heard, softly at first and gradually becoming the song 'Ich bin von Kopf mis Fuss' which is the theme-tune of the film. The credits come up in plain white lettering on a black background, at the end of which the music ceases as the first image fades in.
Long shot from above of the steep-pitched roofs and smoking chimneys of an old town.
Cut to a narrow street: it is early morning and a number of men and women are hauling loudly cackling geese out of cages in preparation for the market. In the background, on the other side of the street, a woman is washing the glass door of a tobacconist's shop. There is a bucket on the ground beside her. Medium shot of the woman from the back as she turns a handle to raise the iron grill over the window. Close-up of the grill rising to reveal a cabaret poster showing a girl in provocative pose with the name 'LOLA-LOLA'. The camera tracks briefly backwards to frame the woman as she picks up the bucket and hurls its water at the window. The poster, being stuck to the inside of the window, remains untouched. The woman starts to wipe the window with a rag, then suddenly pauses to examine the outstretched legs of the girl in the poster. She takes a step backwards, turns towards the camera and, with her eyes still fixed on the poster, clumsily imitates LOLA'S *pose.*
Insert in close-up of a plate fixed to a door, which reads 'PR. DR. RATH'.
Long shot of the staircase of a house leading up to the landing, on which the schoolmaster RATH'S *apartment is situated. Outside* RATH'S *door, a* MAID *takes a bottle of milk from a little girl who hurries past. The girl leaves another bottle at the door of a neighbouring apartment and hurries on up. The* MAID *watches her for a moment*

267

and then goes back into RATH's *apartment, banging the door behind her.*

In the entrance hall of RATH's *apartment, the camera pans briefly towards the* MAID, *who goes over to a large mirror and puts down a tray of breakfast things on a small table in front of it. She pours some milk into a jug, lifts the tray and opens a door.*

In RATH's *study, the door is seen opening from the inside. The* MAID *passes in front of a stove with an old-fashioned flue running right across the room and goes towards another door. She knocks twice.*

MAID : Breakfast, Herr Professor.

Pan as she goes to a table in the middle of the room, clears a place among the litter of books on it, and puts down the tray. There are piles of books and papers all over the study, all covered in dust.

The MAID *grumbles as she looks round at the general disorder.*

MAID *to herself* : What a filthy mess!

The camera pans after her as she goes out of the door. At the same time, the door of the bedroom opens and RATH *appears. He glances round the room, feels in the pocket of his frock coat, hesitates, and finally goes towards his desk. Medium shot of* RATH *looking at the clutter of books. He picks up a small notebook, leafs through it, and puts it in his coat pocket. He takes his watch from his waistcoat pocket, looks at it, puts it back, and, buttoning the top of his frock coat, goes towards the middle of the room. Pan, then medium shot of* RATH, *facing the camera, as he sits down to breakfast. He pours coffee into a bowl, glances away and whistles. He pours out a small quantity of milk, then looks up and whistles again.*

Close-up of a birdcage hanging by the window in a ray of sunlight. The cage appears to be empty. Cut to RATH, *who puts down the milk jug and with a sly smile, takes a sugar-lump and gets up. Medium close-up of the cage as* RATH, *still whistling, appears beside it and holds up the sugar-lump. Suddenly, he stops whistling and his*

*smile fades: he slowly opens the cage and takes out a
dead bird, which he strokes sadly.* He
*looks at the cage again. A door is heard opening off. Cut
to the* MAID *coming through the doorway behind* RATH,
*carrying the rest of the breakfast — including two boiled
eggs — on a tray. Pan after her as she puts down the tray
on the table and approaches* RATH, *still standing, mourn-
ful and silent, with the bird in his hand. The* MAID *sees
the bird and takes it from him.*

MAID *shrugging*: Well! . . . It didn't sing any more, anyway.
*She moves out of frame. A new shot, shows her opening
the stove and throwing in the dead bird. Cut to* RATH,
*who gazes at the stove with a horrified expression. Finally
the camera pans across as he returns to the table, still
holding the sugar-lump intended for the bird. He sits
down, looks at the sugar-lump, and then drops it into
his bowl of coffee. Sadly, and with bowed head, he stirs
his coffee.*

*Long shot of a classroom. The teacher is not there. Some
boys of about fifteen to sixteen years old are gathered
round the window, talking and laughing. In the background, by the master's desk, the form leader is cleaning
the blackboard. Medium close-up of the form leader who
turns round several times and looks over the top of his
spectacles at the group of boys with a furtive and
frightened expression. Clean, combed, seeming timid;
he is excluded from the rowdy clan formed by his fellow
pupils. Medium shot of the group of pupils: they crowd
round a youth,* LOHMANN, *who is brandishing a post-
card-sized photograph, only the back of which is seen.*
LOHMANN *holds up the photograph and blows on it. The
boys crowd round with interest,* LOHMANN *lets some of
the others blow on the photograph. Another pupil pushes
forward.*

LOHMANN : Oh . . . get off!

LOHMANN *blows again on the photograph, while another
pupil —* GOLDSTAUB *— who is standing beside him, leaves
the group and moves out of the picture.*
Medium shot, slightly from above, of one corner of the

269

master's desk. GOLDSTAUB *approaches cautiously, takes the schoolmaster's exercise book and a pencil. Insert close-up of the label on the cover of the book, on which is written ' PROFESSOR RATH.'* GOLDSTAUB *writes ' UN ' in capitals over the name, since the German word UNRATH means excrement. He also adds a quick caricature of the schoolmaster. The pencil lead snaps just as he is finishing the drawing.*

Long shot of the stairway and landing outside the schoolmaster's apartment. The door opens and RATH *emerges, followed by the* MAID, *who inspects his clothing. He is wearing a cape and a wide-brimmed hat, and is carrying a cane and briefcase. He stops on the landing, pats his pockets as if looking for something, turns round and back again and finally goes down the stairs. The* MAID *goes in and shuts the door. A clock begins to strike in the distance.*

Close-up on the enormous face of the town-hall clock; the hands show eight o'clock. After the first note of the carillon, a white dove flits across the shot. The carillon turns out to be the tune ' Ueb immer Treu und Redlichkeit' (Be always faithful and honest). Meanwhile the camera tracks slowly backwards to reveal the whole of the clock face, including a set of symbolic figures which move round the clock face in time to the music. The figures disappear and the clock strikes eight.

Long shot of the classroom, still without the schoolmaster, as the eighth stroke of the clock dies away. A number of boys are fighting.

A PUPIL : Let me go. . . . Let me go !

The form leader is still at the blackboard by the master's desk.

ANGST, *the teacher's favourite* : Be quiet ! . . . Silence ! . . . Be quiet ! Rath's coming.

His orders have no effect and another pupil knocks into him. He just manages to avoid falling, and at that moment, GOLDSTAUB *bursts into the room.*

GOLDSTAUB : Look out, here comes the old man.

Immediately the boys rush to their places and sit down.

270

Silence falls. Long shot down the length of a corridor in the school. On the right are windows; on the left, the doors of the classrooms; between them, the pupils' caps and coats hang on stands. There is also a wash basin. In the foreground, seen from behind, the schoolmaster RATH *has taken off his coat and is walking towards the door of his classroom.*

Wide-angle shot of the classroom, seen from the back row: RATH *enters. The pupils, backs to the camera, get up.* RATH *shuts the door and the camera pans as he goes across to the desk. He pauses in stepping up to the rostrum and inspects the class.*

RATH : Sit down!

Noise of the pupils sitting down, while RATH *carefully puts down the three books he has in his hand. Medium shot of* RATH, *sitting down. The camera pans briefly downwards. Keeping his eyes on the class, he extracts a handkerchief from the back pocket of his frock coat, unfolds it carefully, blows his nose noisily, clears his throat, wipes his nose, and returns the handkerchief to a different pocket. After this performance, he turns round the exercise book lying on the desk in front of him, starts to open it, but pauses as his eye falls on the cover. Medium shot of* ANGST, *sitting rigidly at his desk. He looks at* RATH *who is looking at the label of the exercise book. He raises his head slightly and eyes the class over the top of his spectacles. Medium shot of* LOHMANN *and* GOLDSTAUB *sitting at their desks.* GOLDSTAUB *is looking towards the window with an innocent expression;* LOHMANN *is looking at* RATH. *Cut back to* RATH, *who turns his gaze on* ANGST *again. Cut to* ANGST, *grinning stupidly. Cut back to* RATH, *who gets up from his seat.*

RATH *severely* : Angst, come here!

Medium shot of ANGST, *who gets up and hurries nervously to the front. He is seen again in front of* RATH'S *desk.* RATH *hands him the exercise book, together with a rubber.*

RATH : Erase that!

271

ANGST *bends to pick up the book and the rubber, glancing rapidly at* LOHMANN *and* GOLDSTAUB. RATH *follows his gaze. Cut to* GOLDSTAUB, *seen slightly from above, who grimaces ironically, then suddenly freezes as he notices that* RATH *has his eye on him.* LOHMANN *adjusts his bow tie, then looks at the ceiling and twiddles his thumbs. Return to* RATH *and* ANGST. *The latter rubs out the marks on the book, then hands it and the rubber back to* RATH.

ANGST : Please, Sir. . . .

RATH *bellowing*: Silence! *Waving his hand.* Go and sit down. *Close-up of* GOLDSTAUB, *who smirks with satisfaction, then suddenly assumes a falsely innocent air. Resume on* RATH, *who is now leafing through the exercise book, fiddling with the broken pencil in his right hand. He looks up slowly.*

RATH *sarcastically* : Well, gentlemen. . . . Now we shall see what else you have learnt. *Bending over the book again.* Yesterday we left off at Hamlet, Act Three, Scene One.

RATH'S *gaze wanders round the class again and comes to rest. Cut to a pupil —* ERTZUM *— who is buried in a book which he has under his desk. Cut to* RATH, *who narrows his eyes and points a finger at the schoolboy.*

RATH : Ertzum!

Medium shot of ERTZUM, *slightly from above: he rises nervously to his feet, looking embarrassed. Return to* RATH, *who gestures to him to recite.*

RATH : Well . . . out with it!

Quick shot of ERTZUM, *looking more and more embarrassed and visibly searching his memory. Cut back to* RATH, *turning the pencil in his fingers. The camera cuts from one to the other several times.*

RATH *in English* : To be . . . well? To be or not . . . *Cut to* ERTZUM *while* RATH *continues off* : . . . to be!

ERTZUM *repeating hesitantly in English* : To be . . . or not . . . to be . . . that is ze . . . *he pronounces English very badly.*

RATH *waving the pencil* : Stop. No good.

He gets up, steps down from the rostrum and goes

272

towards ERTZUM. *Medium shot of the two of them together.*

RATH : You never pronounce the English article right. *He waves the pencil at him.* Say after me . . . ' The.'

ERTZUM *mispronouncing it* : ' Ze.'

RATH, *in desperation, shakes his head and almost bellows at* ERTZUM, *showering him with saliva.*

RATH : ' The ! '

ERTZUM *wiping the spittle from his cheek* : ' Ze.'

In his turn, ERTZUM *showers* RATH *with saliva.* RATH *wipes it from his nose, moves slightly backwards and resumes in a more cautious tone of voice.*

RATH : ' The.'

ERTZUM *copying him* : ' Ze.'

RATH : ' The.'

ERTZUM *concentrating furiously* : ' Ze.'

RATH *with increasing irritation* : Open your mouth. *He puts the pencil between the boy's teeth.* ' The.'

ERTZUM *is embarrassed at being put through this performance in front of the other pupils.*

ERTZUM : ' The ! '

RATH *more calmly* : ' The.'

ERTZUM *likewise* : ' The.'

RATH *shrugs his shoulders and snatches the pencil from* ERTZUM'S *mouth.*

RATH : Sit down.

ERTZUM *does as he is told and* RATH, *discouraged, returns to his desk. Group shot of the class, the pupils with their backs to the camera, and* RATH *in the background, returning to his desk.*

RATH : Get out your composition books.

The pupils, seen from behind, do as they are told. RATH *puts down the pencil, cups his chin in his hands and looks at them with a malicious air. Cut to* ERTZUM, *who is gazing expectantly at* RATH.

RATH *off* : Now. . . . *Cut back to him.* Write this down: ' Julius Caesar '. . . . *A pause.* What would have happened if . . . er . . . Mark Anthony . . . *He puts on his glasses* . . . had failed to deliver his oration?

273

RATH *straightens up and, with an affected gesture of the right hand, stands triumphantly over his pupils. The camera tracks backwards, framing the whole class hard at work. Hands behind his back,* RATH *walks nonchalantly towards the window. Cut to* LOHMANN *and* GOLDSTAUB. RATH *passes in front of them and opens the window wide; through it float strains of the song* 'Aennchen von Thorau,' *sung by a choir of schoolgirls somewhere nearby.* RATH *walks up and down the classroom as the song continues. Group shot of the class, slightly from above: as soon as* RATH'S *back is turned, several pupils copy from their neighbours. One in particular, in the front row turns to* ANGST, *the form leader, who immediately covers his work with a piece of blotting paper.*

Close-up of RATH *leaning against the wall at the back of the classroom.   He takes off his glasses and wipes them carefully with a handkerchief, meanwhile glancing slyly at the pupils whose backs are towards him. Close-up of* GOLDSTAUB *from behind, seated at his desk. He leans forward and looks over* LOHMANN'S *shoulder. Cut to* RATH, *who notices the movement and puts on his glasses. Return to* GOLDSTAUB, *seen from behind; still in the same position. Cut back to* RATH, *who advances with a determined air. Group shot of* LOHMANN, *holding the photograph, and* GOLDSTAUB. RATH *comes up, leans over and snatches the photograph from* LOHMANN. *He holds it up and looks at it in horror, then looks sternly from one pupil to the other. Suddenly, he turns round, still holding the photograph. Pan after him as he goes to the window, and shuts it with a bang. The sound of the girls' choir is muted.* RATH *hurries back to his desk.*

Medium shot of RATH *sitting down and looking severely at* LOHMANN.

RATH : Get up!

Cut to LOHMANN, *who gets up uneasily. Resume on* RATH *who examines the confiscated photograph closely and inserts it carefully in a small note-book. He then addresses*

274

LOHMANN, *his arm outstretched.*
RATH : Sit down!
Cut to LOHMANN, *who does as he is told, and cut back
to* RATH, *who waves the notebook, menacingly in the
air.*
RATH : This will be discussed later.
*He stuffs the notebook in the inside pocket of his jacket
and fumbles as he fastens the top button of his coat.
He then takes out his handkerchief and blows his nose
noisily as before. While he is doing this, the camera cuts
to* LOHMANN, *who is looking at* ANGST. *Sound of* RATH
blowing his nose, off. Shot of ANGST *smirking with
satisfaction. He dips his pen in the inkwell and starts
to write. Fade out.*
Fade in : LOHMANN *and* ERTZUM *are crouching in front
of the school entrance. They are clearly hiding, and
remain unnoticed as the other pupils pass in front of them.
The scene is shot from the eye-level of the two boys, so
that only the legs of the other pupils and the briefcases in
their hands are visible. After a moment,* RATH *walks past
with measured tread, followed immediately by* ANGST.
ERTZUM *sticks his foot out and trips up* ANGST. ANGST
*falls flat on the ground, dropping a pile of books in the
process, while* ERTZUM *and* LOHMANN *disappear. Medium
close-up from above of* ANGST *sprawled on the ground.
He lifts his head, looking dazed.* RATH, *in medium close-
up from below, has turned round on hearing the noise of*
ANGST'S *fall and is looking back at him. Shot of* ANGST
from above with dishevelled hair and his cap on crooked.
RATH *stares at the ground in surprise.* ANGST, *shot from
above, follows* RATH'S *gaze and swallows uneasily. Close-
up of the books strewn on the ground. Pan across some
exercise books from which have fallen photographs of*
LOLA. *Fade out.*
Fade in : The entrance hall in RATH'S *apartment, the
dismayed* ANGST *is standing in front of the study door,
clutching his books.* RATH *hangs up his cane, then takes
off his hat and coat and hangs them up. He then picks
up a book and a file of papers from the side table, and he*

275

points at the study door.

RATH *severely*: Inside!

ANGST *opens the door and enters the study, followed by* RATH. *Inside* RATH'S *study*, ANGST *is seen entering, followed by* RATH. RATH *goes to the table, takes a chair, moves it near to an armchair and sits down in the latter. He then turns and beckons peremptorily off shot.*

RATH: Come over here!

ANGST *is seen still standing by the door, twisting his cap in his hands.*

He advances nervously across the room. Medium shot of the two of them, as RATH *relieves him of his books and puts them on the table. He then indicates the empty chair by his side.*

RATH: Sit down!

ANGST *sits down and looks at the floor. Close-up of the two of them.*

RATH *bitterly*: You as well! *Shaking his head.* My form leader!

ANGST *plaintively*: Please, sir. . . .

RATH *interrupting*: Be quiet! *A pause.* RATH *studies his pupil.* Aren't you ashamed of yourself?

ANGST: But, Sir, I . . .

RATH *interrupting*: Silence! Look at me. ANGST *looks up.* RATH *continues severely.* Where did you get those photographs?

ANGST *miserably*: I don't know. . . .

RATH: You're lying! Where did you get them?

ANGST *hesitantly*: Someone must have planted them on me.

RATH *dubiously*: Really? *He leans closer to* ANGST *and raises his left eyebrow.* You think I'm going to believe that?

ANGST *finally bursting into tears*: They all hate me . . . because I won't go with them in the evenings.

RATH *seizing him by the lapels*: Where won't you go with them?

ANGST: The others . . .

RATH: Come on, the truth now.

ANGST *hesitantly*: Every night they all go to THE BLUE ANGEL. . . . There are females!

276

RATH *beside himself* : Where?

ANGST : At THE BLUE ANGEL.

RATH *staring at* ANGST *in astonishment and letting him go*: At THE BLUE ANGEL? . . .

Without taking his eyes from ANGST, *he falls back in his chair. After a pause, he leans in front of his chastened pupil and takes the notebook from the table. He opens it, takes out the photograph confiscated from* LOHMANN, *and examines it closely, addressing* ANGST *as he does so.*

RATH : Off you go. We'll see about this later.

From his chair, RATH *watches* ANGST *shuffle towards the door.* ANGST *bows and goes out.*

Close-up of RATH, *full face. He looks closely at the photograph, then takes from his pocket the other two photographs confiscated from* ANGST. *He fans out the three photographs. After a moment or two, he glances towards the door to reassure himself and then studies the photographs again. He blows on the middle one, as* LOHMANN *and the other pupils did earlier. He glances round again, first at the window, then the door. He blows on the photograph, a little harder.*

Close-up of the three photographs in RATH'S *hand. They represent LOLA-LOLA. In the middle photograph, her skirt is made of pieces of feathers which lift when* RATH *blows on them, revealing her thighs.* RATH *blows again and again. The first notes of a popular tune are heard off.*

A night-club is seen in medium shot, shot slightly from below. LOLA *stands in the centre of the stage of* THE BLUE ANGEL. *She is swinging in time to the music, while behind her several other girls, all on the fat side, are sitting drinking beer. The décor, only party visible, is rather crude and consists of a sun throwing out long rays with cardboard clouds floating in front of it.* LOLA *is dressed in a close-fitting black costume covered in sequins and has a brightly-coloured ribbon in her hair. Hands on her hips, she gazes at the audience with a disinterested and contemptuous look.*

*Medium shot of a cardboard 'angel' which forms part
of the décor: he has movable wings and his expression is
more fatuous than angelic.*
In long shot in the foreground, LOLA *stands with her
legs apart, her stockings and suspenders well displayed;
behind her, the other women drink their beer. Other
parts of the décor are now visible, including a sailing
boat, fishing nets and anchors.*
*Group shot of the stage with the first few rows of the
audience seen from the back in the foreground. Gauze
curtains hang to right and left of the stage; cardboard
clouds and angels swing to and fro, crudely suspended
from the flies.*
A WAITER *off, very loud* : Pig's knuckles and sauerkraut . . .
and one beer !
LOLA *singing* :

Ich bin die fesche Lola	(My name is naughty Lola
Der Liebling der Saison	The fav'rite of the gang
Ich hab ein Pianola	I have a pianola
Zu Haus, in mein Salon	At home with lots of tang
Ich bin die fesche Lola	My name is naughty Lola
Mich liebt ein jeder Mann	The men all go for me
Doch an mein Pianola	But for my pianola
Da lass ich keinen dran	That's only there to see
Doch will mich wer	If you wish to play it
begleiten	You in this cabaret
Hier unten aus dem Saal	I'll bang you on the shins
Dem hau ich in die Seiten	And make you rue the day)
Und tret ihm auf's Pedal	

LOLA *turns and goes nonchalantly back to her place with
the other girls; she sits down, re-arranging her hair.
There is a satisfied murmur from the audience. The
waiters can also be heard shouting their orders: 'Beer !
. . . Sausage ! . . .' A medium shot, slightly from below,
shows* LOLA *seated on the stage. She takes a glass of
beer from her neighbour, drinks, and hands it back.*
MAN'S VOICE *off* : Three more beers.
Long shot of the stage as LOLA *gets up, wiping her
mouth with the end of her hair-ribbon. She advances*

once again to the centre of the stage and continues to sing in the same blasé manner as before.

Long shot, slightly angled, of an ill-lit alley-way; it is night time. Recognisable by his cape, RATH *hurries along. He is wearing the same hat as before and brandishing his cane. The camera tracks, then pans to follow him as he goes along.*

RATH *stops under a street lamp, as if uncertain of his way, and looks around in some embarrassment. He hesitates. In a doorway on the other side of the street, a prostitute waits for a client, smoking a cigarette.*

The camera tracks with RATH *and pans with him as he crosses the street; he stops very briefly, turns up his collar and hurries off. The prostitute bursts out laughing.*

Long shot of the stage of THE BLUE ANGEL: *the scenery is being changed. A stage-hand stands in the middle of the platform and looks up. The band begins to play 'Ach! Du lieber Augustin,' and at the same time, there are impatient shouts from the audience. A middle-aged woman,* GUSTE, *gets up from her place on the stage, comes towards the footlights and begins to sing.*

LOLA'S *dressing room:* LOLA *is seated at her dressing table, facing the camera. She is powdering her face, watched intently by the seated* LOHMANN *and the standing* GOLDSTAUB *and* ERTZUM. *They are wearing their school caps and smoking.*

LOLA *hands* GOLDSTAUB *her powder-puff and takes* LOHMANN'S *cigarette from his mouth; she draws on it and then gives it back to him.*

LOHMANN, ERTZUM *and* GOLDSTAUB *look on, fascinated, as* LOLA *straightens her wig.*

A long shot of the stage shows GUSTE *still singing. She finishes her song and is greeted by whistles from the audience.*

Outside in the ill-lit street, RATH, *shot from above, walks past houses with overhanging walls. As he passes a lamp-post, a ship's siren echoes in the night. A policeman, leaning against a poster of 'LOLA-LOLA' stuck on the*

wall, turns to watch RATH *as he disappears into the distance.*
Inside THE BLUE ANGEL : *a long shot of the stage with scenery representing a fountain. On the left is a bentwood chair, to the right a spotlight. The 'girls' are still seated on the stage, drinking their beer. The band strikes up, and* LOLA *appears to general applause, wearing a blonde wig topped by a small three-cornered hat and a crinoline dress with transparent skirts which displays her thighs and legs.* LOLA *bows to the audience with a smile and sways provocatively in time to the music, her hands behind her back.*

LOLA *singing* : Frühling kommt, der Sperling piept
Duft aus Blüten Kelchen
(Spring is here, sparrows chirp
Fragrant blossoms flower)

As she sings, LOLA *flutters her hands and cups one of them to her ear as if listening. The clarinet responds with an imitation of the sparrow. The audience laughs. In a group shot,* ERTZUM, LOHMANN *and* GOLDSTAUB *are seen leaning against the bar, drinking and smoking cigarettes. All three are gazing at the stage in fascination. A little further back, the* PROPRIETOR *is seen behind the bar, close to the till.*

LOLA *off* : Bin in einen Mann verliebt
Und weiss nicht in welchen
Ober Geld hat ist mir gleich
Denn mich macht die Liebe reich
(Love someone who is a man
But can't tell who is he
I don't care if he's well off
Love alone enriches me)

GOLDSTAUB *moves out of frame. Cut to* LOLA, *shot slightly from below, with her arms outstretched, as if in invitation to the schoolboy.*

LOLA : Kinder, heut abend, da such ich mir was aus
Einen Mann, einen richtigen Mann
(Children, tonight, I look for someone real

280

A he-man, the right kind for me)
*One of the girls goes over to the spotlight and turns it
on the audience.*

LOLA *still singing, moving towards the spotlight* :
Kinder, die Jungs häng mir schon zum Halz heraus
Einen Mann, einen richtigen Mann
(Children, the young are a pain in the neck !
The real man, the right kind for me)
*She turns round: the crinoline only covers one side of
her, the other reveals black-stockinged legs and lacy
briefs. There are hurrahs from the audience. She throws
back her head, smiles, and continues with her song.*

LOLA *singing* :
Einen Mann dem das Feuer aus den Augen glüht
Einen Mann dem das Feuer aus den Augen sprüht
(One whose heart still glows with thoughts of love
One whose eyes shoot out passionate fire)
Cut to the glass door of THE BLUE ANGEL. *The
camera is on the inside; on the outside,* RATH *is seen in
close-up. He peers through the misted window, then opens
the door.*

Another shot shows RATH *coming hesitantly into the
club. In the background,* LOLA *continues her song.*
RATH'S *glasses become misted; the fishing nets that hang
in the entrance and in the aisles bar his way.*

LOLA *off* : Kurz einen Mann der noch lieben will und kann
Einen Mann, einen richtigen Mann
(In short, one who's willing to love and be held
The real thing, and not a fraud)
Cut to the bar. ERTZUM *has just seen* RATH *and hastily
removes his cap, pushes against* LOHMANN *and disappears.
Taken aback,* LOHMANN *throws away his cigarette and
follows* ERTZUM. *Near them a* CLOWN *observes the
audience. Pan from his gaze past several provocative
posters of* LOLA *towards* RATH, *who is seen picking his
way through the nets down the side of the club. Close-up
of* RATH *caught in a net as in a gigantic spider's web.
A raucous sound from the clarinet seems to mock his
predicament.*

281

LOLA *still singing off* : Männer gibt es dünn und dick
Gross und klein und kräftig
Andere wieder schön und schick
schüchtern oder heftig
Wie er aussieht mir egal
Irgend einen trifft die Wahl
(Men there are, thin and thick
Large and small and hefty
Others may be nice and quick
Bashful or aggressive
How he looks means nought to me
Someone here will fill the bill)

Medium close-up of LOLA, *smiling, as she stops singing and goes towards the spotlight. Taking the place of the other girl, who goes and sits down beside* GUSTE, *she directs the beam of light on the audience, who shout invitations at her.*

MAN IN THE AUDIENCE *off* : Hey! Look over here! . . . Over here!

Others follow suit with cries of ' Oh me, me! ' — ' Over here, darling! ' — ' This way, Lola! Here's the cash.' Close-up of RATH, *who turns round suddenly as the beam hits him. He blinks in confusion, the light reflecting off his spectacles.*

LOLA *singing off*: Kinder, heut abend, da such ich mir was aus
Rapid pan to her standing by the spotlight.
Cut back to RATH, *furious and bewildered, looking wildly from the stage to the audience and back again. There are shouts and mocking laughter off, while* LOLA *continues relentlessly with her song.*

LOLA *off* : Einen Mann, einen richtigen Mann
Medium close-up as she leans on the spotlight.

LOLA *off*: Kinder, die Jungs häng mir schon zum Halz heraus
Resume on RATH, *in medium close-up, gazing wide-eyed at the stage. Suddenly he turns and stares in the direction of the bar.*

LOLA *off* : Einen Mann, einen richtigen Mann

The camera shows RATH's *view of the bar. In front of it,* GOLDSTAUB *stands nonchalantly watching the show. Behind the bar near the till stands the* PROPRIETOR *of* THE BLUE ANGEL, *a large bulky man who is listening with evident satisfaction to the reactions of the audience.* GOLDSTAUB *suddenly catches sight of* RATH, *panics, snatches off his cap, and runs off towards the wings.*

LOLA *off* : Einen Mann dem das Feuer aus den Augen glüht

RATH, *shot from above, stands in the midst of the seated audience, still in the glare of the spotlight. The sight of* GOLDSTAUB *making off galvanises him into action. He waves his cane and struggles to find a way through the crowd.*

RATH : Stop ! . . . Stop ! . . . Stay where you are !

LOLA *off, simultaneously with* RATH : Einen Mann dem das Feuer aus den Augen sprüht

Cut to GOLDSTAUB, *disappearing backstage. There are shouts and laughter from the audience drowning* LOLA's *song.*

In medium shot, RATH *rushes towards the door which leads backstage, and bumps into the* CLOWN, *who is standing in his way. After a moment's deliberation, the* CLOWN *lets him through and closes the door behind him. The camera following* RATH *backstage, pans across a wall covered with mirrors, posters and photographs.* RATH *looks around him in confusion. In the background on the stage,* LOLA *invites the audience to sing with her in* THE BLUE ANGEL.

LOLA : Come on, all together, now ! *They all sing.*

RATH, *seen from behind, strides up to a door backstage and flings it open, revealing several of the chorus girls in various states of undress. He looks round in embarrassment and goes out again, shutting the door.*

RATH *now finds himself in* LOLA's *dressing room, which he examines. There are two doors, one leading to the dressing rooms of the other performers, the other giving directly onto the wings. A spiral staircase leads up to* LOLA's *bedroom. The stage door opens and the* CLOWN *appears. A girl passes by behind him. He watches* RATH

*for a moment and then stands motionless. The audience
is heard in the background, singing with* LOLA.
RATH *advances across the room until he is standing by
a screen in front of* LOLA'S *dressing table. He listens.
Applause is heard off, marking the end of* LOLA'S *act,
and he immediately hurries over to the staircase and
goes up it out of sight. Cut to* GOLDSTAUB, *shot from
above, crouching behind the screen and reflected in two
mirrors. Cut to medium close-up of the* CLOWN, *who
catches sight of* GOLDSTAUB *and comes back into the
room.*
*Medium shot of the band, seen from above; the pianist
drinks from a glass of beer and then strikes up an oriental
melody, followed by the trumpet and the saxophone. A
large fountain is painted on the backdrop behind them.
A very fat girl comes onto the stage in medium close-up;
she sways in time to the music, rolling her eyes.*
Pan on LOLA'S *entrance into her dressing room. She
goes to the table, takes off her hat and, suddenly hearing
a strange noise, turns towards the staircase leading up to
her bedroom.*

LOLA *sharply* : What are you doing in my bedroom?
Very slowly, RATH *comes down the stairs with* LOLA
watching.
RATH *brandishing his cane* : So you're Lola-Lola?
Somewhat surprised, but also reassured by RATH'S
general appearance, LOLA *goes to her table, takes off
her wig and starts to brush her hair.*
LOLA : You're from the police?
RATH : Indeed not, madam! I am . . . *He puffs out his chest.*
. . . Doctor Immanuel Rath, schoolmaster of this town.
Shot of LOLA *and* RATH *both together.* LOLA *examines*
RATH *with curiosity. She smiles ironically, then bends
down at her dressing table and continues brushing her
hair.*
LOLA *contemptuously* : In that case you might at least take
off your hat. . . .
Close-up of RATH, *who jumps backwards in embarrass-
ment and hastily removes his hat.* A

284

man and a woman are heard quarrelling violently off.
Their voices become suddenly louder as the door to the
other dressing room opens to reveal the CLOWN. *He shuts*
the door and the voices fade. Cut to LOLA *applying lip-*
stick. Return to the CLOWN *passing in front of* RATH,
who looks at him uneasily. He opens the stage door and
the room is filled with oriental music. The CLOWN *eyes*
RATH *without any expression and then disappears through*
the door, shutting it behind him. RATH *turns towards*
LOLA. *A new shot shows them facing one another.*
LOLA *putting on her lipstick* : What are you doing here, then?
RATH *pompously*: I am here in an official capacity. *He points*
at LOLA. You are corrupting my pupils!
LOLA : Really! You think I run a kindergarten?
Pan after LOLA *as she rises and goes behind the screen,*
undoing the back of her skirt. She sees GOLDSTAUB. *Cut*
to a high shot of GOLDSTAUB, *crouched by the mirror.*
Return to LOLA, *who smiles at him and moves the screen*
slightly to hide him better. She then removes her skirt
and drapes it over the screen. Medium close-up on RATH,
who has been following her movements closely. In
medium shot, LOLA *comes out from behind the screen*
wearing the upper half of her costume and a petticoat.
She puts one foot up on the chair and takes off her
shoe, showing her thighs in the process. Medium close-up
of RATH *watching her with interest. He suddenly pulls*
himself together and turns his head away, still watching
LOLA, *however, out of the corner of his eye. Cut back to*
LOLA, *who takes off her stockings, smiling at* RATH *as*
she does so. Then she throws the stocking she has just
taken off, over her shoulder, and addresses him.
LOLA : Now, you don't say anything any more.
Cut to RATH, *now staring openly at* LOLA. *He turns,*
and, with as much dignity as he can muster, he goes
towards the door, which suddenly opens. The music
marking the end of the act onstage is heard and the girls
troop through, bumping into RATH *and eyeing him*
curiously. Finding him blocking her way, one of the girls
complains.

GIRL : For god's sake! . . . You're obstructing the traffic.
After the girls comes the CLOWN, *who pushes* RATH *back
into the room and shuts the door. On the other side of
the room by the door, two girls are sneering at* RATH.
GIRL : Just look what's crawled in!
They go out, shutting the door.
Return to LOLA, *who is watching* RATH *and playing with
her stocking.*
RATH *off* : I really can't stay here . . . *Shot of him by the
door* . . . I am compromising you.
LOLA *moves into the shot until she is standing face to face
with* RATH. *He draws back a little.*
LOLA *smiling* : If you're . . . very good . . . *She speaks very
slowly* . . . you can stay.
With a mischievous air, she gently takes RATH'S *hat
from him and puts it on the table. Then she passes in
front of* RATH, *brushing against him, and the camera
pans after her as she goes up the staircase.* RATH *stands
mopping his brow, while in the background* LOLA'S *legs
are still visible at the top of the staircase. A pair of briefs
slides down her legs.*
LOLA *partly off* : Look out, below . . . I'm taking everything
off now!
*Taking off her briefs, she throws them down from the
top of the stairs, and they land on* RATH'S *shoulder. He
takes the garment and tries unsuccessfully to fold it. At
this moment,* GUSTE *comes in through the stage door,
looks at* RATH *dubiously, and takes the briefs from him.*
GUSTE *wagging a finger at him* : You! You! I don't want to
hear any complaints from you.
Briefs in hand, she moves away from RATH, *leaving him
speechless. Music is heard in the club.* GUSTE, *in front
of the other door, looks alternately from* RATH *to the
briefs, then throws the garment under the screen. More
music from the club. A high shot of* GOLDSTAUB *catching
the briefs behind the screen. Return to* RATH *who looks
nervously in the direction of the stage. He has obviously
not seen* GOLDSTAUB. GUSTE *glances at* RATH *once more
and goes out, shutting the door. Return to* RATH, *who*

*looks around him and particularly at the staircase, while
music, stage noises and laughter are heard off.* RATH
leans wearily on LOLA'S *dressing table and sits down
heavily. He takes off his glasses, passes a hand across his
eyes, gets out his handkerchief and starts to clean his
glasses. He squints at the stage door which must be open,
judging by the noise. The camera pans as an animal
trainer goes past* RATH, *leading a bear on its hind legs.
In passing, the trainer glances at* RATH, *who shrinks
in his chair in alarm. The trainer goes out of the other
door, followed by the bear. Cut back to* RATH *gazing
after them in stupefaction, still holding his handkerchief and glasses.*

In her bedroom, LOLA *in her black underwear climbs
onto a pile of suitcases to reach a hatbox on top of a
cupboard. A suitcase slips and falls noisily.*

In the dressing room below, RATH *hears the noise and
looks upwards. High shot of* GOLDSTAUB, *seen crawling
out from his hiding place. He puts* LOLA'S *briefs in the
back pocket of* RATH'S *frock coat, without the latter
noticing. Cut to* RATH, *who looks around himself in
increasing bewilderment.*

Up in her bedroom, LOLA *casually gets ready to go
down.* LOLA *comes down the staircase and smiles at*
RATH, *sitting in the chair. Pan as she goes towards him,
takes him by the shoulders and turns him round in his
chair.*

LOLA : Do you like me better like this, then?

She passes in front of RATH, *who turns, moving out of
frame. Close-up on* GOLDSTAUB, *peering out from behind
the screen. Medium shot of* LOLA *standing by the piano;
she puts on a short skirt. The bell calling her onstage
rings.*

Close-up on RATH, *who puts on his spectacles and looks
at* LOLA *while the bell rings again. He raises his head,
and* LOLA *is seen fastening her skirt.*

LOLA : They seem to be in a hurry out there!

*She leans across the piano, striking several keys as she
does so, and reaches for her hat. Cut to* RATH *observing*

LOLA *with astonishment and interest. Return to* LOLA, *who puts on the hat, straightens her skirt and smiles at* RATH. RATH *turns away and gets up. Medium shot of* LOLA *adjusting bonnet.*

RATH *searching around him* : I wonder where I put my hat.
The door opens behind RATH *to admit* KIEPERT, *the manager of the troupe, followed by his assembled artistes.*

A WOMAN *off* : I won't drink any more!

KIEPERT *bellowing* : You'll just have to soak, ladies. You think I give a damn about art? Rubbish! And if you don't want to guzzle, you can get out!

ANOTHER WOMAN : About the commission . . .

KIEPERT *interrupting her* : Shut up! Once and for all, quiet!
He turns and sees LOLA *and* RATH. How did this joker happen to be here?

LOLA : He's only the kids' teacher.

KIEPERT *looks at* LOLA, *takes off and puts on his false moustache, and addresses* RATH *obsequiously.*

KIEPERT : Professor. . . .

RATH *bowing in confirmation* : At the university. KIEPERT *raises his top hat.* Doctor Immanuel Rath.

KIEPERT : Then we're bound to understand each other.

RATH : What do you mean?

KIEPERT *pointing at himself* : Art and . . . *indicating* RATH : Science. *He approaches Rath who draws back slowly.* Allow me to introduce myself! Kiepert, manager and conjurer. *The door closes behind him, as he addresses* LOLA, *who is combing her hair.* Why wasn't I called immediately? *To* RATH, *with an ingratiating bow.* I am delighted to be able to welcome in our midst one of the most eminent personalities of this town.

Pan to RATH, *who draws back slowly, shaking his head.*

RATH : I have come . . .

KIEPERT : I know, because you feel at home here.

RATH *retreating further* : No. I have come . . .

KIEPERT : Indeed, I can see that you have. And I am delighted. . . .

He glares at LOLA, *out of frame. As* RATH *comes back towards him, pan with* KIEPERT *as he strides across to*

LOLA. LOLA *is doing her hair in front of the mirror.*
KIEPERT *appears, putting on his top hat.*
KIEPERT *furious*: I said why wasn't I called? Am I the
manager or aren't I?
LOLA *taking her hands away from her head*: You're a stupid
old bit of beef.
KIEPERT *is speechless. The bell rings again.*
KIEPERT *with a furious gesture*: Get out there! Go and do
your number!
LOLA, *hands behind her back, looks contemptuously at
the two men. She addresses* KIEPERT.
LOLA *full of sarcasm*: Don't overdo it, will you?
As she moves out of frame, cut to RATH, *who has been
watching the dispute indignantly. In medium shot,* LOLA
*opens the stage door, adjusts her costume, and goes out
with a smile of contempt. From a close-up of* RATH, *the
camera tracks backwards to show him retreating as*
KIEPERT *comes towards him again.*
KIEPERT *facing camera*: Fascinating woman! . . . *He strokes
his moustache. A pause.* Herr Professor, I really must con-
gratulate you on your impeccable taste.
RATH *fleeing behind the screen*: I beg your pardon?
KIEPERT *still advancing on* RATH: Come, come, don't get
excited. We can talk man to man.
Cut to the CLOWN *entering from the stage door. Music
filters through from the club.*
KIEPERT *off*: I can fix it up for you. . . . The girl is very . . .
In medium shot, RATH *and* KIEPERT *face each other.*
KIEPERT *insistently*: . . . is very . . .
RATH *raising an indignant finger*: I have come about my
pupils.
KIEPERT: Your pupils?
RATH *furious*: You've been harbouring my pupils!
KIEPERT: Me?
RATH: Yes!
KIEPERT: But we only let in . . .
RATH *beside himself with rage and waving his arms frantic-
ally*: Miserable liar!
LOLA *begins to sing off.*

289

KIEPERT : Liar?

>RATH *takes a step backwards.* GOLDSTAUB, *shot from above, cries out in pain, appears from behind the screen and rushes past* RATH. *The screen falls over.*

RATH : What's this? Stop! . . . Come here, you rascal! Stop! . . . Stop!

>RATH *rushes forward, waving his cane. Rapid pan to follow him, as he runs to the door, knocks into the* CLOWN, *and goes out.*

>*A high-angle shot of the street shows the entrance to* THE BLUE ANGEL. *The walls of the night-club are covered with posters of* LOLA. RATH *comes suddenly from the club, hesitates and looks around him. Applause is heard off, as* LOLA *finishes her song.*

RATH *waving his cane:* Stop! . . . Stop! . . . Stop!

>*He rushes off down the street. Fade out.*

>*Inside the school dormitory,* ANGST *is lying in bed in the darkness. Hearing a curious noise, he sits up nervously in bed. Two figures appear silhouetted against the wall, Ghostly hands rear threateningly over him. Before he can react, the two forms fling themselves upon him, raining blows. He cries out shrilly.*

>RATH *is seen going up the staircase outside his apartment. He reaches the landing, turns, then opens the door of his apartment. Fade out.*

>*In his bedroom,* RATH *sits with a glazed look, his hair dishevelled, exhausted. He passes a hand across his brow, then feels in his pocket after a moment; he draws out* LOLA'S *briefs, wipes his forehead with them as if they were his handkerchief, and looks at them again. Suddenly, aware of them, he lets them fall and slumps in his chair.*

>*A high shot over the roofs of the town.*

>RATH *comes out of his study into the hall of his apartment. He searches in his pockets and picks up his coat. The* MAID *hurries to help him. He thanks her with a dignified wave of the hand and picks up his briefcase and cane, but suddenly realises that his hat is not in its accustomed position on the hatstand.*

MAID, *hands on hips*: Where have you left your hat this time?

Ignoring her question, RATH still searches on the hall table and the hatstand, which he examines for some time. He starts, as if suddenly remembering where the hat is, disappears into his room and comes out again rapidly, wearing a top hat. Ignoring the MAID, he strides out of the apartment. A new shot shows him descending the staircase. The MAID, seen from below, watches him in surprise from the landing.

A series of shots dissolve into one another showing the figures on the town clock, the clock face, and the hands indicating eight o'clock as in a previous sequence.

Inside RATH's classroom, a long shot from the rostrum shows the pupils sitting quietly at their desks. They turn their heads at the sound of the door opening and stand up. Back view of RATH sitting down at his desk; in the background, the pupils stand. He gestures at them wearily.

RATH : All right. Sit down, please.

The pupils sit down. LOHMANN and GOLDSTAUB look at each other, surprised, while RATH, following his customary ritual, takes out his handkerchief. Medium close-up on RATH from the front; he blows his nose, wipes it, puts the handkerchief back in his pocket and opens the exercise book, which he leafs through, looking over the top of his glasses in the direction of ANGST. Medium close-up of ANGST sitting rigidly at his desk, avoiding the schoolmaster's gaze. Return to RATH, who continues to leaf through the book, while his eyes travel across the class. GOLDSTAUB, in medium close-up, looks across at the window with an air of false preoccupation. Cut back to RATH. Still leafing through the book, he looks down the middle row of the class. Medium shot of ERTZUM, who stares back insolently, but finally drops his eyes and twiddles his thumbs. RATH turns over a few more pages, looking at ANGST. ANGST sits gaping with an air of increasing desperation. RATH, totally unmoved, undoes the top button of his coat, takes out his notebook and

291

writes in it, still looking at ANGST. *Cut to* GOLDSTAUB; *he looks surprised, then throws a malicious glance at* ANGST. RATH, *frowning, finishes writing, his eyes still fixed on* ANGST. ANGST, *in medium close-up, swallows uneasily. Fade out.*

A long shot from above shows the street taken by RATH *the previous evening. It is night. A cat sits in the road, miaowing. As* RATH *comes into view, the cat flees to the safety of a window sill. Under the streetlamp* RATH *pauses to check his direction and moves off again. His shadow looms across the wall. The cat miaows.*

A siren is heard. RATH *stops in another street under a streetlamp, walks on, turns back, passes another lamp, and turns back again, his shadow lengthening in the lamplight.*

In her dressing room, LOLA *is seated, facing the camera, at her dressing table. One one side of her stands* ERTZUM, *wearing his school cap; on the other* LOHMANN, *smoking a cigarette.*

LOLA : Oh! . . . And he said nothing at all?

ERTZUM : Of course not. He's afraid of us.

LOHMANN *leaning close and speaking in English in* LOLA'S *ear* : I love you.

LOLA : Cut the English nonsense, sweetie.

LOHMANN *draws back while* LOLA *wipes her hands on a cloth.*

ERTZUM : Now you've upset him.

LOLA : Bah! He'll recover.

LOHMANN *goes and opens the stage door. Music and laughter are heard.* KIEPERT, *the manager of the troupe, comes down the steps from the stage in a fury, brandishing a rabbit and shoving the* CLOWN.

KIEPERT *to the* CLOWN : You stupid old fool, you've messed up the whole number! I ask for a fish so you come out with a rabbit. *He enters the dressing room.* Ah! The young students. Back again already?

LOHMANN *fishes a banknote out of his pocket and holds it out to* KIEPERT, *who examines it attentively.*

KIEPERT *taking the note and putting it away* : One more time

I'll let you in . . . But watch out. You'll make me lose my license.

Cut to the dressing room window seen from the outside. GOLDSTAUB leans out, suddenly looks away in alarm and hurriedly shuts the window. In medium shot, inside the dressing room, GOLDSTAUB rushes towards ERTZUM and LOHMANN.

GOLDSTAUB : He's coming!

ERTZUM *flinging himself at* GOLDSTAUB : Who?

GOLDSTAUB *tearing off his school cap* : Unrath!

ERTZUM snatches off his cap and rushes towards the door where KIEPERT is standing.

KIEPERT *holding them back* : No, no! No, no! Not through the hall, gentlemen, if you please. Into the cellar.

The camera pans on LOHMANN, ERTZUM and GOLD-STAUB as they hurry to the trap door leading down into the cellar, fling it open and disappear.

RATH arrives at the club entrance with a small parcel in his hand.   Music and singing off

Pan on RATH walking down a corridor backstage. As he passes a poster of ' LOLA-LOLA,' his top hat knocks against a lamp bracket sticking out from the wall. He straightens his hat. Medium shot outside LOLA'S dressing-room; on the left, the CLOWN. KIEPERT is standing by LOLA'S door holding his rabbit. On seeing RATH, he raises his top hat.

KIEPERT : 'Evening, Professor. This *is* a surprise.

RATH also raises his hat, then turns towards the CLOWN. KIEPERT motions RATH into the dressing room. RATH starts forward; but before he finally enters the room, he looks once more at the CLOWN, who remains silent. Music and singing are heard off.

Inside her dressing room, LOLA is arranging her costume in front of her mirror. She turns and smiles. In a reverse shot, RATH stands in the doorway; behind him, KIEPERT and the CLOWN.

LOLA *off* : You can always come straight in, Herr Professor. You're very welcome here.

With great ceremony, RATH removes his top hat, gives

a little bow, shuts the door and turns towards LOLA. *He gazes at her.*

LOLA *off* : I knew you would come back.

Shot of LOLA *removing the ribbon from her hair.*

LOLA *smiling* : They all come back to see me !

LOLA *lifts up her skirt, which is open at the front, and her petticoat, as* RATH *enters the picture, carrying his parcel. A new shot shows the pair of them face to face.*

RATH : Madam . . . in my haste . . . yesterday evening . . I seem to have taken . . . instead of my hat . . . this . . . this . . . *he hesitates* . . . garment.

LOLA *takes the parcel, opens it and finds her briefs inside. Letting the underclothing slip through her fingers, she smiles at* RATH *with her head on one side.*

LOLA *caressingly* : Ah, I see. . . . And you didn't come because of me at all?

She drops the briefs, takes RATH'S *hat and cane and puts them down behind her. Sudden music from inside the club indicates that the stage door has been opened.* RATH *stands still, highly embarrassed.* LOLA *pushes a chair towards him as he turns to look in the direction of the door. Cut to the* CLOWN *who comes into the room holding a rabbit. In a group shot,* LOLA *helps* RATH *off with his coat, while the* CLOWN *advances in the foreground, his back to the camera.* RATH *continues to stare at this silent witness, while* LOLA *goes and hangs up* RATH'S *coat. A new shot shows the* CLOWN *looking at* RATH *with a sad and weary expression before going out of the door. Cut to a shot of the dressing table:* LOLA *sits* RATH *down in the chair close beside her.*

Long shot of the stage, slightly from below: GUSTE *is singing, swaying her hips and holding a glass of beer. The other chorus girls are visible in the background.*

GUSTE *singing* : And if you all go together . . . forwards . . . backwards . . . down . . . up . . . from right to left.

She invites the other girls and the audience to sing, which they do. There is loud music and applause.

In a long shot across the dressing room, LOLA, *standing by the door with her hands on her hips, looks at* RATH *slowly up and down. The music and applause can be heard in the background.* LOLA *glances outside the dressing room, then smiles and shuts the door, cutting off the noise.*

In medium shot in front of the dressing table, LOLA *sits down beside* RATH, *who is fiddling with his bow tie and watching her. She hands him the box of mascara.*

LOLA : Here, hold that a moment.

RATH *holds the box open in front of him while* LOLA *spits in it. She then rubs a small brush in it, which she applies to her eyelashes.*

LOLA : I have beautiful eyes . . . don't you think? RATH *turns away as* LOLA *leans towards him.* They're not beautiful, then?

RATH *embarrassed* : Oh yes . . . yes. . . . They're very . . . very beautiful.

Medium close-up from above on the trap door leading to the cellar; it lifts gently. ERTZUM, GOLDSTAUB *and* LOHMANN *watch* LOLA *and their schoolmaster in great amusement. Cut back to the pair of them, facing the camera.*

LOLA : So you're not here in an official capacity today?

She smiles at RATH'S *embarrassment. He replies after a long pause.*

RATH *embarrassed* : I am afraid I did not behave very properly yesterday.

LOLA *takes the mascara from him, puts it down and picks up a packet of cigarettes.*

LOLA : That's quite true. Today, you're much nicer . . .

She puts a cigarette between her lips and hands the packet to RATH, *who fumbles and drops it on the floor.*

RATH : Oh . . . I'm sorry.

He bends down to pick up the cigarettes. Insert of the three schoolboys quietly closing the trap door. RATH *is on all fours under the table by* LOLA'S *stockinged legs.* RATH *picks up the cigarettes scattered on the floor. In a medium shot,* LOLA *lights a cigarette, pulls at it and looks down.*

LOLA : Hey, Professor, when you've finished, send me a postcard, will you?

RATH, *under the table, keeps his eyes on* LOLA'S *legs.*
He misses two cigarettes as a result and turns round.
Close-up of RATH's *head appearing above the table, on*
which he puts the cigarettes. He looks grotesque, his hair
dishevelled and his glasses crooked. In a medium shot,
RATH *kneels in front of* LOLA, *who smiles.*

LOLA : You are a sight! *She runs a comb through his hair*
and he recoils. No, keep still!
Holding his head with one hand, she combs his hair.
RATH *looks flustered. Steeply angled shot of the three*
boys looking through the trap door again.

LOLA *off* : Your boys should see you now!
A medium shot of the dressing room shows RATH *still*
kneeling in front of LOLA, *who hands him a box of*
powder.

LOLA *smiling* : And now to work.
Taking RATH *by the elbow, she helps him up and sits*
him down beside her. She powders her face while RATH
looks nervously around him.

LOLA : You really are . . . *She leans towards him; they appear*
face to face in medium close-up . . . rather sweet.
RATH *cannot bring himself to look at* LOLA. *He says*
nothing, but finally smiles at her; he is very flattered and
closes his eyes, shyly turning his head to one side. LOLA
immediately blows hard on the powder-box, covering
RATH's *face and jacket with a thick cloud of powder.*
He jumps up and starts to cough as though about to
suffocate. LOLA *gaily brushes his coat and face, caressing*
his beard as she does so. RATH, *still coughing, takes off*
his glasses and wipes them. LOLA *tickles him under the*
chin.

LOLA *ironically and pityingly* : Does that hurt?
RATH *stops coughing. He blows, then realises that she*
is tickling him and smiles with childish satisfaction.

RATH *smiling* : No.
LOLA *pinching his cheek* : Is that better now?
RATH *laughing* : Oh yes!
Medium close-up from above on the half-open trap
door, as the three schoolboys look out. Suddenly, the

door opens and music is heard. The boys look towards the door. Kiepert is seen framed in the doorway.

Another shot shows Rath and Lola, Rath looking very embarrassed at the sight of Kiepert. He gets up. Lola smiles. Rath moves back until he is next to the long mirror. He wipes his glasses and puts them on again, looking once more at Kiepert. In *increasing embarrassment, he dusts his coat, on which traces of powder can still be seen. Kiepert approaches Lola. She starts to do her hair while Kiepert bows to Rath.*

Kiepert: I am sorry to interrupt, Herr Professor. *He bends over Lola.* What's going on here? Why aren't there any drinks being served? . . . There's a sailor out there with a wallet that's fit to burst.

Lola: What's it got to do with me? Send out Guste!

In medium shot, Rath, still dusting himself, listens to the conversation. Cut back to Lola and Kiepert.

Kiepert: Are you crazy? Who's going to buy champagne for Guste? It's you he wants.

Lola: I won't. I'm an artiste, not a . . .

Kiepert *speechless*: You're what?

Lola: An artiste.

Kiepert *looking at Rath*: Well, well . . . What do you make of that . . . *Cut to Rath as Kiepert continues off* . . . Professor? The girl's got some crazy ideas about her profession!

A long shot towards the doorway shows the Proprietor, a large cigar in his mouth, carrying a bottle and an ice-bucket. He draws aside to admit a seaman, a Captain in uniform. The Captain almost fills the doorway. Obviously drunk, he makes his way towards the dressing table, while the Proprietor shuts the door. Shot of the three of them together; the Captain moves towards Lola while the Proprietor puts down two glasses beside her.

Captain: Good evening. . . . Here I am.

Cut to Rath, who looks at Kiepert in astonishment as the Captain speaks.

Captain *off*: I've just arrived from Calcutta.

Cut to Lola and the Captain, facing one another. The

CAPTAIN *produces a pineapple and deposits it on the table.*

CAPTAIN : Part of my cargo. . .

He takes LOLA'S *hand and tries to kiss it, but she snatches it away hastily.*

LOLA : Leave me alone.

The PROPRIETOR *uncorks the bottle and fills the glasses.*

LOLA : Get out !

The PROPRIETOR *glares at her and nudges her furiously with his elbow. The* CAPTAIN *leans towards* LOLA.

CAPTAIN : But I haven't done anything to you !

Medium shot of RATH *and* KIEPERT. *The latter restrains* RATH *from hurling himself at the* CAPTAIN. RATH *breaks free and pushes the* CAPTAIN.

RATH : Wretch ! . . . Get out !

CAPTAIN *very surprised, to* LOLA : Who's this, your papa?

RATH *scandalised* : How dare you molest this lady !

CAPTAIN *ironically* : Are you the lady's father?

Members of the troupe appear in the doorway.

KIEPERT *off* : But . . . Herr Professor !

RATH *off* : Silence . . . Silence, I say ! *Resume on* RATH *and* KIEPERT . . . Miserable procurer !

CAPTAIN : Who me? A procurer?

RATH : Yes. Get out ! . . . Out ! . . . Out !

The camera pans as RATH *pushes the* CAPTAIN *out of the dressing room and shuts the door. Medium close-up of the* CLOWN *standing at the other door with the chorus-girls. All have been watching the scene in silence. Cut back to* RATH *and to* LOLA *at her dressing table.* KIEPERT *throws himself on* RATH.

KIEPERT *beside himself with indignation* : But what right have you to . . . ?

RATH slaps him violently a couple of times. Cut to the CLOWN *and the girls looking on in astonishment. They disappear behind the door. Return to* RATH *and* KIEPERT, *face to face.*

RATH : Miserable procurer !

The PROPRIETOR *enters the picture, pushes* KIEPERT *out of the way and plants himself in front of* RATH.

298

PROPRIETOR: Just what the hell's the idea of chucking everyone out, eh? *He brandishes the champagne bottle.* The fellow had paid for the bottle!

As he waves the bottle, he manages to pour some of its contents over KIEPERT.

RATH *haughtily*: I'll pay for everything!

In medium shot, LOLA *looks on in astonishment. She leans back and stretches out one leg, revealing her stocking on her thigh.*

RATH *off*: Get out!

Noises outside the dressing room: the voice of the CAPTAIN *can be heard.*

CAPTAIN *off*: He called me a procurer!

In medium shot outside LOLA'S *dressing room, the* CAPTAIN *is standing on the steps which lead up to the stage, waving his arms and shouting. The* PROPRIETOR *rushes towards him and tries to restrain him.*

CAPTAIN *bellowing*: Procurer!

PROPRIETOR: You're crazy, Captain . . . Don't make a racket here! *He bangs the palm of his hand on the stair-rail.* You'll have the police on my neck.

CAPTAIN *as loudly as ever*: Yes, the police . . . I'll go and get the police . . . You old crook!

He struggles with the PROPRIETOR, *breaks free and goes up the steps.* GUSTE *is seen standing at the entrance to the stage, holding a glass of beer. The* CAPTAIN *knocks into her, upsetting the beer.*

The stage is seen from the front: the CAPTAIN *leaps into view.*

CAPTAIN: The crook! Call the police!

The PROPRIETOR *follows him on. Long shot of the stage as the* CAPTAIN *staggers forward, waving his arms, and divides the front and hind part of a stage horse.*

CAPTAIN *bellowing*: He tried to knock me over!

KIEPERT, *in front of the door into* LOLA'S *dressing room, buries his head in his hands in despair. In* LOLA'S *dressing room,* RATH *is sitting down, holding the bottle.* LOLA *stands beside him, wearing a black costume with a transparent skirt revealing black-frilled knickers.*

299

LOLA *impressed* : Someone fighting over me? *Surprised and genuinely pleased.* That hasn't happened for a long time! *She takes the bottle from* RATH.
RATH *very sure of himself* : I only did my duty.
LOLA *puts the bottle on the table and goes up to* RATH. *The camera pans as she turns around him, caressing his shoulders with her hands. He fidgets.*
LOLA : Now, now, there's no need to get worked up again, Professor. *She picks up the two glasses and hands one of them to* RATH. Now we must wash it down. *She raises her glass and smiles.* Cheers!
RATH : May I . . . ? *He drinks.* Your health . . . Your very good health!
They drink. Still standing, LOLA *looks at* RATH *and smiles.*
The camera pans, then tracks forwards from the entrance of THE BLUE ANGEL *into the club itself, following the arrival of a policeman. He moves towards the stage, increasingly concealed by fishing nets and decorations. The audience, sitting around him, drink and smoke and talk loudly. In the background is a poster of ' LOLA-LOLA ' on the wall. In medium shot, the* PROPRIETOR, *aided by a waiter and some stage hands, tries to remove the* CAPTAIN *from the stage. In a long shot across the club, the audience is seen in the background, with the* POLICEMAN, *his hands behind his back, advancing slowly towards the stage. Cut to* KIEPERT *in the wings. He looks out at the stage and the audience, hesitates, then rushes towards the door to the dressing room and goes through. Inside* LOLA'S *dressing room,* KIEPERT *comes face to face with* RATH *and* LOLA, *and raises his hat.*
KIEPERT *very excited* : I'm sorry . . . Herr . . . Herr Professor, but . . . the police are here.
RATH *uneasily* : The police! . . . The police. . . .
KIEPERT *hands* RATH *his hat.*
KIEPERT : They musn't find you here!
RATH *pulling himself together* : I have nothing to fear from the authorities.
KIEPERT : You haven't, but we have.

300

KIEPERT *moves rapidly out of frame.* LOLA, *who has been listening at the door, takes* RATH *by the arm.*

LOLA : You'd better disappear, Professor.

Pan as she pushes him towards the trap door into the cellar, which KIEPERT *has just opened.* LOLA *pushes* RATH *down through the trap door. Half-way through, he turns round to protest once more.*

RATH : I have nothing to fear from the authorities.

He disappears.

LOLA *and* KIEPERT *shut the trap door and breathe a sigh of relief.* KIEPERT *mops his brow.*

LOLA *amused* : We'll end up opening a boarding-house down there !

In the wings, in front of LOLA'S *door,* GUSTE *tries to keep back the* POLICEMAN. *Standing nearby are the* PROPRIETOR, *the* CAPTAIN, *now a little more sober, the* CLOWN, *stage-hands and various onlookers, all talking at once. There is general pandemonium.*

POLICEMAN *severely* : Keep calm for a moment, can't you?

The POLICEMAN *opens the door into* LOLA'S *dressing room, and goes in. From inside the room, medium shot of the* PROPRIETOR *and the* CAPTAIN *standing in the doorway, the latter containing his rage with difficulty. They both move forward and a stage-hand shuts the door behind them. In a group shot,* LOLA, KIEPERT *and the* POLICEMAN.

POLICEMAN *indicating the* CAPTAIN : This gentleman claims he was assaulted in this very room.

Group shot of all four.

CAPTAIN : He tried to knock me down. . . . Knock me down, I tell you !

LOLA *puts on a gleaming white top hat, apparently indifferent to the whole proceedings.*

KIEPERT : Who?

POLICEMAN *very calm* : Yes, who?

GUSTE *enters the picture, carrying a glass of beer. The* CAPTAIN *looks around, searching for* RATH.

CAPTAIN : What's happened to the . . . er . . . gangster?

GUSTE *pointing at the* CAPTAIN : That's the one, Officer. He

301

attacked me on the stage.

POLICEMAN *moving away from her* : All right, that's enough. I don't want any more wild accusations.

> *He pushes past* GUSTE *and* KIEPERT *and goes to the other end of the room. Pan as he crosses the room and passes in front of the mirror.*

CAPTAIN *off* : Where have you hidden him, you crook?

PROPRIETOR : How should I know, you crazy drunkard, I wasn't even there!

> *The* POLICEMAN *goes to the staircase, glances upwards and climbs a few steps towards* LOLA'S *bedroom.*

RATH *off, in a muffled voice* : Here! Come here!

> *The* POLICEMAN *stops and turns round. Medium shot of the* CAPTAIN, *who also looks round, and realises that the voice is coming from under the floor.*

RATH : Little wretches! . . . I've caught you at last!

> *In the centre of the room, the trap door opens and* LOHMANN *emerges, followed by a furious* RATH *pulling* GOLDSTAUB *through the opening.*

RATH : Come on, come on, out you come! At last I've caught you. It's all over. Come on, up! *He turns back and catches hold of* ERTZUM. You too, up! Rascals! *He pushes them against the wall and bellows.* Guttersnipes!

> *The* POLICEMAN *goes over and looks down into the cellar, then lowers the trap door, while the* CAPTAIN *points an accusing finger at* RATH. *The latter, covered in dust, puts on a dignified air and pulls down his cuffs.*

CAPTAIN : That's him. He's the one who tried to knock me down! It's him, officer, it's him!

> *The* POLICEMAN *goes up to* RATH *and salutes.*

POLICEMAN : Excuse me, Herr Professor.

CAPTAIN *coming forward and pointing at* RATH : He called me a procurer!

POLICEMAN *pushing him away* : Silence. *To* RATH. Excuse me, Herr Professor . . . This man wants to prefer a charge.

> *Group shot of the three men and the schoolboys.*

RATH *gesticulating* : Prefer a charge! *He turns to his pupils standing behind him.* I've got a charge or two to prefer as well!

CAPTAIN *to the* POLICEMAN : What's all this about preferring charges? Arrest the man.

POLICEMAN *pushing him back* : Will you shut up once and for all!

CAPTAIN : Nobody's going to make me shut up!

POLICEMAN *taking him by the arm* : We'll see about that. Come on, off to the police station.

CAPTAIN *towards* RATH : He tried to knock me down!

A new angle shows LOLA *and the* CLOWN *standing to the left, watching the scene. On the right,* GUSTE *looks on sadly, still holding her glass of beer. Behind stands* KIEPERT.

CAPTAIN *off* : He called me a procurer!

Waiters and stage-hands stand in the wings outside LOLA'S *door. Loud music. The* POLICEMAN *passes through, pushing the* CAPTAIN *in front of him.*

Back in LOLA'S *dressing room* RATH *strides to and fro in front of the three schoolboys, who are lined up against the wall. They — and particularly* LOHMANN — *do not look especially worried, but stand watching* RATH *rather contemptuously.* LOHMANN *produces a cigarette.*

RATH *indignant* : You realise what the consequences of this incident will be for you? *He stops, furious, in front of* LOHMANN, *who is nonchalantly lighting his cigarette.* Take that cigarette out of your mouth! LOHMANN, *looking amused, blows smoke in* RATH'S *face;* RATH *seethes with anger.* Take that cigarette out of your mouth!

LOHMANN stares insolently at RATH, *who strikes the cigarette from his mouth and turns to the other two, who are standing and sniggering.*

RATH : Confess! . . . What do you come here for?

Cut to LOLA, *who turns first to* KIEPERT, *then to* GUSTE.

GOLDSTAUB *in medium close-up* : The same thing as you, Herr Professor!

A new shot of RATH *with the three schoolboys shows the schoolmaster slapping* GOLDSTAUB *violently, then* ERTZUM, *before pushing them towards the door.*

303

RATH *shouting*: Out! . . . Out! . . . Out!
The schoolboys flee towards the exit.
In long shot outside LOLA'S *dressing room, the school-*
boys run down the corridor, silhouetted against the wall.
Music.
RATH *off*: You haven't heard the last of this!
Back in LOLA'S *dressing room, the* CLOWN *leans against*
the mirror. He turns round with a bitter expression and
goes out, shutting the door behind him. Medium shot
of RATH *coming back towards the middle of the room,*
straightening his glasses. Pan to GUSTE, *who goes to-*
wards him and pats him on the shoulder.
GUSTE : You did the right thing, ducky! Now push this drink
behind your necktie.
She hands him her glass of beer; he takes a large gulp
from it. There is a loud noise outside, as the window
is flung open. Cut to the window and the faces of the
three schoolboys yelling in its frame.
SCHOOLBOYS : Unrath! . . . Unrath! (Excrement!)
They disappear. Cut back to RATH, *who puts down his*
glass and snatches it up again, upsetting some beer in the
process; he then bumps into GUSTE *and rushes to the*
window.
RATH *leans from the window and waves his hand with*
the glass, threateningly after the boys, who have disap-
peared. As he bellows after them, his gestures become
more and more jerky and mechanical. The beer spills on
the ground.
RATH *uncontrollably*: Little devils! You haven't heard the
last of this! . . . You have . . . *His voice breaks, he tries again.*
You ha . . . *Much less loudly* . . . You haven't heard the last
of this! *His voice fades away.* You haven't heard . . . You
haven't . . .
He puts his hand to his heart, groans and staggers.
Cut back to the dressing room from the inside; LOLA
runs across to RATH *and holds him up, helped by* GUSTE.
Pan as they carry him to a chair. Medium shot of RATH,
slightly from above. He sits in a chair, his eyes closed,
gasping for breath. The two women lean over him.

304

LOLA *takes his hat off.*
LOLA *anxiously*: But . . . for heaven's sake, what's the matter?
He tries to reply. GUSTE *looks towards the* CLOWN.
RATH: It will soon pass . . . It will . . . *He puts his hand to
his heart.* I feel better already.
GUSTE: The little hooligans! *A pause.* You've certainly chosen
a fine profession.
LOLA *patting him on the back*: You just got overexcited . . .
You shouldn't do that . . .
She strokes RATH'S *hair. The bell rings to call her on-
stage.* RATH *leans towards her, but she moves away.*
LOLA: Damn that bell!
Cut to the PROPRIETOR, *who strides in angrily through
the stage door. Music is heard off, and there is a loud
discontented hubbub from the audience. The* PROPRIETOR
addresses KIEPERT.
PROPRIETOR: What's going on here? The place is half empty!
KIEPERT: Oh, quit complaining! Who brought the Captain
in, anyway? *To* LOLA. Come on! *He gestures towards the
door.* Get moving.
*LOLA *nods, goes up to* RATH *and looks him in the eye.*
LOLA: Come outside, Professor. . . . Come and listen. *She
leans towards him and tickles him under the chin, smiling.*
I'll soon put you right. *Pan as she moves
towards the door.* Yes! . . .
The PROPRIETOR *is seen standing outside* LOLA'S *door.
*LOLA'S *leg appears stretched out horizontally through
the doorway. He looks at it with interest.* LOLA *herself
appears and shuts the door, smiling. There are whistles
from the audience, off, and the band begins to play the
tune of* 'Falling in Love Again' (Ich bin von Kopf bis
Fuss). LOLA *taps her top hat and goes onstage, smiling.
Sitting at* LOLA'S *table,* RATH *looks at* KIEPERT, *who
goes over to an upended suitcase on which there are
several bottles. He fills a glass and addresses* RATH.
KIEPERT *filling the glass*: You gave me a bit of a punch, but
I'm not the kind to bear a grudge . . . *He comes towards
RATH *holding the glass; the* CLOWN *can be seen in the back-
ground, watching them.* I'm going to give you a bit of my own

305

personal medicine . . . *He picks up one of the champagne glasses and empties into it the glass, which he already has in his hand.* There we are. Drink it, it'll put soup in your bones.

RATH *looking curiously at the glass and then at* KIEPERT: You really think it will do me good?

KIEPERT: Right! It'll bolster you up a bit.

RATH *empties the glass in one gulp and starts to cough violently. The* CLOWN *and* KIEPERT *watch him as he takes a deep breath and smiles.*

KIEPERT: Okay?

RATH *nodding, slightly hoarse*: Yes!

KIEPERT: Right, now you can show your face again. *He takes* RATH *by the arm.* Come on!

RATH: Where to?

KIEPERT: To the celebrities' box.

RATH: What for?

KIEPERT: Don't you want to hear Lola sing?

RATH: Lola?

KIEPERT: Yes.

RATH *happily*: Ah yes, Lola!

KIEPERT *takes him by the arm and leads him out.*

Inside the club, the camera pans from the audience towards the stage, where LOLA *is singing in her white top hat. Behind her sit* GUSTE *and the other woman. Fishing nets and an anchor are hanging over the stage.*

LOLA *singing*: Ein rätselhafter Schimmer,
　　　　　　　Ein je-ne-sais-pas-quoi,
　　　　　　　Liegt in den Augen immer
　　　　　　　Bei einer schönen Frau!
　　　　　　　(An enigmatic glimmer
　　　　　　　A je-ne-sais-pas-quoi
　　　　　　　Shines always in the glance
　　　　　　　Of a pretty woman.)

From a distance, the camera pans to follow RATH, KIEPERT *and the* CLOWN *coming into the club from the side.* KIEPERT *pushes* RATH, *who is listening and watching in fascination, past a statue in front of the band and past some standing people, towards a reserved table in a box at the top of some steps. On the way up,* RATH

306

stops, his eyes glued to the stage. Pan upwards as KIE-
PERT *pushes him on.*

LOLA *singing off* : Doch wenn sich meine Augen
     Bei einem vis-a-vis
     Ganz tief in seine saugen,
     Was sagen dann die?
     (But when my eyes look deeply
     At my vis-a-vis
     And gaze intently at him
     What does it mean?)

KIEPERT *off* : Stop! . . . Your attention, please!
  LOLA *looks up towards* RATH. *In a reverse shot,* RATH
  is seen sitting in the box on a balcony, with his hands on
  the balustrade. KIEPERT *stands behind him, holding his*
  top hat.

KIEPERT *coming forward* : Ladies . . .
  Medium close-up on a bewildered RATH. *He squints*
  down at the audience.

KIEPERT *partly off* : . . . and gentlemen, may I have the
pleasure . . .
  Cut to a long shot of the stage, then pan as LOLA *moves*
  across the footlights, shielding her eyes from the glare.
  She looks up at the balcony. The camera, following her
  gaze, pans back to RATH *and* KIEPERT.

KIEPERT *continuing* : . . . of presenting to you this evening's
guest of honour, Doctor Immanuel . . .
  Medium close-up of RATH *looking a little self-conscious,*
  but nevertheless proud. He gives a little wave to the
  audience.

KIEPERT *continuing* : . . . Rath, Professor. *Pan towards the*
audience, all looking up expectantly at the balcony . . . at the
local university.

VOICES IN THE AUDIENCE : Oh! . . . Well! . . . Oh! . . . Well
now! . . . Hurrah!
  The camera tilts down onto the audience, who are laugh-
  ing and clapping noisily. Close-up of RATH, *smiling and*
  much flattered by his ovation. A pause, then a shot of
  LOLA *on the stage, also clapping. Long shot of the stage,*
  slightly from below, as GUSTE *raises her glass in a toast*

to RATH, *while* LOLA *applauds. Then pan with* LOLA *as she thrusts her hips forward and goes nonchalantly back to the centre of the stage, winking at one of the girls at the back, who immediately gets up.* LOLA *takes her chair and sits astride it, leaning on the back. Crossing her legs and throwing a suggestive glance up at the balcony, she begins to sing, underlining each phrase with a provocative gesture.*

LOLA *singing* : Falling in love again
　　　　　　Never wanted to . . .

In a medium shot of the celebrities' box, the enthralled RATH *listens as* LOLA *continues to sing.* KIEPERT *stands beside him, his hands in his pockets, noting* RATH's *reaction.* 　　　　　　*After a few moments, he taps his head and moves away, unnoticed by* RATH.

LOLA *off* : What am I to do
　　　　　　Can't help it
　　　　　　Love's always been my game
　　　　　　Play it how I may
　　　　　　I was made that way
　　　　　　Can't help it

She throws her head back, eyes half-closed.
　　　　　　Men cluster to me . . .

In a long shot, the CLOWN *stands by the band, looking on.*

LOLA *off* : Like moths around a flame . . .

Pan upwards, taking in a life-size wooden statue of a naked woman in the form of a figurehead. The camera comes to rest on RATH, *who is smiling.*

LOLA *off* : And if their wings burn
　　　　　　I know I'm not to blame.

RATH *looks with interest at the statue, which almost reaches the top of the box.*

LOLA *off* : Falling in love again,
　　　　　　Never wanted to —
　　　　　　What am I to do?
　　　　　　Can't . . .

RATH *turns his attention back to the stage . . .*
　　　　　　help . . .

308

Cut to LOLA, *smiling . . .*
    it.

As RATH *smiles happily in medium shot, the audience applauds off. Looking embarrassed, he puts a hand to his face, to hide his pleasure from the audience and smiles at* LOLA, *who starts to sing an encore, as the room hushes.*

LOLA *off* : Falling in . . .
    She taps her top hat in medium shot.
      . . . love again,
      Never wanted to . . .
    She opens her arms wide.
      What am I to do?
      Can't help it.
Cut back to a delighted RATH, *then back to* LOLA.
      Love's always been my game
      Play it how I may
      I was made that way
      Can't help it
      Men cluster to me
      Like moths around a flame,
      And if their wings burn,
      I know I'm not to blame.
She shakes her head and smiles.
      Falling in love again,
      Never wanted to . . .
Cut to RATH, *attentive and smiling. He runs his fingers round under his collar, then puts a hand up to hide his self-satisfied smile from the audience. His smile becomes almost a grimace.*

LOLA *off* : What am I to do?
      Can't help it.
      (Ich bin von Kopf bis Fuss auf Liebe eingestellt
      Denn das ist meine Welt und sonst garnichts
      Das ist- was soll ich machen meine Natur
      Ich kann halt lieben nur und sonst garnichts
      Männer umschwirren mich wie Motten um
        das Licht
      Und wenn sie verbrennen dafür kann ich nichts

Ich bin von Kopf bis Fuss auf Liebe eingestellt
Denn das ist meine Welt und sonst garnichts)

In RATH's *bedroom, close-up on a motto hanging above the bed with the inscription, '* Be just and fear no one.' *There is a knock at the door.*

MAID *off* : Herr Professor?

The camera tracks backwards to reveal the bed, which has not been slept in. A ray of sunlight falls across it from the window. On a shelf above the bed is a row of books; there are more books piled on the bedside table.

MAID *insistently, off* : Breakfast ! . . .

Cut to a shot of the MAID *as she opens the door and goes to the bed. Finding it empty, she looks around her in bewilderment.*

In LOLA's *bedroom,* RATH *is stretched out on the bed, snoring, with a doll in his arms. His waistcoat is hanging loosely from his right arm, his shirt collar is undone and he is still wearing his trousers. After some moments, he wakes, sits up on the bed and looks around the room, as if wondering where he is. He sits on the edge of the bed, looks at the doll which he still has in his hand, and pushes its arm down, letting off a musical chime. He puts the doll to his ear; the chime stops. Intrigued, he picks up his glasses. The chime starts again and then stops.* RATH *throws the doll down on the bed behind him. The chime starts again for a few seconds, then a bird is heard singing.* RATH *looks up and smiles. Cut to a shot of a bird cage, in which a small bird is twittering and hopping about. A new shot shows* LOLA *in a dressing gown, standing by the table in the centre of the room; breakfast is laid. She is holding a coffee pot and turns towards* RATH *and smiles.*

LOLA : 'Morning, Immanuel.

RATH *in medium close-up* : Good morning.

He gives a little bow and straightens his bow tie. Cut back to LOLA, *who strikes a cup with a teaspoon, making it ring.*

LOLA : Breakfast is served, Herr Professor !

RATH *has got up. He puts on his waistcoat, buttons it up, runs his fingers through his hair and picks up his coat from the back of a chair. The bird is heard chirruping off. Pan towards* LOLA, *who goes towards* RATH *and takes him by the hand.*

LOLA : Come on, sweetie, the coffee'll be cold.

She leads him across to the table, helping him on with his coat. He combs his hair.

LOLA : There, sit down.

As he sits down, she goes round behind him, takes the comb from him, sits down, puts the comb on the table and picks up the milk jug. Medium shot of the two of them sitting together at the table. LOLA *pours* RATH *some milk. He looks at her and smiles. She smiles back.*

LOLA : Tell me, sweetheart, do you always snore so much?

RATH *rubbing his eyes* : I'm afraid I rather overdid it last night.

LOLA *pouring herself some milk* : Ah yes! Two bottles of champagne. You held it very well.

RATH *smiles, flattered.* LOLA *takes some sugar.* RATH *gazes at her, fascinated.*

LOLA *taking a lump of sugar and holding it over* RATH's *cup* : One?

RATH *gazes at her without replying, so she drops the lump into the cup and takes another one.*

LOLA : Two?

RATH : Three!

She drops another lump into the cup.

LOLA *winking at him* : You really are a sweet one.

The bird chirrups. RATH *stirs his coffee and drinks.*

LOLA : Is it all right?

RATH : Excellent! Remarkably good!

LOLA *waving a knife* : You see . . . you could do this every day.

RATH *looks at her lovingly. The bird chirrups again.*

RATH : There's no reason why not. *He ponders.* . . . Since I'm a bachelor.

LOLA *leans back in her chair astonished.* RATH *drinks his coffee. At that moment the carillon of the town clock, playing* ' Ueb immer Treu und Redlichkeit ' *can be heard in the distance.* RATH *looks over the edge of his cup at the camera. He puts the cup down. The clock strikes eight. He takes out his watch and looks at it.*

RATH *excitedly* : I must be off to school. *He gets up.* I must hurry.

In the class-room, LOHMANN, *seen in long shot with his back to the camera, is drawing a caricature of* RATH *on the board. He represents him as an angel with a halo, floating among clouds and playing a lyre, from which emerge the words ' LOLA-LOLA '. As he draws,* LOH-MANN *glances continually towards the door. A shot of one corner of the classroom shows* ANGST, *gagged and struggling, being firmly held down by* ERTZUM. *Cut back to* LOHMANN, *who finishes his drawing, adding long hairs to* RATH'S *legs.*

Back in LOLA'S *bedroom,* RATH *stands with his hat and coat on, cane in hand; he looks excited.* LOLA *comes up to him with a carnation in her hand.*

LOLA : Come here ! *She draws him to her.* Keep still. *She puts the carnation in his buttonhole.* There, that's so you'll think of me.

She tries to kiss him on the cheek, but he hurries away. The camera pans after him as he goes past her out of the room and down the stairs.

LOLA : Aren't you going to say good-bye to me?

RATH *does not raise his head.* LOLA *kneels down and leans over the stair-rail.*

LOLA : Kiss me once more !

RATH *puts his head between the bars of the staircase. She kisses him.*

LOLA : Do you still love me?

RATH *plaintively* : Yes . . . yes, of course . . . yes. Good-bye. *He goes on down.*

LOLA *watching him go* : And be careful of the trams !

Long shot across LOLA'S *dressing room: two maids watch* RATH *coming down the stairs.*

ONE OF THE MAIDS : 'Morning, Herr Professor.

RATH : Good morning.

He looks round, annoyed, and goes out. Fade out.

A long shot of the school clock shows the time as ten past eight. Above the clock face is the motto ' ORA ET LABORA.' Pan downwards as RATH *hurries into the main entrance of the school.*

RATH, *having taken off his coat, goes towards the door of his classroom in long shot. He hesitates for a moment before entering, bends down, puts his ear to the door, straightens up, looks around him, then finally goes into the room.*

A long medium shot across the room from the inside catches RATH *as he comes in through the door. All the pupils get up. Pan as* RATH *goes to his desk.*

RATH : Sit down!

The pupils sit down. The camera pans across one side of the blackboard which has another drawing on it showing RATH *in frock coat and top hat, carrying one of* LOLA'S *legs over his shoulder. Very slow pan across the blackboard to* LOHMANN'S *drawing of* RATH *as an angel. The words ' LOLA-LOLA ' have been repeated several times.* RATH, *having seen the drawings, now looks furiously at the class, obviously controlling himself with difficulty. He takes the board rubber and begins to rub out the first drawing with hasty, sweeping strokes. At that moment,* ERTZUM, *his back to the camera, gets up from his desk at the front of the middle row.*

ERTZUM *shouting* : Please Sir . . . this place stinks of Unrath! (Excrement!)

He turns to the rest of the class, seeking their agreement.

ERTZUM *very loudly* : Unrath! . . . Unrath!

Seen in a long shot with his pupils, RATH *stands with the board rubber in his hand.* *The situation seems beyond his control and he gapes at the class which is now yelling in a frenzy. There are whistles and laughter, and the word ' UNRATH ' is shouted again and again. A long shot down the corridor outside the classroom, shows several other masters, alarmed by the shouting, as they gather outside the door and listen to the uproar inside. After a few moments, the* HEAD-

313

MASTER *appears at the top of a staircase. He hurries up to the door.*

Inside the classroom, the camera pans across, as the HEADMASTER *comes in through the door. The pupils are still yelling and whistling, while* RATH *is standing beside his desk as before, trembling with rage and shouting at the boys.*

RATH *shouting*: Be quiet! . . . Be quiet! I'll have you all locked up, you devils!

On seeing the HEADMASTER, *the pupils fall silent and go back to their places.* RATH *also stops shouting and looks at the* HEADMASTER.

HEADMASTER *to the class*: Outside, all of you. You'll be dealt with later.

Very quietly, the pupils leave the room.

Outside in the corridor, they are seen emerging, while the other masters turn and go back to their classes.

Inside RATH'S *classroom, pan towards* RATH *and the* HEADMASTER, *who have been watching the pupils file out of the room. The* HEADMASTER *then turns towards* RATH *and watches him as he puts the board rubber down on the desk, takes out a handkerchief and cleans his hands. The* HEADMASTER *walks round the desk to the blackboard and looks at the drawings.*

HEADMASTER: Not without talent!

As he speaks, the HEADMASTER *goes up to* RATH, *looks him up and down, and removes the carnation from his buttonhole. Medium shot of the pair of them face to face.* RATH *puts on his glasses, while the* HEADMASTER *sniffs at the carnation and then hands it back to him.*

HEADMASTER *taking off his pince-nez*: I understand the situation completely . . . but how can you risk your whole career for the sake of a creature like that?

RATH *angrily*: Headmaster, I must forbid this . . . You are speaking of my future wife!

HEADMASTER *incredulously*: You can't be serious!

RATH *puffing out his chest*: I couldn't be more serious. I won't hear another word.

The HEADMASTER *gives* RATH *a long and searching look,*

314

*then turns away with a gesture of resignation. A new
shot shows him near the door.*

HEADMASTER : I am extremely sorry, my dear colleague . . .
but in that case, I am afraid we can hardly let the matter
rest there.

*He goes out, his face serious and decided. Pan towards
RATH standing at the blackboard, in front of the caricature of himself as an ' angel'. Slowly he goes to his
chair, puts the carnation down on the desk and sits down
heavily. After a while, he opens a drawer and puts into
it the class exercise book. A new shot of RATH, full face:
he takes from the drawer his little black notebook and
an open penknife, which he puts on the desk. He looks
at the notebook for a few moments, then puts it in the
inside pocket of his coat. He pauses, then picks up the
penknife, closes it and puts it in his trouser pocket.
Finally, he gathers up his books. In a medium long shot
across the empty classroom, RATH is seen standing behind
his desk. He puts down the books and, looking at the
carnation, sinks back onto the chair. He seems very tired.
The camera tracks backwards, taking in the empty seats.
Fade out.*

LOLA'S *dressing room is in complete disorder. There are
suitcases everywhere.* KIEPERT, *a cigar between his teeth,
walks up and down the room. A woman passes, her arms
full.* GUSTE *is scurrying about. All three are in travelling
clothes.*

KIEPERT : Get a move on and pack your things, will you?
. . . You'll make us miss the train.

GUSTE *shrugs and takes a cigarette. There is a knock at
the door.*

KIEPERT : Come in.

The door opens on RATH, *looking very formal. He is
wearing a top hat and carrying a large bouquet of
white roses.*

KIEPERT : 'Morning, Professor. *Bumping into* GUSTE. Haven't
you got anything better to do than stand around here? . . .
I really wonder why I ever married you.

GUSTE *tossing her head* : I've racked my brains asking myself that, too!

KIEPERT *to* RATH: What are you standing around for? *Indicating the staircase.* Go on up. You know the way, don't you?

> *Very slowly,* RATH *climbs the stairs.*
>
> *In her bedroom,* LOLA *is seen from behind, bending over the bed and packing a suitcase. She is wearing travelling clothes. Medium shot of* RATH'S *head as he appears at the top of the staircase. He comes up into the room and looks around. Cut back to* LOLA, *who hears him and turns round.*

LOLA: How nice of you to come and say good-bye to me.

> *She carries on packing. Cut back to* RATH, *standing stiffly, holding his flowers.*

RATH *hesitantly*: Dear Miss Lola, I . . .

> *Return to* LOLA *who straightens up and comes towards* RATH. *A new shot shows the pair of them face to face.*

LOLA: Oh! What lovely flowers! *She takes them and kisses him on the cheek.* Thank you.

> LOLA *moves out of the picture. Another shot shows her by the bed; she turns and smiles. Medium shot of* RATH, *twisting his hat in his hands; he looks extremely embarrassed. Return to* LOLA, *who sniffs the bouquet; feels that she has thanked him too little, and puts the flowers on the bed and comes towards him. Shot of the pair of them face to face.*

LOLA: There's no need to look so sad! I'll return next year.

RATH: Dear Miss Lola, I have brought you something else.

> *He feels in his pocket and brings out a small box, which he holds out to her.*

RATH: Would you . . . *Medium shot of* LOLA, *looking very surprised, as he continues off* . . . accept this present from me?

> LOLA *takes the box and opens it. There is a ring inside. She is amazed. She takes the ring out of the box and slips it onto her finger.*

RATH *off*: And may I at the same time ask . . . *Medium shot of both of them* . . . for your hand?

LOLA *looking frankly sceptical*: You want to marry me?

RATH *sincerely*: Yes.

316

LOLA *immediately doubles up with laughter. The camera pans as she puts her hand over her mouth and moves a short distance away from* RATH. *Still laughing, she opens her arms and comes back towards him, then takes his hat and cane and puts them on the table. She calms down slightly and tries to take him in her arms. He draws back and gazes at her intently.*

LOLA : God, you are sweet!

RATH : I hope, my child, that you are fully conscious of the gravity of this moment.

LOLA *calms down completely and for the first time seems extremely embarrassed. She looks at* RATH *for a moment in silence. He puts his arm round her shoulders and draws her to him.* LOLA *smiles and presses herself against him. They kiss.*

With a group, LOLA, *dressed in bridal costume is leaning on* RATH'S *shoulder, and smiling at him as they listen to a piano playing Mendelssohn's 'Wedding March.' They are seated at a table covered with bottles and glasses. Voices are heard off — particularly* KIEPERT'S *— singing and cheering. The next shot shows the company assembled round the table, which is loaded with the remains of the wedding feast. All the members of the troupe are present with* KIEPERT *acting as cheer-leader.* LOLA *and* RATH *are on his left and* RATH *has his arm round his wife, who looks very happy and takes his hand tenderly. Several times the guests rise to their feet with glasses in their hands and toast.* LOLA *and* RATH *rise, too. They all sit down again, except for* KIEPERT, *who remains standing. The piano stops.*

KIEPERT : Ladies . . . and gentlemen. To-day, it gives me very great pleasure . . .

GUSTE *getting up* : Stop! *Weeping with emotion.* Can't you stop blathering for one moment?

KIEPERT *sitting down with a shrug* : Here we go again!

Medium shot of GUSTE, *who is now standing behind* RATH *and* LOLA.

GUSTE : It was wonderful when I got married, too. *To* RATH. If I'd known you then, perhaps I'd have been a school-

master's wife, too. Now all I've got for a husband is a conjuror.
KIEPERT *leaping to his feet* : Yes, I am indeed a conjuror!
GUSTE : Now we're in' for some more of his pathetic tricks.
KIEPERT : Sit down, will you? *She sits.* You're not going to
prevent me giving the Professor a demonstration of my art.
To RATH. I will now take the liberty . . . of producing a few
eggs from under your nose. Look, my hands are empty.
*He takes hold of RATH's nose, and suddenly an egg
appears in his hand. There is a fanfare, followed by
applause.*
KIEPERT *giving* RATH *the egg* : There, take it! Now, I'll
produce a second egg. Now, Professor, watch carefully.
He produces another egg from under RATH's nose.
Again there is a fanfare and applause.
KIEPERT *gives* RATH *the second egg and sits down. LOLA
looks sideways at RATH and begins to cluck like a hen.
RATH sits holding the two eggs. At first he looks surprised,
then grinning happily, he suddenly crows like a cock.*
RATH *upright in his seat* : Kick-a-rick-ki!
*A new shot of RATH, smiling happily at LOLA, who clucks
away.*
RATH : Kick-a-rick-ki!
*Applause and laughter, as RATH looks pleased with
himself and crows again for effect.*
*LOLA, watching KIEPERT, bursts out laughing. RATH
hugs and kisses her. Fade out.*
*In a hotel room, RATH walks up and down near a curtain
behind which LOLA is changing her clothes. She can be
seen in silhouette. RATH goes and looks through the
curtain. He smiles, looking very pleased with himself
and puffing out his chest. Then, scratching the back of
his neck, he sits down on a divan, takes a puff at his
cigarette and inhales deeply. In medium close-up, LOLA
pokes her head out from behind the curtain.*
LOLA : Give me the small case, will you, sweetheart?
*RATH scrambles to his feet. A second shot shows him
standing in front of a pile of suitcases. Taking the top
one, he turns out the contents on the floor. The camera
tilts down onto postcards of LOLA scattered on the carpet.*

318

Cut to LOLA, *half-hidden behind the curtain. She watches* RATH, *smiling.*

LOLA : You are hopeless!

High-angle shot of RATH *kneeling on the floor. He puts his cigarette in his mouth and picks up the cards.*

RATH : Why did you bring these postcards?

Cut to LOLA.

LOLA : What a stupid question! They're sold every evening.

RATH *shot from above* : So long as I have a single penny . . .

Cut to LOLA, *as* RATH *continues off* . . . they will not be sold!

LOLA : All right . . . but you'd better pick them up . . . one never knows.

She disappears behind the curtain. Fade out.

A night-club interior: RATH *is sitting at a small table by a poster of ' LOLA-LOLA '. Sounds of applause. He turns his head towards the camera and puffs at the fag-end of a cigarette. His hair and beard are dishevelled, and he looks generally in a pitiful state.*

LOLA *singing off* :

> Nimm Dich in Acht vor blonden Frauen
> Die haben so etwas gewisses
> S'ist ihnen nicht gleich anzuschauen
> Aber irgend etwas ist es
> (Take care of women who have blonde hair
> They have a special flair
> They have no way of being fair
> They'll strip you and leave you bare)

RATH *turns round. He looks weary.*

LOLA *singing off* :

> Ein kleines Blickgeplänkel sei erlaubt Dir
> (Stare all you please but do no more than look)

RATH *pulls a packet of photographs of* LOLA *from his pocket.*

LOLA *singing off* :

> Doch denke immer — Achtung vor dem Raubtier
> (For if you do you'll end up on the hook)

RATH *spreads the photographs of* LOLA *out on a tray in front of him.*

LOLA *singing off* : Nimm Dich in Acht vor blonden Frauen

Die haben so etwas gewisses
(Take care of women who have blonde hair
They have a special flair)

Cut to a shot of the stage as LOLA, *her song finished, bows to loud applause and goes offstage. Return to* RATH, *who stubs out his cigarette, buttons his now slightly worn-looking coat, picks up the tray, and gets up slowly from his seat. A bowed figure, he wanders through the club, trying to sell the photographs, but he is met with catcalls. The camera pans after him for a few moments, as he makes his way among the audience.*

Medium shot of LOLA'S *dressing room. In the foreground,* KIEPERT *is sprawled on a divan, smoking a cigar.* LOLA *enters and undoes her skirt. The general hubbub from the club itself can be heard in the background.*

Cut to RATH, *trying without success to sell his photographs to the audience.*

Back in the dressing room, LOLA *is sitting at the dressing table, applying cream to her face.* KIEPERT *is still smoking his cigar in the foreground.* RATH *enters, puts down the tray of photographs on a case and drains a half-empty glass of beer.* LOLA *crosses her legs, polishes her finger nails and starts to peel an apple.*

LOLA *with a hint of irony*: How's business?

RATH *putting down the glass*: Only two cards! What an ignorant bunch.

KIEPERT *jumping up*: An ignorant bunch! You're a fine one to talk! You'd do better to go and have a shave. What do you think you look like? RATH *takes a cigarette.* You can't expect to do any business looking like that. Yes, that's right, look dumb. . . . *His voice rises.* You're not at the university now!

He goes out, slamming the door. Insert of KIEPERT *outside the door, walking away. Inside the dressing room,* RATH *sits down behind* LOLA. *He has a glazed look.* LOLA *continues to peel her apple.*

LOLA: He's quite right, you know. You might at least let a razor see your face. Anyway, what's the matter with you? What do you have to call them an ignorant bunch for? After all, we make a living out of them.

LOLA *puts the apple peelings on the table, cuts a slice out of the apple and starts to eat it.*

RATH *in resignation and despair*: Oh yes! We make a living. We make a living!

LOLA: If you don't like it, you can always go.

RATH *mumbling*: Yes, I'll go away . . . I'm going . . . I'm going. . . . *He jerks upright, quivering, and shouts.* I've had enough! Enough! I'd rather die like a dog than carry on like this.

The camera pans rapidly as he rushes out of the room, slamming the door. Cut back to LOLA, *who has watched him go, smiling and munching her apple. Pan as she gets up and goes over to a gas-ring beside the door, which she lights, putting a pair of curling tongs on it to heat. She returns nonchalantly to her chair, puts one leg up on it and starts to take off her stocking. Long shot as the door of the dressing room opens slowly to admit a repentant* RATH. *He looks in an even more pitiful state than at the beginning of the scene. He shuts the door, and stands motionless in front of it.* LOLA *turns towards him, a contemptuous smile on her lips, and sits down on the divan.*

LOLA *as if nothing had happened*: Ah! . . . yes . . . pass me my stockings, will you?

RATH *gets the stockings, then kneels in front of* LOLA, *who stretches out her left leg. As he is pulling the stocking onto her leg, the bell rings to call her onstage.*

LOLA *pushing him*: Quick, get me the curling tongs.

RATH *goes to the gas-ring, while* LOLA *puts on the second stocking herself. He takes the tongs and hands them to* LOLA, *who has sat down again in front of the mirror. She takes the tongs, protests, and hands them back to* RATH.

LOLA *sharply*: But they're too hot!

RATH *looks around for something to bring down the heat. He goes up to a calendar hanging over the gas ring and tears off a sheet which spells out the day, 27. As he puts it on the tongs, it catches fire. He blows it*

*out and tears off another sheet marked 28. Close-up on
the calendar: three shots dissolve one into the other as
three more sheets are torn off, the last of which bears the
date 2 December, 1925. Dissolve to a close-up of a new
calendar, showing the year, 1929.*

In another dressing room, RATH *sits in medium close-up
at a dressing table lit by a flickering candle. He looks at
himself in the mirror with a disillusioned air. He is even
more unkempt than before and his forehead is covered
with wrinkles. He applies make-up laboriously, drawing
a vertical line through each eyebrow, then examines the
result in the mirror.* Apparently
*satisfied, he puffs at a cigarette, coughs, puts the cigarette
down and picks up a large, bulbous false nose. He puts
this on, and then a clown's wig. Looking sad and weary,
he checks his appearance once more in the mirror and
takes another puff at his cigarette. He then picks up a
very broad false collar, which is many times larger than
his neck, and passes it over his head.*

Pan to KIEPERT, *who comes up behind him wearing top
hat and tails. He has just emerged from a staircase, which
can be seen behind him with one of* LOLA'S *skirts hanging over the rail.*

KIEPERT : Well, Professor . . . And how are we to-day? *He
takes out a cigar and offers it to* RATH. You want a cigar?
It's Havana . . . the wrapper, Sumatra leaf !

LOLA *comes into view with a towel round her waist and
busies herself in the background.* RATH *takes the cigar
and smells it, turning as he does so towards the candle
so that one can see that his make-up is like the* CLOWN'S
in the beginning, in ' THE BLUE ANGEL.'

RATH *wearily* : You seem in a very good mood to-day.

KIEPERT : As well I might be . . . I have a very good
reason . . .

RATH *mouths a vague 'Ah!,' while* LOLA, *in the background, turns her head towards the two men.*

KIEPERTH You should be pleased too . . . You're becoming
my star.

LOLA *genuinely indignant* : Don't make fun of the old man.

322

He hasn't done anything to you.

KIEPERT: You can just shut up! . . . Your husband has become a very important part of the act. Look . . . *He takes something out of his pocket.*

LOLA *has come towards* KIEPERT. *Her face appears near his hand, which is brandishing a piece of paper.*

KIEPERT *partly off*: A contract! . . . All arranged by telegram. *A pause.* And where do you think it's for?

A new shot shows LOLA *reading the contract with interest, while* KIEPERT *turns towards* RATH.

KIEPERT: At 'THE BLUE ANGEL.'

RATH *starts imperceptibly, puffs at his cigarette, and raises his head slowly to look at* KIEPERT.

RATH: 'THE BLUE ANGEL'?

KIEPERT: Yes, we're going back to your home town. *Raising his arms.* There'll be lots of publicity: 'Professor Immanuel Rath.'

RATH *hotly*: Never! . . . I will never go back to that town!

KIEPERT *somewhat surprised*: You must think about it . . .

RATH: I already have!

KIEPERT: Isn't that just like you? For five years you've lived off this woman . . . *He indicates* LOLA, *who is wiping her hands* . . . and now the first time you have the chance to make a bit for yourself . . . *Mincingly* . . . the Professor says, 'No, I won't go.'

A new shot of the three of them together. RATH, *in his clown's outfit, is still seated.*

LOLA *to* KIEPERT: Leave him alone . . . You know very well he'll go.

RATH: No, I won't go!

KIEPERT: We're leaving tomorrow. It's all fixed.

RATH *quivering*: No, I won't go. Never! You can demand what you like of me, but that . . . I won't do it!

LOLA *patting him on the shoulder*: There's no need to get worked up.

RATH *putting his cigar in his mouth*: No, no, I won't do it! Never!

LOLA *losing patience*: But you don't have to go!

RATH *not listening to her and looking at himself in the mirror*:

Never! . . . Never! . . .

It is evening in a street. Medium close-up of a man with his back to the camera, passing a poster of 'LOLA-LOLA' on the wall. He pastes the front of the poster and sticks diagonally across the lower half of it a label which reads in gold lettering: 'PERSONAL APPEAR-ANCE OF PROFESSOR IMMANUEL RATH.'

Behind the scenes in THE BLUE ANGEL, *the camera tracks sideways past the dressing rooms, following a couple of performers. In the foreground are nets, columns and beams. Nearby, the* PROPRIETOR *of* THE BLUE ANGEL *is standing against a column, saying goodbye to the outgoing performers, and welcoming the first arrivals from* KIEPERT'S *troupe.* KIEPERT, *a cigar between his teeth, comes up to him.*

KIEPERT *very sure of himself*: Good morning, Herr Direktor.

PROPRIETOR: Good morning to *you*, Herr Direktor . . . You finally made it!

The two men shake hands and GUSTE *appears.*

GUSTE: 'Morning . . . Well, I never thought I'd be crawling about this hole again!

PROPRIETOR: My establishment . . . a hole?

Several girls greet the PROPRIETOR. *People pass continually in front of the camera.*

KIEPERT *with irony*: You haven't got any slimmer, I see.

PROPRIETOR: No, but you can hardly complain of that yourself.

A member of KIEPERT'S *troupe enters the picture, raises his hat and greets the* PROPRIETOR.

PROPRIETOR: Good morning.

The performer goes off; the camera tracks along beside him.

KIEPERT: Why should I be losing weight? *Off.* Business is good. How are things with you?

PROPRIETOR *off*: Bah, we'll be all right now. The last three weeks though . . . I've never seen anything like it! No, Sir!

The camera has arrived at the entrance to the dressing rooms. The strong man MAZEPPA *comes out, wearing an overcoat and carrying a suitcase on his shoulder. He*

passes in front of the camera, which pans after him.
MAZEPPA *goes up to the* PROPRIETOR *and* KIEPERT.
MAZEPPA : Au revoir, Herr Direktor.
PROPRIETOR : Be seeing you, Maestro — but not in the next
ten years, I hope. *He turns away disdainfully.*
MAZEPPA *somewhat put out and very haughty*: Your tin-pot
establishment may be all right for the usual run of second-rate
turns . . . but not for a high-class act like mine! . . .

> *Cut to* LOLA *coming into the club. She is dressed in a fur
> coat, the collar of which is turned up against the snow
> falling outside.*
> *Return to* KIEPERT, MAZEPPA *and the* PROPRIETOR.

MAZEPPA *in French*: Au revoir, mon petit . . . cochon!
> *He goes off.*

KIEPERT *to the* PROPRIETOR : And who was that turn?
PROPRIETOR : Oh him! . . . One more week with him and I'd
have been bankrupt.

> *Cut to* LOLA *coming in through the doorway.* MAZEPPA
> *stands back to let her through, following her with his
> eyes.*

MAZEPPA : Good morning, Lola!
LOLA *off*: Good morning.

> MAZEPPA *stands for a moment looking after* LOLA, *who
> has gone by. Instead of going out of the door, he unloads
> his suitcase.*
> LOLA *has arrived between* KIEPERT *and the* PROPRIETOR.
> *She looks at the two men, then in the direction of*
> MAZEPPA.

LOLA : So many handsome men in one place.
KIEPERT *shrugging*: Good hunting!

> *He moves out of frame, while* LOLA *puts her hands on
> her hips and looks provocatively towards* MAZEPPA. *Cut
> to* MAZEPPA, *who smiles and raises his hat. Cut back
> to* LOLA, *who turns and goes towards the entrance to the
> dressing rooms.*

GUSTE *off*: Don't put all the cases on top of each other . . .
Oh! I've never seen anything like it . . . All over the floor!

> LOLA *pauses in the doorway, turns to smile at* MAZEPPA,
> *and goes in. Cut back to the* PROPRIETOR *as* MAZEPPA

passes him.

PROPRIETOR : Don't miss the train!

MAZEPPA *with a contemptuous grimace* : What do you know about love?

> *Medium shot of* LOLA *in her dressing room, arranging her hair in front of a mirror. A noise is heard. Cut to* MAZEPPA, *who appears in the doorway and goes boldly towards the staircase leading up to the bedroom. He stops and smiles at* LOLA. *In another shot,* LOLA, *after noticing* MAZEPPA, *adjusts her coat and goes towards him. A new shot shows the pair of them at the foot of the stairs.* MAZEPPA *stands back to let her go up. She looks at him while, with an air of complicity, he raises his hat in a sweeping gesture.*

MAZEPPA *in French* : Permettez-vous, Madame . . . *In German* . . . Allow me to introduce myself. Mazeppa, Hans Adelbert Mazeppa.

LOLA *leaning back and smiling at him* : Yes . . . so what?

MAZEPPA *leaning on the stair-rail* : I'm staying here . . . for you! That's how I am . . . a man of action! *He raises himself on the rail and tries to kiss her.*

LOLA *pushing him back* : Don't be so impetuous! . . . *Seductively.* We've got plenty of time . . . haven't we?

> *She smiles at him and goes up the stairs.* MAZEPPA *gazes after her in fascination and then cups his hands to his mouth.*

MAZEPPA : For me, it's not a question of hours!

> *It is evening. A medium shot from above shows the entrance to* THE BLUE ANGEL. *A* POLICEMAN *is standing in front of the door, holding back a noisy crowd.*

POLICEMAN : Now then . . . go home quietly . . . All the seats are sold . . .

> *A band strikes up. Dissolve to a shot of* LOLA *and* MAZEPPA *behind the scenes in the club.* MAZEPPA *is carrying a bunch of flowers and smoking a cigar. He smiles at* LOLA, *who smiles back. They move on.*
>
> *In a long shot of the stage, six girls are seen dancing in a line, each one with her hand on the hips of the girl in front. There are loud cries from the audience.*

AUDIENCE *shouting off*: The Professor! . . . The Professor! . . .
> LOLA *appears, hands on hips. Smiling at the band she moves to the middle of the stage and starts to sing.*
LOLA *singing*: Take care of women who have blonde hair
> They have a special flair
> They have no way of being fair
> They'll strip you and leave you bare
> *Medium shot of* LOLA *behind the line of girls.*
> Stare all you please but do no more than look
> For if you do you'll end up on the hook
> Take care of women with blonde hair
> They have a certain flair

A high shot of the audience shows the club completely full. The audience applauds.

Medium close-up of RATH *in* LOLA'S *dressing room. He is sitting inert in front of the mirror.* KIEPERT'S *hands come into view. He spreads make-up on* RATH'S *wrinkled forehead.* RATH *does not react, but closes his eyes from time to time.*

KIEPERT *partly off*: This will be the decisive evening of your career. To-day, if we're well received, we'll be a success! . . . La Scala! . . . Berlin! The Alhambra! . . . London! . . .

> *A new shot shows* RATH *still seated, while* KIEPERT *stands over him, making him up as a clown.* GUSTE *is standing by the mirror.*

KIEPERT *to* GUSTE: The brush! . . . GUSTE *hands it to him.* The Hippodrome! . . . New York! . . .

GUSTE: Stop romancing! You're getting delusions of grandeur. Right now, we're at 'THE BLUE ANGEL.'

KIEPERT: You're just a killjoy!

GUSTE: And what do you think you are?

KIEPERT: Stop squawking! Where's the nose?

> *He puts the clown's collar on* RATH.

GUSTE: The nose?

KIEPERT: That's what I said, the nose. You had it, didn't you?

GUSTE: I had it? You had it, you mean!

KIEPERT *taking the nose from the box which* GUSTE *is holding*: I had it, did I?

GUSTE *to* RATH: There's no need to get nervous, ducky. I know exactly how you feel. I was just like you, just as nervous, twenty years ago . . . the evening I had my first big success.
KIEPERT *putting the false nose on* RATH: Will you shut your mouth for a few minutes?

Pan towards the door. The PROPRIETOR *rushes in.*
PROPRIETOR: Chairs! . . . More chairs! . . . Even the Mayor is here! *He goes out.*
GUSTE *proudly*: The Mayor! . . . Then I'm going out there, too! *She goes out.*

The PROPRIETOR *reappears, carrying two chairs.*
PROPRIETOR: Now there's no need to get nervous, Professor. We're sold out! . . . Everybody's here! Your colleagues, your pupils, everyone! What a crowd!

He moves out of the picture, while the camera stays on RATH *and* KIEPERT.
KIEPERT: Quite right! He's absolutely right. Keep calm. Look at me, for example. Now we'll go out and really give them the works!

He slaps RATH *on the shoulder and moves out of shot. The camera holds on* RATH, *who sits staring into space, utterly depressed. Outside the dressing room, a fireman and a stage hand stand in front of* LOLA's *door, while the girls from the revue hurry past followed by* LOLA *and* MAZEPPA. *Back in* LOLA's *dressing room,* RATH *is still sitting motionless in front of the mirror. He does not react when the girls enter and pass through the room.* LOLA *and* MAZEPPA *come in. A new shot shows the three of them together,* RATH *sitting at the dressing table on which are a bottle of champagne and some glasses.* LOLA *looks at* RATH *and smiles at* MAZEPPA.
MAZEPPA *taking his cigar from his mouth and putting his arms round* LOLA: When I see a beautiful woman, I don't waste a minute. I'm well known for that!

LOLA lowers her eyes coquettishly. RATH *looks up, and* LOLA, *her head tilted slightly back, addresses him.*
LOLA: Well, what's the matter? What are you looking like that for? Every time I have a bit of fun, you act like a stuffed shirt!

MAZEPPA *putting his cigar back in his mouth* : What's going on here? The atmosphere's electric! Oh! . . . Well, it happens in the best of families. *To* RATH. Allow me to introduce myself. My name is Mazeppa . . . Hans Adelbert Mazeppa . . .

> RATH *does not look up.* LOLA *smiles arrogantly. The warning bell rings.*

LOLA *to* RATH : What are you sitting there for? Go on . . . go and do your number.

> MAZEPPA *picks up the bottle of champagne.*
>
> > LOLA *moves out of the picture, but her reflection can still be seen in the mirror.*

MAZEPPA : Have some of this, my dear colleague. *He pours* RATH *a glass of champagne.* It can't do you any harm.

> *He takes the bottle and the second glass and moves out of frame. Cut to* LOLA *and* MAZEPPA *cautiously mounting the staircase which leads to* LOLA'S *bedroom.*

MAZEPPA : The boy seems a bit off!

> *Cut to* RATH, *who turns round with a glazed expression.* LOLA *laughs, off.* RATH *gets up and, seen in medium close-up, goes over to the staircase and looks up.* LOLA *laughs again, off.* MAZEPPA'S *voice is heard.*
>
> *In another shot of the dressing room,* RATH *still stands at the bottom of the staircase. The door opens and* GUSTE *appears. Through it can be heard music and the impatient shouts of the audience.*

GUSTE *intrigued* : What's going on? Where are you hiding? *She approaches* RATH. What's the matter with you?

> *Medium close-up of* RATH, *who turns towards her.*

GUSTE *off* : But . . . but what's the matter?

> *Medium shot of* GUSTE *looking at* RATH, *who is still standing at the bottom of the staircase.*

GUSTE : Lola, come down!

> *She moves out of sight. The camera stays on* RATH, *who shakes his head.*

RATH : I won't go onstage!

> *At these words,* KIEPERT *appears.*

KIEPERT : What's come over you? . . . Are you crazy? . . . You're not going to let me down now? . . . One minute before we have to go on. . . . You can't do that to me!

> LOLA *comes slowly down the staircase. Medium close-up of her looking towards* RATH.

LOLA : What's the idea? . . . You don't want to go onstage?

> *Medium close-up of* RATH, *completely distraught.*

LOLA *off* : You're going to go on.

> LOLA *is seen taking the clown's wig from the table. She holds it out to* RATH.

LOLA : Put on your wig.

> *It is* KIEPERT *who takes the wig from* LOLA *and puts it on* RATH'S *head. At that moment, the door opens to admit the* PROPRIETOR.

PROPRIETOR *furious* : What's this I hear? You don't want to go on?

KIEPERT : Yes, of course he'll go on!

PROPRIETOR *to* RATH : Have you gone mad? That kind of thing just doesn't happen in my establishment.

KIEPERT *pushing* RATH *towards the door* : Come on, move!

> RATH, *looking completely shattered, turns towards* LOLA.

PROPRIETOR : Outside!

> RATH *is pushed towards the door. Medium close-up of* LOLA *watching him. She looks sad and distressed.*
>
> RATH, KIEPERT *and the* PROPRIETOR *are seen at the door of the dressing room.* RATH, *supported by the two other men, turns once more towards* LOLA, *while* KIEPERT *straightens his top hat for him. Cut to* LOLA, *hands on hips, walking nonchalantly across the room with a cold and disdainful smile. Return to* RATH, *now standing in the wings supported by* GUSTE *and the* PROPRIETOR. *There is a fanfare and applause.*
>
> *Cut to* KIEPERT, *going onto the stage.*
>
> *In a long shot of the stage seen from the front,* KIEPERT *draws aside the curtain and addresses the audience.*

KIEPERT : Ladies and Gentlemen! Please excuse this short interruption. A slight technical hitch! *Derisive shouts from the audience, mixed with laughter and applause.* But you will be amply recompensed by our next number . . . a display of conjuring which is truly international in character! *Shouts of 'Bravo!' and applause, as the curtain opens and the house lights go down.* In this number, I should like to present to you, as an altogether exceptional attraction, a man whom you all know already through his long and remarkable educational activities . . . *Shouts of derision* . . . his educational activities at this town's university.

There are shouts from the audience, particularly cries of ' Onstage, Professor ! ' . . . ' Come on, Prof ! '

Close-up on RATH *behind the curtain in the wings. He looks haggardly from the stage to the dressing room and back again. The audience continues to shout for* ' The Professor.'

KIEPERT *off* : I can see, Ladies and Gentlemen . . . *He appears before the camera* . . . that I need say no more. I shall therefore try your patience no longer. It is indeed our . . . *Long shot of the audience* . . . well-loved Professor Immanuel Rath !

The audience reacts with laughter, whistles and applause. Cut to RATH, *still standing at the side of the stage, looking towards the dressing room.* KIEPERT *comes and takes him by the arm.*

KIEPERT : Watch out now . . . or you'll mess up the whole number !

PROPRIETOR *agitated* : Come on ! Come on !

KIEPERT *drags* RATH *away. The* PROPRIETOR *watches them go.* GUSTE *goes past the camera in the direction of the audience. In another shot, the* PROPRIETOR *is seen arriving at the bar. A long shot of the stage through transparent gauze curtains shows* KIEPERT *making his entrance and bowing.* RATH *appears at the back of the stage and* KIEPERT *indicates him to the audience. Another shot of* RATH *looking out through the transparent gauze curtains. As he moves slowly upstage, accompanied by shouts from the audience, he throws a glance in the direction of the dressing room.*

Medium shot of LOLA *as she comes out of the dressing room and leans on the balustrade by the stage entrance.* MAZEPPA *follows her. Cut back to* RATH, *who turns back and continues to move upstage. Long shot of the audience, shouting and applauding. Return to* RATH, *as he draws aside the final curtain and comes out at the front*

331

of the stage, his eyes wide, looking completely bewildered by what is going on around him. Long shot of the stage from the front. KIEPERT *goes up to* RATH *and raises a hand for silence. The audience falls quiet.*

KIEPERT : Ladies and Gentlemen, may I present to you . . . Auguste, my apprentice sorcerer. *He indicates* RATH *and hitches up his sleeves.* As you will observe, ladies and gentlemen, I work without props . . . only with my two hands . . . my ten fingers. What I am going to show you, ladies and gentlemen, is just a hat . . . a perfectly ordinary top hat. *He takes* RATH'S *hat from his head and shows it to the audience.* No false bottom, no secret opening, no trap door. This hat, ladies and gentlemen . . . I now place it . . .

Cut to LOLA *and* MAZEPPA, *seen from above. He tries to kiss her; she is watching the stage.*

KIEPERT *continues off* : . . . on the head of my assistant Auguste . . . *Cut back to the stage, seen from the front.* And from the hat, I will make so bold as to produce for you, by magic, here and now, a live dove! No doubt, ladies and gentlemen, you are all convinced that the conjuror has already put the dove inside the hat. Oh no! You are quite wrong. *He turns the hat round, showing it to the audience from all sides.* Look, I pray you . . . Empty! *He taps the hat.* Empty! *He taps on* RATH'S *head.* Quite empty!

The audience is seen from above, laughing uproariously. Resume on KIEPERT, *who puts the hat back on* RATH'S *head and goes over to a small table.*

KIEPERT : One moment, please. Here is further proof! *He brandishes a knife.* A knife, if you please!

Medium close-up on RATH *and* KIEPERT. KIEPERT *walks round* RATH *and plunges the knife into the hat on* RATH'S *head several times.*

KIEPERT *plunging in the knife* : One . . . two . . . three . . . four . . .

During this performance, RATH *looks at the audience in bewilderment.* KIEPERT *returns to the table, exchanges the knife for a pistol and comes back towards* RATH. *The camera pans briefly to follow his movement.*

KIEPERT : Ladies and gentlemen . . . Do not be alarmed by

the sight of this revolver in my right hand. *He aims at* RATH's *hat and fires, then goes and lifts the hat to reveal a dove perched on* RATH's *head.* Voila! Now Auguste has got the bird!

> *Cut to a section of the audience, seen from the side. A man in top hat and tails gets up, looking angry and disgusted.*

THE MAN: This is revolting! ... Call the police!

VARIOUS VOICES: Sit down! ... Sit down! ...

> *Applause. The* PROPRIETOR *is seen from above, sitting behind the bar. He smiles with satisfaction at the applause.*

PROPRIETOR *calling across to* KIEPERT: Herr Direktor, I've run out of eggs. Would you like to produce some magic ones for me?

> *Resume on* KIEPERT, *who bows to the* PROPRIETOR, *while* RATH *glances into the wings.*

KIEPERT: Of course, Herr Direktor . . . Indeed, I shall be delighted to do so. Ladies and gentleman, I shall now make so bold as to produce some eggs, here and now . . .

> *While he is speaking,* RATH *moves towards the wings. The camera catches him between the transparent gauze curtains, more bowed than ever. The audience laughs and whistles. Cut to* RATH's *view down into the wings:* LOLA *is watching the stage, while* MAZEPPA *flirts with her. Cut back to* KIEPERT *as he catches up with* RATH.

KIEPERT: . . . from under my assistant's nose! *He tugs at* RATH's *tail coat and speaks to him in an undertone.* Think what you're doing, Auguste . . . After all, you were once a schoolmaster! *Close-up on* RATH, *gazing stupidly.* No doubt, ladies and gentlemen, you are all convinced that friend Auguste has the eggs all ready inside his hat. A gross mistake! *He lifts the hat from* RATH's *head to show a second dove.* Oh! Another bird . . .

> *Fanfares. The camera tilts down onto the audience, who are yelling and whistling, then returns to the two men on the stage.*

KIEPERT: Right away, ladies and gentlemen . . . At your service! *He makes passes in front of* RATH's *face.* One . . .

333

two . . . three . . . hup! an egg. *He shows the egg to the audience, then turns to* RATH *and speaks to him in an undertone.* What's happened to your kick-a-rick-i? *Louder.* An ordinary common hen's egg . . . *He breaks it on* RATH'S *head.*

Group shot of the audience from above. Several people get up and leave in indignation. The majority laugh and clap.

SHOUTS : Lay another one!

Cut back to the two men on the stage.

SHOUTS *off* : Lay another one!

In another shot of the wings as seen by RATH, LOLA *looks at the stage while* MAZEPPA *takes her in his arms and kisses her.* LOLA *keeps her eyes on the stage as he does so. Cut to the audience shouting ' Lay another one ! ', then cut to* RATH *and* KIEPERT.

KIEPERT *to* RATH : If you don't crow this time, I'll finish you off. *Louder.* Once again, then!

He makes passes in front of RATH's *face.*

KIEPERT : One . . . two . . . three . . . An egg! *He shows it to the audience.* I'll prove he's laid an egg. *He breaks it on* RATH's *head.*

Cut to the audience laughing, seen from above. Cut back to the two men.

KIEPERT *losing his temper, but still keeping his voice down*: Crow, will you! . . . Kick-a-rick-i! If you don't crow now, I'll kill you! . . .

Cut to a close-up of RATH *looking down. He has moved back slightly and is clinging to the curtain. Medium close-up from above of* LOLA *in* MAZEPPA's *arms. They are still kissing.* LOLA *is looking onto the stage as before.* MAZEPPA *draws away and also looks up. Cut back to the stage.* KIEPERT *drags* RATH *violently away from the curtain and hauls him to the front of the stage.*·

KIEPERT *brutally* : Crow.

RATH *staggers, wild-eyed. Cut to* LOLA *and* MAZEPPA *looking up at the stage.* MAZEPPA *has an ironic smile on his lips. Return to the two men on the stage.* KIEPERT's *face is set in a grim expression.* RATH, *staggering, crows hoarsely at the top of his voice like a madman. His*

*crowing sounds mad, like a groan of despair. His hands
tremble as he returns to the back of the stage and takes
hold of the curtain, uttering another crowing as
anguished as the first. He clings to the curtain and
spins round, wrapping himself up in it. Medium close-up
of* KIEPERT, *who looks anxiously out at the audience.
Medium shot of the stage from the front.*

RATH *seen through the curtains, bellowing*: Kick-a-rick-i!

The camera tilts down to a medium shot of LOLA *and*
MAZEPPA. LOLA *is beginning to look really alarmed. The
camera pans with her as she retreats towards her dressing
room.*

MAZEPPA *watches her, then glances uneasily up at the
stage. Medium shot of* RATH *as he parts the curtains and
gazes down into the wings. In the background,* LOLA
can be seen going into her dressing room, followed by
MAZEPPA, *who glances several times in* RATH'S *direction
and shuts the door behind him. Angry shouts can be
heard from the audience. Cut to* RATH, *shot slightly from
below, as he rushes down the steps from the stage and
throws himself against the locked door of the dressing
room. He batters the door with his head.*

RATH *bellowing*: Kick-a-rick-i!

*He breaks open the door. There are shouts and whistles
off from the audience, getting louder and louder.
Seen from inside* LOLA'S *dressing room,* RATH *stands in
the doorway and crows again, choking as he does so.
In medium close-up,* LOLA *looks at him, anguished.*

LOLA : What's the matter with you? I haven't done anything!
Cut to MAZEPPA *watching* RATH *closely, then cut to*
RATH.

RATH *puffing out his chest and bellowing*: Kick-a-rick-i!

He slams the door and leaps at LOLA. *Insert of* MAZEPPA,
surprised, then a medium shot of RATH, *who throws
himself on* LOLA *and tries to strangle her. She screams
loudly, her screams mingling with* RATH'S *repeated
crowing. In his madness,* RATH, *gripping* LOLA'S *throat,
knocks her head against a suitcase, then against the piano,
and drags her to the nearby divan, still throttling her.*

335

MAZEPPA *intervenes and hauls him off. There is a short battle which ends in* RATH, *the stronger of the two, throwing* MAZEPPA *furiously against the piano. Then, still crowing madly, he rushes into the chorus girls' dressing room where* LOLA *has taken refuge.* LOLA *screams off.*

Her screams continue as the camera cuts to KIEPERT *and the* PROPRIETOR, *who have come into the dressing room. They walk across and enter the other room. A chorus girl rushes out, followed by all the other girls. There is general confusion.* MAZEPPA *and the various members of* KIEPERT'S *troupe are gathered round the door as* LOLA *rushes out, terrified.* GUSTE *appears beside* MAZEPPA, *who leans against the wall, smiling with relief. The* PROPRIETOR *springs at him waving his arms. The fireman forces his way through the crowd. Furious voices are heard. Bystanders enquire what is going on. In the background, a dishevelled* LOLA *looks frantically at the staircase, then retreats slowly up it backwards, her face frozen in terror. A new group shot centred on* MAZEPPA *shows him opening a large trunk. He takes out a straitjacket which he uses in his act and comes back to the doorway.* GUSTE, *looking in alarm at what she sees in the room beyond, draws back to let him pass . . . The* PROPRIETOR *rushes out calling for a doctor.* GUSTE *goes out of the dressing room. The* PROPRIETOR *shuts the door behind her, then goes back into the room where* RATH *is. Fade out.*

Close-up on RATH *in the straitjacket, pale-faced with a vacant expression, his hair in disorder. He raises his head and looks slowly around him. Cut to* KIEPERT *outside the door. He hesitates, then makes up his mind and goes in. Return to* RATH *in a corner of the room, imprisoned in the straitjacket. He is gazing blankly at the floor, but turns towards* KIEPERT *on hearing the door open. His face suddenly changes, showing fear. Cut to* KIEPERT, *who shuts the door behind him and comes purposefully towards* RATH. *Medium shot of* RATH, *who closes his eyes and rests his head against the wall.*

Cut to KIEPERT *untying* RATH.

KIEPERT: Come here!

KIEPERT *undoes the straitjacket and throws it on the floor.*

KIEPERT: You asked for it! . . . I don't understand you . . . After all, you're an educated man! . . . And all that for the sake of a woman!

RATH *looks at him almost sympathetically, while* KIEPERT *pats him reassuringly on the shoulder.*

KIEPERT: Just take it easy . . . I'll take care of everything . . . *He gives* RATH *a final pat on the shoulder and goes off. Another shot of* KIEPERT *by the door, as he turns to look at* RATH *before going out of the room. Cut back to* RATH, *who has watched him depart. His face has changed, the weary expression giving way to one of cunning as he sees his coat hanging up. The camera pans to follow his hands as they reach up and take the coat. It pans down again to show* RATH *putting on his coat, looking anxiously at the door. He then puts on his battered hat, and hurries to the door.*

Outside the dressing room, the door opens and RATH'S *face appears. He looks from side to side. Laughter and applause come from the audience.* RATH, *in medium close-up, looks out at the audience while* LOLA *is heard singing off.*

LOLA *singing off*: Falling in love again
                      Never wanted to
                      What am I to do? . . .

Medium shot of LOLA, *sitting astride a chair in the middle of the stage, which is hung with white drapes, but otherwise empty. She is wearing a close-fitting black costume and a broad-brimmed black hat; she sits astride the chair as she sings.*

LOLA *singing*: Can't . . .

Emphasising each word.

              . . . help it!
              I know I'm not . . .

She leans back, still holding onto the back of the chair.

              . . . to blame . . .

337

Long shot of RATH *as he slips away, looking back all the time over his shoulder. He moves out of the picture.*

LOLA *off* : Love's always been my game
  Can't help it !

Cut back to LOLA *as she leans forward with a crooked smile and, propping one arm on the back of the chair, caresses her shoulder with the other hand.*

LOLA *singing* : Men cluster to me
  Like moths around a flame
  And if their wings burn
  I know I'm not to blame.

She continues to sing.
  Falling in love again
  Never wanted to
  What am I to do?
  Can't help it !

Medium shot of RATH *sidling along the wall of the club towards the exit. He is half bending down and hiding his face. The camera pans after him, while the audience is heard applauding.*

Cut back to LOLA, *leaning on her chair and smiling down at the audience with a cool expression.*

It is night, as RATH *staggers down a narrow and ill-lit street, stopping frequently to support himself against the wall. The camera pans after him as he approaches a small square with a fountain in the foreground. A foghorn echoes, sinister in the distance. Exhausted,* RATH *stops and leans against the wall of a building, and laboriously scrapes away the thin coating of snow on it. He moves off again, staggering drunkenly. The foghorn is heard again.* RATH'S *shadow looms across a wall as the scene begins to fade.*

Dissolve to a long shot, from above, of the entrance to the high school. It is night. RATH, *seen from the back, staggers towards the porch and rings a bell. Close-up of the bell ringing. In medium shot,* RATH *rings again impatiently.*

Down the dark staircase of the school, a flickering light

338

comes towards the camera. A limping CARETAKER *appears in the foreground carrying a lamp. Cut back to* RATH *outside. The door opens and the lamp lights up his face as he enters. Pan as he passes in front of the* CARETAKER *and goes unsteadily up the stairs, followed by the latter and lit from below by the beam of his lamp. Medium shot of* RATH *advancing down the corridor to his classroom, leaning against the wall for support. He gets there with difficulty, opens the door and enters.*

Cut to the CARETAKER *following* RATH *in surprise up the staircase. Music. A second shot shows the* CARETAKER *arriving in the corridor. The light of his lamp falls on the half-open door of the classroom. He advances and hesitates for a moment, while the music changes to an orchestrated version of the tune played by the town clock, ' Be always faithful and honest.'*

Medium close-up of RATH *in his classroom. He is sitting sprawled over his desk. In the light of the lamp, he appears inert; but with his arms wide apart, he is gripping the edge of the desk in a final spasm. Between his arms, his head rests lifeless on the desk. The* CARETAKER *appears. Close-up of* RATH *followed by a medium shot of both. The* CARETAKER *panics and tries with all his might to release* RATH'S *hand from the grip on the desk, but in vain. Close-up of the hand, as the* CARETAKER *tries vainly to pull it away. In medium close-up, the* CARETAKER *looks at the dead* RATH *in horror and retreats to the door. The music stops abruptly. The final scene shows the inert slumped figure of* RATH, *lit by the* CARETAKER'S *lamp, gripping the corner of his desk in his last gesture to regain security. He has found peace in the classroom he once abandoned. The camera tracks slowly backwards disclosing the empty desks of his pupils, while outside the clock tolls twelve. On the final stroke of twelve, the words: THE END*

In a final and more menacing rendition of "Falling in Love Again" by composer Friedrich Holländer, Marlene Dietrich, as Lola-Lola, cooly surveys the theater audience.